10633337

Books by C. L. Sulzberger

THE
FALL
OF
EAGLES

C. L. SULZBERGER

CROWN PUBLISHERS, INC.

NEW YORK

© 1977 by Crown Publishers, Inc.

All rights reserved. No part of this book may be reproduced or utilized in any form or by any means, electronic or mechanical, including photocopying, recording, or by any information storage and retrieval system, without permission in writing from the publisher. Inquiries should be addressed to Crown Publishers, Inc., One Park Avenue, New York, N.Y. 10016.

Printed in the United States of America
Published simultaneously in Canada by
General Publishing Company Limited

Designed by Ruth Kolbert Smerechniak

Produced in cooperation with Time-Life Films, Inc.

IN MEMORY OF
PRINCE PAUL KARAGEORGEVIĆ

Most cultivated of sovereigns, who ruled Jugoslavia seven years with selfless patience. When betrayed and traduced by his Allied friends, he behaved according to chivalrous tradition, sans peur et sans reproche.

ACKNOWLEDGMENTS

I wish especially to thank Linda Lamarche for her enormous help in getting this book together; also Eda Pallier. As always, my wife, Marina, was of perceptive assistance in editing until just before her tragically premature death, and I am grateful to her as always and know not how I shall produce future books without the help of her wise and tolerant judgment, and her loving encouragement.

I also wish to thank Professor Charles Maier of Duke University for looking through the manuscript with shrewd percipience.

But particularly I am grateful to Princess Olga of Greece and Denmark and her husband, Prince Paul of Jugoslavia, for their helpful observations concerning the Romanovs and also for making available to me private letters of the period of Czar Nicholas II as well as a rare instruction of Czar Peter the Great to his ambassadors.

I am equally thankful to Archduke Otto von Habsburg, legal heir to his dynasty's claims, and to Prince Louis Ferdinand of Prussia, the Hohenzollern claimant, both of whom were most generous and helpful with their time and observations.

CONTENTS

Habsburg

Hohenzollern

Romanov

THE
FALL
OF
EAGLES

I THE EAGLE PEOPLE

With his hooked beak, cruel talons, and keen, piercing eyes, the eagle has gained a martial reputation that far exceeds the truth. Indeed, ounce for ounce, even the dove and certain species of the lascivious quail are braver and more bellicose. Nevertheless the eagle is history's most familiar symbol for warriors on the march. He transcends the lion, the tiger, or those dragons devised by heraldry from early imagined snakes.

Although the Tatars summoned their marauding troops of cavalry behind horsetail standards bobbing on poles, not kingly birds, they used the golden eagle to capture antelopes. During the height of falconry as a noble sport, only kings (arms strengthened by wielding lance and broadsword) were entitled to fly eagles on the chase.

For some reason, men, looking up at the eagle's crude twig-nests perched among barren crags, or admiring the vast glides and swoops of this farsighted hunter capable of making off with an entire sheep, endowed the eagle with a myth transcending all reality. Since the Roman legions, behind their gilded eagle standards, tramped from Scotland and the Rhine to the deserts of northern Africa and western Asia, army after army has marched to death under the heraldic spread of aquiline wings. Even the peaceful American colonists, isolated as they hoped to be from world battlefields, succumbed in the end to the eagle's token values and selected him over the turkey as their symbol.

For centuries the eagle, as a royal or military emblem, was rendered with surprising accuracy and in surprisingly naturalistic form. It was only when adopted as the imperial emblem of the east Roman Empire that the eagle entered the domain of fantastic bestiaries already inhabited by unicorns, griffins, rocs, and other fabled creatures; he was depicted with two heads looking, like the twin faces of Janus, in opposite directions. This double-headed eagle of Byzantium became the most famous heraldic sign of all time.

Scholars disagree on why the eastern emperors abandoned the single-headed eagle of imperial Rome in the West. Some say the change betokened claims of the new Rome that was to become Constantinople and that sought to spread its administrative wings over both Europe and Asia, covetously regarded by the twin-headed bird from the point where the continents joined.

Others believe the heraldic change came about only after two great Byzantine ruling families, the Paléologues and the Lascaris, united and reigned above the Golden Horn. The third and perhaps most vainglorious theory originated with a discovery on the Greek Cycladic island of Kea. There, a carven stone was found bearing the two-headed royal bird and a verse describing one head as representing the human sovereignty of the emperor, the other as representing his link to the divine as holy chief of Christendom represented by Constantine's eastern church.

It is not unnatural that this haughty double-headed eagle should have flown on through time. It became the ruling mark of succeeding great imperial dynasties. It was assumed by the Romanov czars of Russia who, like their predecessors of earlier Slavic royalty, continued to eye Constantinople with greed. Russia has, ever since the Ottoman Empire sickened in the eighteenth and nineteenth centuries, been the largest Middle Eastern state.

Like the suzerains of Byzantium, the two-headed eagle looks both toward dawn and dusk across the earth. The Ottoman sultans who conquered Constantinople stole from them that city's earlier device, the crescent moon, which still adorns the Turkish flag. The Russians, who, since medieval days, had been mounting expeditions aimed at the capital of Byzance, which they called Czarigrad, City of the Emperors, stole instead the double-headed eagle.

Over the long span of history Russia dreamed of itself as the Third Rome, successor to that of the Caesars and to Constantinople. It is possible to conjecture that this vision helped develop a national case of schizophrenia, a split between Westernizers and Slavophiles, which eventually undermined the national psyche long before the final wave of revolutions came. As Professor Arnold Toynbee was to write:

> A classic case of the idolization of an institution bringing a society to its grief is the fatal infatuation of Orthodox Christendom with a ghost of the Roman Empire, an ancient institution which had fulfilled its historic function and completed its natural term of life in serving as the apparented Hellenic Society's universal state.

And still today, under the hammer and sickle, no longer the double-headed eagle, Russia continues to seek universality. The commissars who replaced the czars have turned their ideological creed into a kind of ecclesiastical basis for imperialism. Thus they preserve (as did the Romanovs with their orthodoxy) that relationship between church and state established by Constantine and maintained by his descendants until Justinian.

But Russia and its ambitious emperors were not alone in aspiring to such glory. The Habsburgs farther west created a vast imperial domain with the combined blood of battlefield and marriage bed, a domain that at its apogee included many areas once ruled by Constantinople, and they too stole that capital's twin-headed symbol. Even Skanderbeg, the fifteenth-century Albanian chieftain who carved a kingdom out from Turkish Constantinopolitan rule, hoisted the double-headed eagle standard. This was a poetically suitable bit of posturing. The Albanians call themselves shqiptar in their own cacaphonous language, a word which means "eaglemen" or "sons of the eagle."

Finally the Hohenzollerns, a tribe of south German robber barons who gained their first major foothold in Franconia and then pushed northward into Prussia, adopted the glowering eagle. But theirs was the single-headed bird of western Rome, not that of Kea. And its glance was not intercontinental but focussed only across the sandy plains and forested valleys tenanted by Teutonic people. But its regard always faced eastward (toward Slavdom) according to Prince Louis Ferdinand of Prussia, today's Hohenzollern heir.

There have been other, scarcely remembered dynasties which sought to embellish their slight renown with this same device. A minor branch of Hohenzollerns accepted the throne of Romania as a result of a deal among Europe's statesmen and brought the eagle along. A still more distant arm (or twig) of that family dispatched a cadet member, Prince Wil-

Until its adoption as the imperial emblem of Byzantine Rome, the eagle, rendered natu-ralistically, had been a common royal or military emblem. Then, depicted with two heads looking, like the twin faces of Janus, in opposite directions, the double-headed eagle of Byzantium became the most famous heraldic sign of all time. Pictured here is the double eagle on the fence of the Russian Museum, which was formerly Mikaylovsky palace.

helm of Wied, to become sovereign of Albania shortly before World War I. Soon he discovered neither pleasure in sheltering under the wings of Skanderbeg's imperial bird nor an aptitude for the job. He resigned to become a major in the German Kaiser's army.

Of the principal dynasties succeeding to the double-headed eagle of Byzantium or that of Rome, Romanov, Habsburg, Hohenzollern, all three spawned emperors of increasing pomp who knew the court ceremonials developed in their names as intimately as they knew the bodies of their mistresses. And all three shared certain rudimentary resemblances.

Each (even the Romanovs) had German blood. Each attributed to itself a divine right that encouraged autocracy and arbitrary rule. Each had as one overpowering aim the increase of its wealth and territory. Each, on the whole, dealt in an amateurish, unsuccessful way, with politics, diplomacy, and war. Each sought to deceive fellow imperial sovereigns by appealing to the obligations of cousinly kinship while arranging successful betrayals. And each collapsed abjectly at the end of World War I.

At their apogee the three crowns they wore would have controlled together more of the earth's surface than the great British empire that Victoria built: a Russia extending from Poland to the Pacific and from the Arctic to Afghanistan; a

The upper panel shows the "three aging empires" which occupied much of central and eastern Europe in the seventeenth century. Though maintaining themselves with growing difficulty under modern conditions, the Polish Republic lasted until 1795, the Holy Roman Empire until 1806, the Ottoman Empire until 1923. Meanwhile, beginning in the seventeenth century, the political leadership in this area was assumed by three states of more modern type, organized around the institutions of monarchy, the standing army, and the professional bureaucracy or civil service—the reorganized Austrian empire of the Habsburgs the Hohenzollern kingdom of Prussia, and the Russian empire of the Romanovs. These are shown in the lower panel. All three figured prominently in the affairs of Europe for more than two hundred years; all perished in the First World War, 1914–18.

1660
*Three Aging
Empires
and . . .*

. . . *the
Powers that
Grew
at Their
Expense.*
1795

Map (top, 1660):

NORTH SEA

BALTIC SEA

• MOSCOW

REPUBLIC OF POLAND

BERLIN •

• WARSAW

HOLY ROMAN EMPIRE

VIENNA •

• BUDAPEST

KINGDOM OF HUNGARY

OTTOMAN

ADRIATIC SEA

BLACK SEA

CONSTANTINOPLE •

EMPIRE

MEDITERRANEAN SEA

300 Miles

Map (bottom, 1795):

NORTH SEA

BALTIC SEA

• MOSCOW

PRUSSIA

RUSSIAN EMPIRE

BERLIN •

WARSAW •

HOLY ROMAN EMPIRE

VIENNA •

AUSTRIAN

• BUDAPEST

MONARCHY

OTTOMAN

ADRIATIC SEA

BLACK SEA

CONSTANTINOPLE •

EMPIRE

MEDITERRANEAN SEA

POTENTISSIMVS MAXIMVS E
QVI CVNCTOS SVI TEMPO
MAGNANIMITATE LIBERALI
ANIMI FORTIDVDINE SVPERA
M CCCC LIX DIE MARCII
DECESSIT VERO ANNO M D
OPT MAX IN NVMERVM V

The arms of Maximilian I.

Germany going from the lower Rhine to East Prussia and Silesia and including colonial appanages in West Africa, East Africa, and the Pacific; and an Austro-Hungarian hodgepodge taking in Bohemia, part of Poland, and Transylvania, through northern Italy and on down to the Bosnian border with surly little Montenegro, an area once pertaining to Byzantium.

Of these lordly houses, the Habsburgs were the earliest on the ceremonial lists: archdukes of Austria from the thirteenth century, Holy Roman emperors from the fifteenth. They originated in German Switzerland at the castle of Habichtsburg on the Aar River, near its confluence with the Rhine. Habichtsburg, which means the Hawk's Fortress, was built in 1028 by the bishop of Strasbourg, now the capital of French Alsace.

For generations the Swiss, not notably humorous, have referred to the Habsburgs as their most successful emigrant family. Today even that claim might be considered dubious. An early forebear, Rudolf, acquired leadership of the first four-cantonal league of Switzerland. Perhaps this experience helped foster the family's original contribution to monarchic rule: institution of a condominium system in which the senior male members could share enjoyment and government of their domains. This idea of consanguine responsibility runs as a wavering thread through Habsburg history. At its peak, the ambitious house specialized in greedy statesmen who preferred weddings to war as a means of expansion.

The most brilliant Habsburg marriage-maker was Emperor Maximilian I. He took the heiress of the duke of Burgundy as his own bride, and she brought with her dowry the Netherlands and two provinces of France. Their son, Philip I, was married to Joanna, daughter of Ferdinand and Isabella of Spain. The vast lands she gave her husband more than made up for the fact that she was insane. Their son, Karl (Carlos) V, was the greatest sovereign of his time: Holy Roman Emperor, lord of Spain and the Netherlands, Sardinia, Sicily, and southern Italy, Alsace, Austria, Hungary, Bohemia, and the huge colonies of Spanish America whose gold and precious stones poured copiously into Europe.

The Habsburgs produced no geniuses, except perhaps Charles V, and not many statesmen of great ability. Several of their scions showed distinct evidence of madness (at least in part traceable to Joanna). Most of them were decidedly eccentric and addicted to scandal. They contributed two lasting dynastic traits: the adage "Let others wage war, you, happy Austria, marry—*Bella gerant alii, tu, felix Austria, nube*"; and an unattractive, pendulous lower lip that marks so many of the solemn portraits great painters made of them, with the notable exception of those rare competents, Maria Theresa and Joseph II.

By way of contrast, their imperial cousins (a courtesy title empires bestowed upon each other) the Romanovs, were more violent, emotional, uncontrolled, reckless, and disorganized. They too stemmed from a Teutonic nobleman who, early in the fourteenth century, had emigrated to Moscow. His fifth son was nicknamed Koshka (the cat) and became chief of a family called thereafter the Koshkins, many of them prominent Muscovites of the era.

One of these, whose first name was Roman, took to calling himself Romanov. In the early sixteenth century he married off his prosperous daughter, Anastasia, to Czar Ivan the Terrible. Their son, Theodore, was the last ruler from the dynasty of Rurik, an early Russian prince who first attacked Constantinople. Although Theodore was forced by the usurper Boris Godunov to divorce his wife and become an eremite monk, his son Michael was propelled to the throne by the *boyars,* or noble chiefs. They fancied that he, a lad of sixteen, would be easy to manage in their own feudal interests.

The Romanovs saw as their destiny the filling out of Russia's own natural frontiers, the expulsion from its main western areas of the Tatars and other Asian peoples, the

Titian's painting of the Emperor Charles V at the height of his power after the Battle of Muhlberg in 1547.

eventual completion of this task by extension to the far Pacific, and the basing of the entire massive complex on Europe, still regarded as the fount of civilization. This was an apt if unconscious fulfillment of the Byzantine double-headed eagle's rule, avarice peering long-sightedly East and West.

The Romanovs, in this respect like the Habsburgs, sired few great figures, but several who were brutally flamboyant. They had a strong streak of Asian authoritarianism in them and, claiming it was divine will, fell increasingly behind the times. As the rest of the world progressed they permitted the development of an uncoordinated, awkward, backward society ready-made for corruption and incapable of either governing itself in peace or efficiently fighting the wars into which it was endlessly led.

The two outstanding Romanovs were Peter the Great and Catherine the Great, of whom only the former truly qualified for history's adjective. Both were built on a superhuman scale of energy and improbability. As is so often the case when Teuton and Slav mix (and there were numerous marriages between czars and German princesses) cruelty became a dynastic familiar. Maurice Paléoloque, perhaps France's most famous ambassador to Russia and also, strangely enough, himself of imperial connection, sharing the twin-headed eagle through his own royal Byzantine blood, wrote long afterward:

> A curious feature of the first Romanovs is that notwithstanding their efforts to rule in accordance with the people's wishes, and though each of them in turn manifested a total lack of personal ambition, circumstances so imperiously demanded a strong hand that autocracy was evolved and imposed upon a succession of totally ungrasping autocrats. The general leaning of the country toward a firm rule prepared the way for Peter the Great's activities.

Peter set the basic pattern for what was to become Russian policy thereafter, under commissars as well as czars. He pushed into the confines of Europe, expelling an intrusive Sweden from Russia, and headed the national dynamism southward toward a slowly crumbling and retreating Turkish empire. He began—if somewhat fruitlessly—the ponderous but immutable drive into Central Asia that finally ended on the Pacific shore. He also used dictatorial means to modernize Russia with the intent of making it strong.

On the one hand he beat his son to death—and then, on the other, he ordered his ambassadors to deny the murder to foreign governments. On June 27, 1718, Peter wrote to his Minister Plenipotentiary in Paris, Baron de Schleinitz: "Once he had been convicted of great crimes committed against us and our Empire and the sentence of death had been announced to him [Alexei, the son, who actually died July 26] he was seized by a kind of apoplexy." He recovered slightly, according to the czar's untrue version, confessed his crimes weeping, then died. "This death caused us great sadness but notwithstanding we believe Divine Providence wished by this to deliver us from uneasiness and tranquilize our empire." The letter was signed "Peter" and witnessed by "Count Golovkin."

Notwithstanding this murder of his own heir, the ruthless czar encouraged westernization, industrial development, religious tolerance, and a primitive form of women's liberation. He was energetic, imaginative, brave, and truly patriotic. Before defeating the fierce Swedish King Charles XII at Poltava, he formally reminded his soldiers: "As for Peter, remember that life is of no value to him unless Russia lives in happiness and glory."

Catherine II (another eighteenth-century sovereign) also displayed broad vision and shrewd talent as a ruler despite idiosyncratic behavior that, generations later, might have been deemed worthy of a psychoanalyst's couch or a mental home. Catherine was born and bred a German princess, but she enthusiastically adopted Slavdom's fulsome embrace. She

Peter the Great set the basic pattern for what was to become Russian policy thereafter, under commissars as well as czars. He pushed into the confines of Europe, expelling an intrusive Sweden from Russia, and headed the national dynamism southward toward a slowly crumbling and retreating Turkish Empire. He began—if somewhat fruitlessly—the ponderous but immutable drive into central Asia that finally ended on the Pacific shore.

Catherine the Great of Russia (Catherine II).

As an eighteenth-century cartoonist pictured Queen Catherine's Dream of Russian imperialism.

CONSTANTINOPLE

WARSAW

QUEEN CATHERINES DREAM,

London Pub. by W. Holland N°50 Oxford St. November 4 1791

threw herself into the raptures of authority and used the mattress not as a means of conquest in the Habsburg sense of marrying for gain but more in the Teutonic sense of battle, a sporting arena. Yet she was far abler than her libidinous ways suggested.

Avid for mental as well as physical stimulus, she injected a fresh intellectual vigor into the barbaric heritage of her newfound land. The liberal thoughts of French Encyclopedists served to stimulate reforms which, although distorted by their Russian background and application, propounded new laws and administrative systems. She wound up quarreling with her most brilliant European friends, like Voltaire, but she did much to promote art and to protect artists, founding the nucleus of the Hermitage Collection which still bedazzles visitors.

Peter, that huge, inquisitive, and practical genius, brutal at home yet unfashionably democratic when abroad—a man of the same stamp as Kemal Atatürk two centuries later—and Catherine, lustful, conscienceless, patriotic, somewhat sordid, and certainly talented, were the two outstanding Romanov sovereigns; and she, after all, was but a minor German princeling's daughter with not a drop of Slavic blood. Yet, Russian by adoption, she assimilated well.

As I have said, there has always been something peculiar about the Slav-Teuton hybrid. One can trace this through Russo-German history, along a borderland of endless clashes, symbolized by Russian Romanovs and Prussian Hohenzollerns. Each nation was renowned for bravery; and also for exaggeration. As my friend Milovan Djilas, a pristine, untainted Slav from Montenegro, says: "A Serb will kill you; that is all. But when a Russian kills you he weeps."

The Romanovs, astride the frontier belt where Germans and Russians fought for centuries when both were not battling Poles, produced on the whole a covetous, thwarted, and uninspired group of rulers except for Peter and Catherine. The

Hohenzollerns were even less interesting, both as nonentities and notables. Their particular knack was making war and their besetting sin was vain pomposity.

Originally obscure Swabian counts invested by a friendly emperor with the electorate of Brandenburg, they subsequently added Prussia, initially only the area along the Baltic in present-day Poland; then northeast Germany and fragments of the peaceable West. By 1870 they had acquired supreme lordship over all Germans save for those under Habsburg rule, in Austria, Bohemia, and among the Balkan and Volga *Volksdeutsche*. Their basic dynastic principle was absolutism, only gentled by the European revolutions of 1848; obedience to their rule was the sole accepted virtue; and militarism came to be seen as the instrument of their foreign policy and the acme of their internal caste system.

Perhaps half a dozen Hohenzollerns were men of unusual character. Even among these, only one, Frederick (Friedrich), the Great, could be seen as a genius. The remainder (except for the worthy Great Elector, Friedrich Wilhelm, who made his mark in the seventeenth century as a fine general and organizer, and an even finer trickster) could be listed as inefficient, vain, sometimes industrious, sometimes weak, squanderers of both success and money. Most of the others, save perhaps Wilhelm I—and this is arguable—were given to little sense of purpose or comprehension of dynastic destiny.

The Brandenburg Margrave Friedrich captured a town called Berlin in the latter Middle Ages and made it his capital. A later successor, the sly Joachim I, dabbled in astrology, opposed Luther (who was to become the Prussian prophet), and publicly burned Jews, a harbinger of the future. In the seventeenth century Elector Friedrich Wilhelm unified the lands his forebears had acquired by violence, then invited French Protestants to settle his domain. He spent his final years personally supervising the splendid flowers and songbirds in his gardens. The Great Elector also built up the first solid army

Leningrad: the Winter Palace, which now houses the Hermitage Museum, the nucleus of which was founded by Catherine II.

that served as a springboard for Prussian militarism in succeeding generations.

His grandson, King Friedrich Wilhelm I of Prussia, an uncouth martinet, distorted this splendid fighting force with a
curious taste for gigantic grenadiers. He called them his "tall
fellows" and spent vast sums of money to acquire huge mon-
sters, often well above seven feet high, buying, stealing, and
kidnaping them when necessary. After this short, fat king,
who hated intellectuals and anything French but who, despite
some bureaucratic ability, had the major historical importance
of siring Prussia's King Friedrich II (Frederick the Great),
finally died in 1740, the roads of the continent filled with
doltish giants lumbering home, dismissed as useless by the
warrant officers of a more efficient service.

Frederick the Great was called effeminate by his stodgy
father. Not surprisingly, he revolted against such stupidity at
an early age. He expressed his opposition by sitting around in
a silk dressing gown and practicing the flute instead of
musketry drill on the parade ground. He so infuriated his
parent by this rebellious spirit that the latter beat him savagely
in public and once almost spitted him on his sword. The
prince reacted by attempting to escape abroad with a friend,
his tutor, Hans von Katte. He was himself sentenced, then
pardoned, but forced to watch Katte's beheading.

This heartless upbringing turned the sensitive and unusually intelligent lad into a cynic. He pretended to obey his
father by studying what was assigned to him, married without
love (the normal royal duty), and spent minimal time with
his wife. Increasingly, whenever he could capture time for
privacy, he read Voltaire and participated in chamber music
concerts.

When Frederick assumed the throne he presented an astonishing contrast to his somewhat boorish, uncultivated,
militarist predecessors. He, too, was increasingly fascinated by
army affairs; but his approach was less crude and more in-

tellectual. He abolished his father's regiments of "tall fellows." He called up more troops and trained them with greater efficiency. He ended the useless brutality that had previously prevailed in the barracks. And, to protect his craving for privacy with friends of his own choice, he built a country house, called it Sans Souci, and often tenanted it with wits and intelligentsia. Many of them spoke French, the king's own preferred language.

Frederick was a strange anomaly. In a dynasty that was on the whole crude, nonintellectual, obsessed with the means of warfare although by no means brilliant in its pursuit, he was originally uninterested in the family avocation but then became its outstanding practitioner. It was a line that, no matter how mediocre its methods, had always succeeded better in destroying than in procreating humanity. Frederick's forebears had been more familiar with managing brigades than households; he moved up the ladder of competence to supervise armies and palaces. His ancestors also—and here he did not interrupt the trend—had proven more adroit at winning battles than in wooing women.

As heir apparent he had studied Machiavelli. While not profoundly understanding the Italian, he at least modeled his own policy on the theory that no state needed to concern itself with morality in the formulation of its policies. He was also vain and thirsty for glory once blooded upon the battlefield.

He picked a quarrel with the Habsburgs early by conquering Silesia, which became the Prussian state's richest province. This touched off a series of conflicts against coalitions possessing forces far larger than his own, especially the Seven Years' War (1756–63). In that ghastly fracas, Frederick maneuvered his troops effectively and speedily to successive victories. Nevertheless, after a million soldiers had fallen (half of them from tiny Prussia) the settlement achieved saw little perceptible change from what already existed. It was, from Frederick's viewpoint, a magnificent *tour de force,* simply to have

survived, much less to have hung on to Silesia.

He eventually concluded: "Glory is vain. Have men ever deserved praise? They have only been praised because they made a stir."

Such should have been his epitaph. All he did, in effect, was create a vast commotion. He realized this negative role himself. During the last third of his life, he quarreled with most of his friends (including Voltaire), lost his interest in music, and spent much of his time sitting or lying about with the sole creatures who adored him, a pack of greyhounds. The belligerent and schizoid king who had worked so hard, thought so much, fought so well, observed not long before his death in 1786: "He who improves his land, makes waste land fruitful, and who drains swamps, he wins victories over barbarism." But for Frederick it was too late.

The Hohenzollern empire over the entirety of Germany originated in the Prussian pressure cooker, but it was not created by any sovereign, only by exceptional statesmen. The first of these notables was Freiherr vom Stein who served the respectable but dreary Friedrich Wilhelm III. Stein oversaw the grant of a constitution and other administrative reforms that followed the spread across Europe of French revolutionary ideas, a cultural seeding accomplished in the wake of Napoleon's armies.

The second was Otto von Bismarck-Schönhausen, a tough, massive, unscrupulous minister with clarity of vision and a precise idea of where he wished his king to go. He led the aged Wilhelm I into three wars, none of which the ruler wanted but which made him emperor of the Germans: one with Denmark over the frontier provinces of Schleswig-Holstein (1864); one with Austria, designed primarily to put that center of Teutonic imperialism in its place (1866); and one with France (1870), diabolically incited by the Prussians. In the last, Prussia succeeded in shattering the vestiges of Bonapartist battlefield tradition. When it had been swiftly and

Frederick the Great. He eventually concluded: "Glory is vain. Have men ever deserved praise? They have only been praised because they made a stir." During the last third of his life, he quarreled with most of his friends, lost his interest in music, and spent much of his time sitting or lying about with the sole creatures who adored him, a pack of greyhounds.

39 ‡

GROWTH OF
PRUSSIA

1417-1918

These maps give a con-
spectus of Prussian history
from the time when
Brandenburg began to
expand in the seventeenth
century. One may see,
by looking at all the
panels together, how
Prussia was really an East
European state until
1815; its center of gravity
shifted westward, in sig-
nificant degree, only in
the nineteenth century.
Panel 2 shows the early
formation of three un-
connected masses; Panel
3, the huge bulk of Silesia
relative to the small
kingdom that annexed it;
Panel 4, the fruits of the
Partitions of Poland.
Napoleon pared Prussia
down. The main crisis at
the Congress of Vienna,
and its resolution, are
shown in Panels 6 and 7.
Bismarck's enlargement
of Prussia appears in
Panel 8. The boundaries
established by Bismarck
remained unchanged
until the fall of the
Prussian monarchy in
1918.

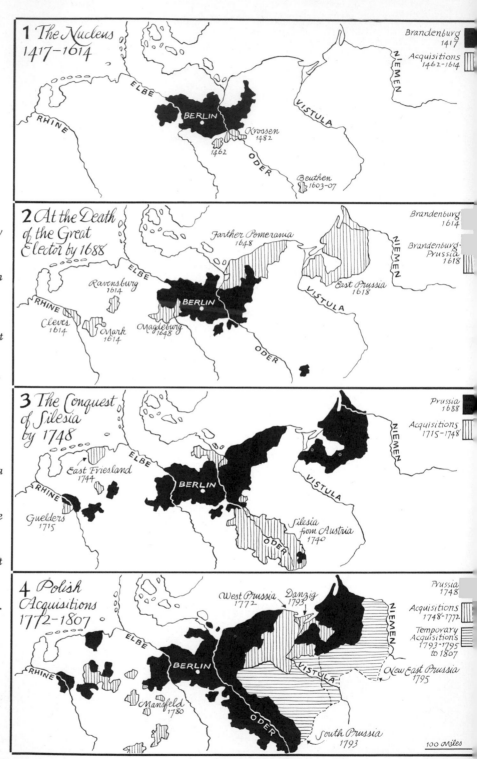

1 The Nucleus 1417-1614

Brandenburg 1417
Acquisitions 1462-1614

ELBE · RHINE · BERLIN · Krossen 1482 · 1462 · ODER · Beuthen 1603-07 · NIEMEN · VISTULA

2 At the Death of the Great Elector by 1688

Brandenburg 1614
Brandenburg-Prussia 1618

Farther Pomerania 1648 · ELBE · Ravensburg 1614 · BERLIN · RHINE · Cleves 1614 · Mark 1614 · Magdeburg 1648 · East Prussia 1618 · NIEMEN · VISTULA · ODER

3 The Conquest of Silesia by 1748

Prussia 1688
Acquisitions 1715-1748

ELBE · East Friesland 1744 · BERLIN · RHINE · Guelders 1715 · Silesia from Austria 1740 · ODER · NIEMEN · VISTULA

4 Polish Acquisitions 1772-1807

Prussia 1748
Acquisitions 1748-1772
Temporary Acquisitions 1793-1795 to 1807

West Prussia 1772 · Danzig 1793 · ELBE · BERLIN · RHINE · Mansfeld 1780 · New East Prussia 1795 · South Prussia 1793 · NIEMEN · VISTULA · ODER

100 Miles

‡ 40

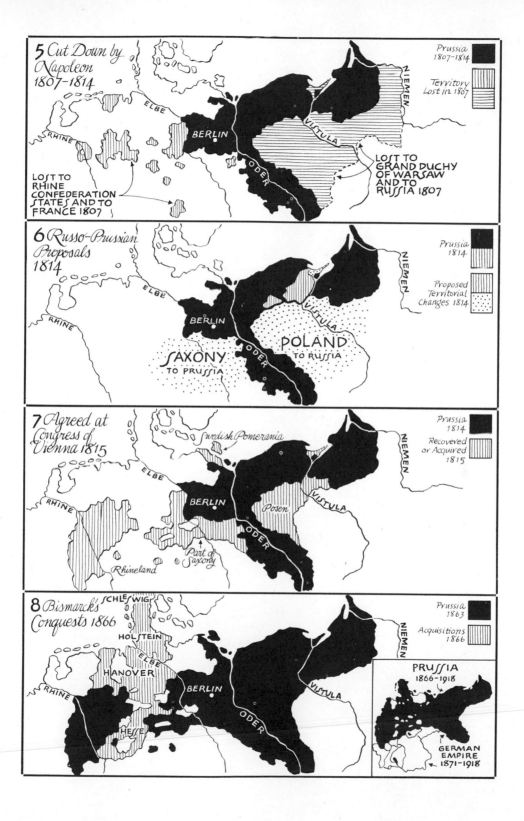

5 Cut Down by Napoleon 1807–1814

Prussia 1807–1814
Territory Lost in 1807

BERLIN
NIEMEN
ELBE
RHINE
VISTULA
ODER

LOST TO GRAND DUCHY OF WARSAW AND TO RUSSIA 1807

LOST TO RHINE CONFEDERATION STATES AND TO FRANCE 1807

6 Russo-Prussian Proposals 1814

Prussia 1814
Proposed Territorial Changes 1814

NIEMEN
ELBE
RHINE
VISTULA
BERLIN
ODER
POLAND TO RUSSIA
SAXONY TO PRUSSIA

7 Agreed at Congress of Vienna 1815

Prussia 1814
Recovered or Acquired 1815

Swedish Pomerania
NIEMEN
ELBE
RHINE
VISTULA
BERLIN
Posen
ODER
Rhineland
Part of Saxony

8 Bismarck's Conquests 1866

Prussia 1863
Acquisitions 1866

SCHLESWIG
HOLSTEIN
HANOVER
ELBE
NIEMEN
RHINE
BERLIN
VISTULA
ODER
HESSE

PRUSSIA 1866–1918
GERMAN EMPIRE 1871–1918

wholly eviscerated, Bismarck arrogantly had his reluctant sovereign installed as Kaiser of all Germany in the Hall of Mirrors at Versailles Palace, most arrogant symbol of the conquered French before their fall.

Unlike Frederick the Great, an astonishing man in many respects and nonpareil in the Hohenzollern family, Bismarck, their servant (who was finally cast off like a useless discard by Wilhelm II, the disastrous final Hohenzollern), left behind something more concrete than a mass of military cemeteries. It was scarcely his fault that the self-inflated final kaiser, Wilhelm, should throw all this away in a needless quest for even greater glory, now called World War I.

I once asked Konrad Adenauer, held by most people (including Churchill) to be the greatest German chancellor since Bismarck, what he thought of his ambitious Prussian predecessor. Adenauer said: "Bismarck was a great foreign politician but a very poor home politician. He persecuted the Catholics and he persecuted the Socialists, thus preventing the creation of a large liberal party in Germany. As a result the German people, in my opinion, were not politically strong enough to bear the power which they suddenly obtained. And that is what led to our collapse."

THEY BECOME ALL BODY AND NO MIND

With the splendid self-assurance and overweening cockiness of a spokesman for what was then the world's youngest ideology, Thomas Jefferson wrote of royal rule:

> Take any race of animals, confine them in idleness and inaction, whether in a stye, a stable or a stateroom, pamper them with high diet, gratify all their sexual appetites, immerse them in sensualities, nourish their passions, let everything bend before them, and banish whatever might lead them to think, and in a few years they become all body and no mind. . . . Such is the regimen in raising Kings, and in this way they have gone on for centuries.

Jefferson was notably passionate on the subject. He had gained his impressions of monarchy from his countrymen's revolutionary prejudices against Britain's George III and by some knowledge of France's Louis XVI who, although he manifestly did a great deal to enable the triumph of the American cause against the British, was not personally an impressive man. Moreover, a hint of Jefferson's jealousy of his first diplomatic boss, Benjamin Franklin, could have exacerbated his views. Franklin was a great favorite at the French court.

Nevertheless, exaggerated or not, there is much truth in the Jeffersonian analysis. He was never acquainted with any member of the three aquiline imperial families dominating this book. Nevertheless, he aptly remarked that "the practice of Kings marrying only in the families of Kings has been that of Europe for some centuries," and he foresaw the inevitable genetic consequences of this habit which notably helps explain not only the decline of Romanovs, Habsburgs, and Hohenzollerns, but also the disappearance of most of the world's dynastic crowns. As descendants of great houses became increasingly "body" and decreasingly "mind," they were less able to deal with changes wrought upon the international and national political scene.

When Jefferson entered the Continental Congress in 1775, virtually every country was ruled by hereditary or designated aristocratic families—with the notable exception of modest Switzerland. The vigor, therefore, of his bias seemed far less logical or capable of realization than it was to appear before his death when the fires of revolution had already been lit in many corners.

Revolution, as a modern political form, first occurred in the English-speaking world. The protorevolution, indeed, was that of Cromwell whose squirearchy overthrew King Charles and then, to insure against his return, decapitated him. From the king's execution in 1649 until the Restoration in 1660, what came to be known as the Commonwealth of parliamentarians, Levellers, Covenanters, Ironsides cavalrymen, and other Roundheads was in power. Few leaders in royal Europe, however, imagined that the regicide republic, for most of the time an autocracy under a lord protector, could endure indefinitely. They were right. Two years after the death of Oliver Cromwell, the great general, described by the king's men as "a brave, bad man," the crown was restored.

Oddly enough, when almost three decades thereafter, William of Orange sailed over with his Stuart queen, Mary, and seized power, his action was described as the Glorious Revolution. The word "revolution" was for the first time introduced into the language of politics. The seventeenth century had become increasingly familiar with the theories and discoveries of Galileo and Copernicus and eventually realized that the planets, including a round earth, revolved about the sun, not vice versa. Thus the "Glorious Revolution" was an expression coined to show that in the political realm things had been restored to where they had been, that planet Earth was, as it were, back in the same place—with specific reference to England—when a Protestant sovereign reigned again.

By going back to old times the symbol implied by revolution meant, in fact, what we now call counterrevolution. But this anomaly in terms was of short duration. The fact that two European counterrevolutions spoiled the dreams of progressive change inspiring the true revolutions that preceded them—in seventeenth-century England and in eighteenth-century France—undoubtedly helped strengthen the monarchic and absolutist idea and to preserve it beyond its normal allotted historic life.

The Thirty Years' War on the Continent, when Christian fought Christian in the name of Protestant and Catholic sovereigns and generals, created such chaos and devastation that authority, if it implied at least minimal stability, was a welcome solution to three agonized decades. This formula,

in turn, made it easy for mediocre sovereigns such as the Habsburgs and Hohenzollerns of their day to maintain and even
increase their role.

Essentially, most rulers had until then—and since truly
feudal days—maintained civil power over their subjects primarily in a kind of landlord function. Following the excruci-
ating and prolonged anarchy that flowed back and forth across
Europe between 1618 and 1648, even hitherto free but now
befuddled and impoverished people were ready to accept the
position of fettered workers or formal serfdom in exchange for
the simple and by no means constant guarantee of some protection. The position of the sovereign and his noble lords, a
collective establishment known as the court, grew and imposed
itself increasingly as dominator or owner of chattels, taxer of
those feeling themselves threatened with oppression.

The people, many of whose ancestors had established strong
positions in early bourgeois communities and free cities, accepted a status reverting to neofeudalism; they became the
virtual property of the court. Thus, it may be noted, serfdom
was legally formalized in backward Russia in 1649, only one
year after the Thirty Years' War ended. Relatively untalented
lordlings as well as indifferent kings managed to cement the
ascendancy of their family heritage in the old familiar name
of law and order.

The next major political upheaval—what soon became
known again as revolution—was not a European phenomenon,
although engineered by people who thought of themselves as
"Europeans." It occurred once again in the English-speaking
world, but this time among Britain's American colonies. Nor,
as in the political argumentation that followed the Cromwellian and post-Cromwellian wars, was there any confusion
about whether the transatlantic events symbolized true change
or a harking back to the past.

Unlike the Cromwellian endeavor, which took place just
off the shores of the European continent with its gallimaufry

of royal families, all of whom were a bit leary about endorsing the disinheritance and murder of one of their colleagues, the revolution that exploded more than a century later in America was far, far away. It didn't seem to matter to them much except as a way of poking a finger in the English king's eye. But raising revolution is an infectious disease. The Americans, feeling oppressed by "taxation without representation," seized upon ideas long pondered by French philosophers and British Whig theorists and put them into practice. When the French themselves saw how well that worked, they decided to ape their students. They too ultimately declared a republic—and decapitated the king who had so generously come to the American colonies' aid.

Europe's worried monarchies saw that this was quite a different thing, a most embarrassing precedent in their own backyard, no longer an occurrence on a nearby island or on a distant, unfamiliar, and unimportant continent across the seas. Yet when they sought somewhat halfheartedly to intervene in favor of the dispossessed royal faction, their attempts were divided and surprisingly ineffective.

France, then a huge, strong, populous power, responded with a zeal and élan that exceeded even the Gallic fury of the troops of Louis XIV, the imperious Sun King, a century earlier. But it was the French themselves who ended the republic they had created. They did so by permitting that exuberant military genius, Napoleon, first to take supreme executive power and then to declare himself emperor of a brand-new dynasty. This he gave international acceptance by marrying off his family on a wholesale basis into European royalty's faded patchwork quilt.

That ascendant amalgam known as the court, which became increasingly familiar on the political scene of seventeenth-century Europe, had been especially powerful—and also useless and wasteful—in the France of Louis XIV and his successors. It was against this institution—where aristocrats paid fortunes to maintain themselves at Versailles and vied to accept the most menial jobs, from supervising the king's kennels to attending his daily exercise on the chamber pot—that intellectuals, liberals, thoughtful nobles, and priests, and irked country gentlemen led increasing masses of the people in a revolt that eventually got out of hand and became the first massive revolution to shake the society of the Continent since ancient Roman days.

The curious result was that Napoleon, who as a self-made emperor aspired to the solid esteem of more established dynasties, committed a form of monarchic mass murder. As his astonishing armies marauded Europe between Spain and Russia, they spread the legend of the "Marseillaise" and of Liberty, Equality, Fraternity even while both they and their supreme commander were themselves violating that credo.

The French Revolution in effect began as an effort to speed up a lagging and but slowly evolving bureaucracy and irresponsible court into an actual responsible government which administered to and guaranteed popular rights instead of simply manipulating policies to suit the taste of monarchs or their crafty principal ministers. Had the original tenets developed as its first inspirers—and even its subsequent, bickering, and murderous successors—sought, the philosophically alien idea of a sort of democratic formula would have taken over all Europe, including that already ruled by the Habsburgs, Hohenzollerns, and even the barbaric Romanovs, to whom these concepts were so unutterably alien. However, in the name of preserving its dogma, Bonaparte seized the Revolution, wholly distorted it, and turned it into that quintessential paradox, a counterrevolution in the revolution's name.

Who can assess what would have happened had the French Revolution with its credo of Liberty, Equality, Fraternity not been betrayed by the brilliant and ambitious Napoleon who traded an idea of which he proclaimed himself initially the servant and whose time might well have come for the short-lived glory of an empire that ravaged Europe and removed France from superpower status. Napoleon himself admitted (May, 1814): "I myself have destroyed the revolution."

Liberty would have freed the serfs and slaves and other forms of forced and semiforced labor that still burdened the Continent. Equality would have destroyed the immense financial advantage of the royal and imperial courts and their servants, the great clerical orders, over the poor masses. Brotherhood would have brought freedom and spiritual ease to the oppressed ethnic and religious minorities: Central and East European Slavs; the Turkish-dominated Greeks; the Italians under Austria; Protestants in Spain, Catholics in the Baltic area, and Jews everywhere.

But Napoleon sold out the *philosophes* to a crown he placed upon his own head. Thereafter, he brutally assaulted one land after another between Portugal and Russia, rallying against him the wobbly assortment of German and Italian states, the archaic Spanish and Austro-Hungarian monarchies, the disorganized, puzzled Russian czardom.

Everywhere they went, although as imperial instead of republican soldiers, Napoleon's armies still brought with them a philosophical ferment. For the first time some of this heady omen of the future shone through Romanov, Habsburg, and Hohenzollern domains. Apart from local and traditionalist nationalism, no such fiery political concepts had ever penetrated there before, save in subdued conversations of intellectual visitors like the French Encyclopedists and Voltaire, who talked much to the autocratic sovereigns but, in fact, accomplished little. The imposed presence of revolutionary methods and ideas spread into every corner of a Europe that had just begun to stir with political discontent and became a revolutionary herald of doom for the prevailing system of royal divine rights. Ultimate change was as inevitable as remorse.

Yet, because of Napoleon's betrayal of the Revolution, a

military and political genius who lacked a soul, this progress was temporarily staved off. The death knell of inherited absolutism reverberated, but the echoes rumbled underground and, in the domains of the Eagle People above all, reaction continued basically to rule. Moribund dynasties were reestablished, adjusting but tardily and wearily to the social and economic explosions of the Industrial Revolution and even managing to crush its political reflection in the insurrections of 1848. If anything all three of the imperial dynasties dealt with in this book were revivified by their success in surviving yet another threatened upheaval.

Together, during this period between Napoleon I and the preparations for Napoleon III in France, the old autocrats won—for a while. They staved off the future by devising a Holy Alliance which was truly the kind of political act the Glorious Revolution meant to describe. Metternich, Castlereagh, the cynical turncoat Talleyrand, and a dazzling clutch of statesmen and sovereigns participated in or approved the effort to resurrect the past and, in the name of keeping Europe's peace, managed astonishingly to do just that for more than an entire generation.

Although rudimentary nationalism and rising popular expectations both sprouted in the post-Napoleonic climate, favoring more modern concepts in keeping with new political thoughts and an explosion of knowledge, the Congress of Vienna, convoked in 1815, sought to paper all this over with decorated parchments of the past. A largely fictitious German Confederation, claiming great pretensions and exerting virtually no authority, was elaborated on the medley of Teutonic principalities and kingdoms.

Britain saw to it that the key Channel ports were kept out of the hands of major powers; France was reestablished under conventional sovereignty; Austria-Hungary and Russia somewhat overconfidently refurbished their creaking empires; and the Hohenzollern-Habsburg-Romanov club agreed to support

The First Consul by Gros is one of the few portraits for which Napoleon ever posed. It was the French themselves who ended the republic they had created. They did so by permitting Napoleon first to take supreme executive power and then to declare himself emperor of a brand-new dynasty.

EUROPE
1815

"Europe, 1815."
Boundaries are those set
by the Congress of
Vienna in 1815.
Outside the Balkans
they remained basically
unchanged until the
Italian War of 1859,
except that Belgium
became independent
and the separate
kingdom of Poland
disappeared in 1830–31.

KINGDOM O
NORWAY
& SWEDEN

OSLO

NORTH
SEA

COPENHAGEN

UNITED KINGDOM
OF GREAT BRITAIN
& IRELAND

EDINBURGH

DENMARK

SCOTLAND

SCHLESWIG

HELIGOLAND
(BR.)

HOLSTEIN

IRELAND

DUBLIN

KINGDOM OF THE
NETHERLANDS

HAMBURG
ELBE

ENGLAND

WALES

HANOVER

BER

LONDON

RHINE

COLOGNE

BELGIUM
(INDEP.
1831)

ENGLISH CHANNEL

HESSE

SAXON
STATES

SAXO

PR

ATLANTIC

ROUEN

METZ

BAVARIA

OCEAN

SEINE

PARIS

LORRAINE
STRASBURG

WÜRT.

LOIRE

TOURS

FRANCE

MUNICH

BERNE
SWITZER-
LAND

TYROL

ALSACE

LYONS

BORDEAUX

GARONNE

SAVOY

LOM-
BARDY

VENETIA

RHONE

MILAN

TOULOUSE

PIEDMONT

BURGOS

EBRO

PYRENEES MTS.

NICE

MODENA

PAR.

LUCCA

PO.

TUSCANY

PAPA
STAT

PORTUGAL

MARSEILLES

TOULON

GENOA

MADRID

BARCELONA

KINGDOM OF
SARDINIA

ELBA

CORSICA
(FR.)

ROME

NAPLE

LISBON

TAGUS

SPAIN

VALENCIA

BALEARIC IS.
(SP.)

SARDINIA

GUADALQUIVIR

SEVILLE

CADIZ

GIBRALTAR
(BR.)

MEDITERRANEAN SEA

PALERM

MOROCCO

ALGIERS

ALGERIA
(FR. 1830)

TUNIS
(TURK.)

MALT
(BR

500 Miles

Boundary of the
German Confederation

FINLAND
(RUSSIA 1808)

ST. PETERSBURG
REVAL
STOCKHOLM
NOVGOROD
VOLGA

BALTIC SEA

RIGA
MOSCOW
BORODINO

SMOLENSK

RUSSIA

LITHUANIA

EAST PRUSSIA

DANZIG
VISTULA
NIEMEN

RUSSIAN EMPIRE

DON

WARSAW

KINGDOM OF POLAND
(1815-1831)

UKRAINE
KIEV

DNIEPER

CRACOW
GALICIA

STRIAN
PRESSBURG

DNIESTER
BESSARABIA
ODESSA
MOLDAVIA
(RUSSIA 1812)

CAUCASUS
(RUSSIA)

CRIMEA
BUDAPEST
HUNGARY
EMPIRE

TRANSYL-VANIA
(AUT. 1819)

DANUBE

ATIA

WALLACHIA
(AUT. 1829)

DOBRUJA

SEVASTOPOL

BLACK SEA

BOSNIA
BELGRADE
SERBIA
(AUT. 1829)

DANUBE

ATIA

SOFIA
BULGARIA

MONTENEGRO

OTTOMAN

CONSTANTINOPLE

EMPIRE

ADRIATIC SEA

SALONICA

AEGEAN SEA

SMYRNA

IONIAN IS.
(BR.)

ATHENS
GREECE
(INDEP. 1829)

NGDOM OF THE
TWO SICILIES

RHODES
CYPRUS

PALESTINE

BEIRUT

CRETE

JAFFA
JERUSALEM

MEDITERRANEAN SEA

TRIPOLI
ALEXANDRIA
EGYPT

53 ‡

its tiny membership against threats to their divinely anointed pretensions.

Largely because of Metternich's skillful diplomacy this wobbly system prevailed through the mini-revolution of 1830. Nevertheless, the vigor of bourgeois families and the boundless importance of industrialization, harnessed to steam power, created a new and restless base for an archaic superstructure. Raw materials and cheap labor became increasingly essential in Europe's developing economy.

When Karl Marx and Friedrich Engels analyzed this change in their *Communist Manifesto* (1848), they helped set alight a bonfire already nearing the point of spontaneous combustion. The following year a full European explosion erupted after the initial "crowing of the Gallic cock" in France.

The French, typically doing the precise opposite of the Cartesian logic they professed to worship, removed an acceptably democratic king and replaced him with what became an undemocratic republic. The latter started with the flamboyant romanticism of a poet, Alphonse de Lamartine, and soon disappeared under the ambitions of a pretentious president named Bonaparte. By clever use of referendum procedures, he soon gained supreme power and made himself a second emperor, Napoleon III.

The impact of 1848 on the three major continental dynasties was more terrifying than substantial. Metternich had used his Holy Alliance of Prussia, Austria, and Russia to oppose political change until, to his surprise, the Revolution achieved astonishing successes in Vienna and Berlin. These forced Metternich's retirement.

However, Prussian and Austrian troops were mustered to beat down the masses hollering for liberty. The hapless Austrian emperor then resigned in favor of his young nephew, Franz Josef, who ruled (amazingly) right into World War I. The czar got the eighteen-year-old Habsburg off to what both

During the period between Napoleon I and
the preparations for Napoleon III in France,
the old autocrats won—for a while. They
staved off the future by devising a Holy Alliance which was truly the kind of political
act the Glorious Revolution meant to describe.
Metternich, Castlereagh, the cynical turncoat
Talleyrand, and a dazzling clutch of statesmen
and sovereigns participated in or approved the
effort to resurrect the past, and, in the name
of keeping Europe's peace, managed, astonishingly, to do just that, for more than an entire
generation.

of them deemed a good start by sending Russian troops to Hungary where they helped put down the last burst of revolutionary fire.

Political revolution is a strangely imitative process, both vertically in terms of time (as with the influence of the American revolt upon that of France and of 1789 upon 1848) and also horizontally in terms of space (as with the spread of 1848's clamorous populism from Paris to Berlin and Vienna and Budapest). Professor Toynbee quite correctly says:

> Revolutions may be defined as retarded, and proportionately violent, acts of mimesis (mimicry). The mimetic element is of their essence; for every revolution has reference to something that has happened already elsewhere, and it is always manifest, when a revolution is studied in its historical setting, that its outbreak would never have occurred of itself if it had not been thus evoked by a previous play of external forces.
>
> An obvious example is the French Revolution of A.D. 1789, which drew its inspiration in part from the events which had recently occurred in British America—events in which the French government of the *ancien régime* had most suicidally assisted—and in part from the century-old achievement of England which had been popularized and glorified in France by two generations of philosophes from Montesquieu onward.
>
> The element of retardation is likewise of the essence of revolutions, and accounts for the violence which is their most prominent feature. Revolutions are violent because they are belated triumphs of powerful new social forces over tenacious old institutions which have been temporarily thwarting and cramping these new expressions of life. The longer the obstruction holds out the greater becomes the pressure of the force whose outlet is being obstructed; and, the greater the pressure, the more violent the explosion in which the imprisoned force ultimately breaks through.

Against this background one can see that 1848 was but a

stepping-stone from 1776 and 1789 to 1917–18. The spirit of the Holy Alliance endured despite the ouster of Metternich. So strong was the instinctive habit of authority still accorded the Habsburg, Romanov, and Hohenzollern rulers, despite their personal mediocrity, that the autocratic institution prevailed once more. Neither the newly influential middle classes nor the newly clamorous working class were sufficiently organized or sufficiently united to impose democratic methods. This was even true in France where republicanism once again rapidly disappeared beneath a pretentious tide of pomp and circumstance.

The enormous delay which thwarted and cramped those expressions of eagerness for a new life in Austria-Hungary, Germany, and Russia made inevitable a degree of violence when the belated revolutionary triumph came. Had 1848 succeeded either in undoing the existing power structure or in frightening the sovereigns of the Holy Alliance to accept the Industrial Revolution's political meaning, it is at least conceivable that a quiet transitional process to modern political methods might have been managed.

But reaction, not progress, was the key. Serfdom continued in backward Russia whose surly popular lassitude prepared her neither to tolerate a continued past nor to welcome an evident future. In Austria the emperor paid slight attention to the unhappy, truculent Hungarians or to the murmurous Slavic and Italian minorities, decreasingly ready to accept Germanic rule. Instead he devoted himself to splendiferous operatic ceremony and a Spartan personal life seasoned by persistent hunts and the comic opera pleasures of his bedchamber. And in Prussia, guided by Bismarck, a genuine and growing liberal sentiment was carefully diverted toward nationalist goals. The imperial dream was nurtured and eventually produced the strutting destiny of vainglorious Kaiser Wilhelm II.

The three great dynasties were each infected by a fatal

malady in 1848. That none succumbed to it earlier than they ultimately did was largely a matter of momentum: their own self-assertive vanity and the habit of popular acquiescence which, among other things, Metternich had prolonged.

To quote Toynbee once again:

> It is evident then that, whenever the existing institutional structure of a society is challenged by a new social force, alternative outcomes are possible: either a harmonious adjustment of structure to force, or a revolution (which is a delayed and discordant adjustment), or an enormity.

The imperial eagle-bearers used the second half of the nineteenth century to make inevitable an "enormity" without either preparing themselves for it—or even being aware of its imminence. Each dynasty's meager potential had worn itself out long before the dynasty itself subsided into history's attic.

Outstanding among the Romanovs had been a creative, brilliant, visionary, half-mad giant and a German nymphomaniac, long since dead. Outstanding among the Hohenzollerns had been the psychopathic heir to a boorish father, one who aspired to the arts and culture of peace and became a familiar symbol of warlike talent, who dreamed of everything and left nothing. As for the Habsburgs, since Charles V, the *Wunderkind* of political marriages, they slowly, steadily, undramatically but with the dignity of great gentlemen, slid down the hill of fame. In each case the flicker of talent was submerged in a night of mediocrity.

None of the three great imperial houses had adjusted to the arrival of political and social democracy imposed by the nineteenth century. Both monarchic England and republican France could have survived defeat in World War I (even though losing their colonial empires) because of their institutional strength. But, of the Habsburgs, Hohenzollerns, and Romanovs, none could even have survived victory. For, in Jefferson's words, they had for too long banished from their own minds "whatever might lead them to think."

III THE WALTZ TOWARD DISASTER

I<small>T IS HARD TO WRITE OF NINETEENTH-CENTURY</small> V<small>IENNA WITH</small>-out using clichés: Blue Danube, waltzing, café, *Torte, gemütlich.* Yet it was certainly a great imperial capital which governed an agglomeration of races and peoples and was given vibrant life by the artistic talents and learned discussions of these lively and contrasting citizens. The Viennese became a nationality of their own: boastful men, flashing-eyed women, representing a mixture of south Germans, Magyars, north Italians, Ruthenes, Czechs, Wends, Slovaks, Tziganes, Croats, Poles, Slovenes, Moslem Bosniaks, and Orthodox Romanians.

The heart of Vienna was a splendid baroque museum, thanks to the industrious pride of emperors and the conceit of their principal liege lords. A museum of humanity, it sought to teach its citizens to coexist by *gemütlichkeit* and *Schlamperei,* special Viennese words implying a charming, sympathetic, and agreeable but idle, inefficient nature.

Outside the city's lovely architectural heart, away from suburban palaces and low, forested mountains to the west, extended a dreary, squalid metropolis, leading along a particularly undramatic stretch of the Danube to the rural hinterland of empire. As the Viennese said to one another with smug satisfaction: the Balkans began at the edge of the Ring, that broad boulevard girdling the baroque center.

Although such world capitals as Paris and London regarded the flamboyant Habsburg domain as a weird, nonnational medley in Europe's continually shifting political kaleidoscope, its own subjects, or those with pretensions to education, considered that theirs was a truly universal state. They saw it not only as bringing under one governing apparatus a diverse mass that had become virtually ecumenical but also as a shield on the flank of Western Christian society.

This attitude had been justified during the heroic age of the Danubian Habsburg realm. That heroic age coincided with the pressure of Ottoman Islamic sultans fighting their way westward with turbaned troops, encouraged by drums and cymbals, and fierce, scimitar-bearing Janissaries.

The first Turkish siege of Vienna came in 1529 when the city was saved by stubborn resistance under the aegis of Ferdinand von Habsburg. The second Turkish assault came in 1682–83. This time a Polish king, Jan Sobieski, came to the rescue, acquiring vast booty from the defeated Moslem regiments. Impressive portions of this loot are still displayed in Poland at the Wawel, ancient citadel of Cracow.

The second Ottoman defeat, which occurred in 1683, had a profound effect upon Vienna. It removed the dynamic threat that had given the city a certain psychological vigor and religious fervor. Also, it provided curious impetus to a new development in Middle European society.

When the Turks were driven pell-mell from the battlefield, huge sacks containing strange aromatic beans were found inside their tents. This proved to be coffee, and within a short time coffeehouses were available to a citizenry that could henceforth relax in unmenaced comfort, exchanging gossip and ideas over the delicious hot syrup brewed in the new cafés. Eventually they even came to be used as clubs where musicians composed their scores and authors scribbled their manuscripts. Vienna discovered a delightfully novel way of life.

As the sultans retreated gradually eastward and southward, Habsburg troops followed on their heels, occupying new areas and acquiring an ever greater subject population of strange peoples. But there were no large further increments of Teutonic *Herrenvolk* to rule them; the gradual strengthening of Prussia and its appanages saw to that, blocking all serious thought of Austrian advances into Germany.

This imbalance of population—the proportionately decreasing ethnic prevalence of German-speaking Austrians as compared with their Slavic and Magyar fiefdoms—inevitably gave increasing confidence to nationalist movements within the empire. The latter movements assumed coherence as French revolutionary ideas began to percolate among the restive subject peoples. The confusion of cultures that mixed in easygoing Vienna represented an ever-sharpening and often bigoted disparity of traditions in the provinces outside. A kind of mutual political unintelligibility impeded organized advance toward the social progress demanded by Europe's new needs. This was the primordial problem that overshadowed the sixty-eight-year-long reign of Emperor Franz Josef from the very moment he ascended the throne in the revolutionary year of 1848.

Following pages:

The Ringstrasse in about 1860. Outside the city's lovely architectural heart, away from suburban palaces and low, forested mountains to the west, extended a dreary, squalid metropolis, leading along a particularly undramatic stretch of the Danube to the rural hinterland of the empire. As the Viennese said to one another with smug satisfaction: the Balkans began at the edge of the Ring, that broad boulevard girdling the baroque center.

*Archduchess Sophie of
Austria, mother of
Franz Josef of Austria.
The entire continent
was aflame when the
willful archduchess
eased Franz Josef to
power ahead of the
rightful heir, his
vacillating, unintelligent
father.*

That December the young sovereign, still eighteen, found himself amid the wreckage of the Holy Alliance and Metternich's long-enduring effort to share out Europe among its major dynasts. The entire Continent was aflame when Franz Josef's mother, the willful Archduchess Sophie, eased him to power ahead of the rightful heir, his vacillating, unintelligent father. The latter, after abdicating his claim, knelt beside the new boy-emperor and murmured: "Bear yourself bravely. God will protect you. It's all right."

Franz Josef inherited a seething mess. In Habsburg-ruled north Italy there were popular uprisings against the peace-keeping forces of Austrian Marshal Radetzky. These were sub-

Louis Kossuth. In the year of European uprisings, Kossuth, the Hungarian revolutionary, demanded the abolition of serfdom and the end of absolute rule from Vienna.

sequently inflamed by King Victor Emmanuel of Sardinia-Piedmont and his shrewd prime minister, Count di Cavour. Kossuth, the spirited Hungarian insurgent, likewise had raised the violent Magyars, always an isolated and rambunctious ghetto amid a sea of Slavs and Germans. They demanded an end to Viennese rule and an end to prevailing serfdom. When fighting surged through Budapest, barricades were soon raised in Vienna itself by the new working class and a motley of indignant minority peoples. Many of them were quite ready to agree by the time they heard of Marx's proclamation: "A specter is haunting Europe—the specter of communism."

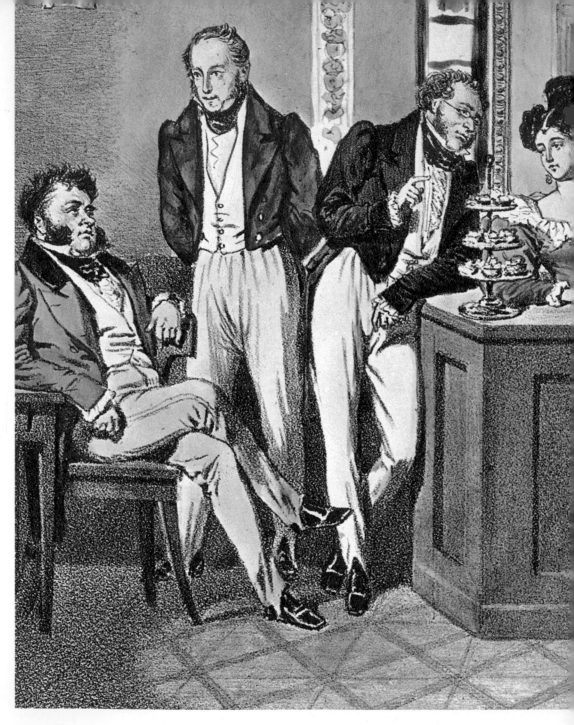

When the Turks were driven pell-mell from the battlefield after their
second attack on the city in 1632–33, huge sacks containing strange
aromatic beans were found inside their tents. This proved to be coffee,
and within a short time coffeehouses were available to a citizenry that
could henceforth relax in unmenaced comfort, exchanging gossip and

ideas over the delicious hot syrup brewed in the new cafés. Eventually, they even came to be used as clubs where musicians composed their scores and authors scribbled their manuscripts. In this lithograph by Katzler, Beethoven, second from the right, enjoys the camaraderie of his favorite Viennese coffeehouse, Das Silbercafe in der Spiegelgasse.

On March 13, street fighting began in Vienna itself and Metternich was dismissed. An independent government was set up in Budapest and claimed to be tied to Vienna only by the Austrian emperor, who was acknowledged as king of Hungary under what was to be called the Dual Monarchy. The Austrian Empire was now severely threatened and the court fled to Innsbruck.

When Franz Josef took over, Metternich had already been dismissed; the Viennese insurrection and the Italian rebellion had been crushed; and, as reaction triumphed elsewhere in Europe, even including Paris where the trouble had begun, Franz Josef set about curbing the tough Hungarians. His predecessor, Ferdinand, had proven incapable of facing the storm as relentlessly as Metternich had wished.

Therefore, as one of his final decisions, he agreed to institute a new ruling arrangement under which an autonomous government was created for Budapest. The autocratic Austrian emperor, however, was still acknowledged by the Magyars as King of Hungary. This administrative fiction resembled in reverse the Habsburg heraldic device of the double-headed eagle; the new formula envisioned an eagle with but one

The coronation of Franz Josef as king of Hungary, 1867. From now on Franz Josef held the title of His Apostolic Majesty the King-Emperor of Austria-Hungary, and in June of that year he and Elizabeth went together in state to be crowned king and queen of Hungary.

head and two bodies, called the Dual Monarchy. It signified little. The revolution continued to bubble and the imperial court even had to flee Vienna temporarily for Innsbruck in the West.

Youthful Franz Josef, enthroned upon chaos, proved to be a courageous, unimaginative man of soldierly tastes and superb, if distant, formal manners. His training, and consequently his habits, were military. He was strict and frugal, lived with stern simplicity, rose at dawn, respected the rules of army protocol and authority, and swiftly adjusted these to court ceremonial requirements, above all to his own position of supremacy. When he relaxed he listened to music, like any good Viennese. He chased stag, boar, and birds or he earnestly

Schloss Belvedere: Imperial Vienna in its most opulent loveliness.

pondered the official army list. He had one weakness, not un-known to professional officers: he was an occasionally en-thusiastic lecher. In his sixties, he was still a triumph of potent vitality.

Prince Felix zu Schwarzenberg, whom the young emperor inherited as prime minister, wrote of Franz Josef: "Physically and morally he is fearless and I believe that the main reason why he can face the truth, however bitter, is that it does not frighten him." Perhaps he did not scare easily; yet wisdom was rarely the better part of his valor. The emperor simply embodied a kind of petrified instinct of the Habsburgs.

When he dispatched new forces to Budapest to quell the rebels, whose concept of liberal nationalism distrusted the Dual Monarchy formula, they resisted with determination. As a consequence, harking back to the moribund Holy Alli-ance, whose creator, Metternich, was gone, Franz Josef asked for help from the Czar of Russia. Nicholas I was only too willing to comply. Already he was afraid the epidemic of European restiveness might spread across his own gloomy borders.

In May, 1849, the Imperial Russian Army marched into Hungary against Kossuth and his gallant rebels. They were joined by Austria's brutal general, Baron von Haynau, re-called from an assignment to crush the north Italian revolt. Haynau proceeded with a heavy hand in Budapest where he earned the contemptuous sobriquet, General Hyena. Kossuth and his principal lieutenants escaped abroad. They were hanged in effigy while hundreds of their associates were shot. In the very first years of his rule the unfrightened Franz Josef blandly approved some two thousand warrants of death.

As a youth, Franz Josef was slender, handsome, with almost poetic features. He was exceedingly active, energetic, addicted to riding, dancing, and able to make do with little sleep on his hard, soldier's cot. While the years marched along, he kept his lean figure, but his face grew tougher, and he

Empress Elizabeth in a painting by the Habsburg court painter, Winterhalter. Her sympathetic understanding of the ethnic question in the Habsburg eastern lands played an important part in Franz Josef's imperial policies, especially in Hungary.

GENERAL HAYNAU.

General Haynau. In May 1849, the Imperial Russian Army marched into Hungary against Kossuth and his gallant rebels. They were joined by Austria's brutal general, Baron von Haynau. He proceeded with a heavy hand in Budapest, where he earned the contemptuous sobriquet, General Hyena. The London Times *of December 1849 said that his "conduct in the late Hungarian war was stained with such acts of atrocity as will only cause his name to be held in execration throughout Europe."*

adorned it with muttonchop whiskers and mustachios.

One thing that did not change, however, was his disciplined habit of work. With rare exceptions he arose before dawn and spent ten hours at his desk. This did not make his cold personality popular with the masses, and, indeed, he was shot at five years after he succeeded to the throne; but he was governed by an enormous sense of duty which, among other things, reminded him of his obligation to produce an heir; and here again his mother played a dominating role.

As a member of the eminently suitable Wittelsbach dynasty of Bavaria, Archduchess Sophie felt in a position to recommend her niece, Helene von Possenhofen, for the task. Helene's father, a duke with a passion for the violin and with homosexual tendencies, had managed to produce two lovely daughters. They were Franz Josef's first cousins, but the Vatican had a convenient habit of ignoring the fact that such a marriage might technically violate canon law. Anyway, the enormously powerful Catholic family of Habsburgs often tended to intermarry when a question of new lands or political allegiances was at stake.

Helene was nineteen when the Archduchess Sophie moved into action. She invited the girl, her mother, Duchess Ludovika von Wittelsbach, and the younger daughter, fifteen-year-old Elizabeth, called Sissi by her family, to the magnificent palace of Bad Ischl, not far from Vienna. The matrimonial plan succeeded with one significant alteration: Franz Josef enormously preferred the younger princess and made no bones about saying so in his forthright, soldierly way. Eight months later they were married, despite Duchess Ludovika's last-ditch fight for her preference, Helene.

The lovely girl with lithe figure and masses of dark brown hair is known to history as the Empress Elizabeth. She arrived on the imperial stage at a moment more or less coinciding with the new development of the ethnic question that was ultimately to dismember the Habsburg empire. This question was always inherently latent after the Ottoman retreat had released millions of non-Austrians to Vienna's rule. It altered in political expression following the events of 1848 and was now heard in a susurrous, underground rumble, above all in discontented and subjected Hungary.

Therefore, it was a strange coincidence that Elizabeth was given special tutoring to round out her youthful appreciation of history for her new responsibilities and that the man chosen for this task was the Hungarian Count Majlath. Majlath was a wholly suitable and cultivated gentleman but with a typical enthusiasm for the Magyars and their individualistic, roman-

Liberty Leading the People, *Eugene Delacroix, 1831. The Romantics, particularly in France, were fascinated by and enthusiastically predisposed toward revolution, not only as a means of emancipating "the people" but as a supreme act of personal liberation. Through revolutionary action, the individual could experience the heroic life and achieve union with the spirit of history.*

Young Franz Josef *by Friedrich Krepp.*

tic way of life. Indeed, he saw to it that his tender charge started to learn Hungarian. This was a difficult if lovely aberration to impose upon an initially problematic marriage. After all, it was her husband who had summoned to quench the flame of Hungarian nationalism the troops of the Russian czar and the Austrian general "Hyena." It was her husband who had coldly consigned hundreds of Magyar patriots to the executioner.

When he married Elizabeth, Franz Josef conventionally insisted that he was "as much in love as a lieutenant and as happy as a god." Since he had never before known either emotion properly, the expressed sentiment might be regarded in due proportion except that he remained touchingly sentimental about this puzzling wife until her tragic death. Nor was the rather restrained and artificial relationship encouraged by his bride's teen-age fantasies—about Hungarian gypsies and wild horsemen ranging the flat, mysterious *puszta*—a prop to marital stability.

Inhibited by her domineering mother-in-law, whom she detested, lonely among relatives and courtiers who were older, remote, and mostly pretending subservience, lacking in the usual evanescent joys of proper girlhood, overpowered by the routine of a peculiarly rigid, formalistic court, the Empress Elizabeth soon became morose. She began to grumble at her courteous, soldierly husband, and had recourse to writing bad, somber poetry. The personal dichotomy of those who bore the twinned crowns of Budapest and Vienna sadly symbolized the relationship of the artificially twinned nations involved.

The very year that Franz Josef accepted the inevitable Habsburg destiny of dynastically suitable marriage, the Crimean War broke out. This conflict had typical nineteenth-century origins. Political convenience was mixed with moral pretensions. Wholly unimportant factional disputes—in this case involving rival religious sects in Ottoman-governed Jerusalem —were allowed to provoke ridiculous campaigns.

The czar, suddenly hoist by the petard of his own stupidity and his eagerness to dismantle the waning Turkish empire, despite Anglo-French opposition to him, called on his Habsburg colleague for assistance. He did not neglect to remind Franz Josef of the generous aid rendered by Russian troops in stamping upon the Hungarian revolt. Franz Josef, however, did not respond. This was the epitaph of the Holy Alliance.

A feud among the eagle-crested dynasts had begun. One may permissibly surmise that the Austrian emperor remembered this decades later when, as an old, old man in 1914, he found himself engaged in fatal war against the Romanovs and their powerful Western allies.

The Crimean campaign in which French and British troops fought stupidly if courageously against equally brave and badly led Russians, while the Turks—a supposed symbol of anti-Christian repression—remained relatively quiescent, was marked by bad tactics, worse strategy, some slight advance in the care of miserable soldiers, and magnificent newspaper reporting which for the first time influenced mass public opinion.

Having ignored his implied Metternichean obligation to repay a personal debt to the czar, Franz Josef tried to consolidate the position in his own imperial domains, a position terribly disrupted by events succeeding the volcanic explosion of 1848. He made a conciliatory tour through northern Italy, taking his empress along to inspect the sullen Habsburg domains of Istria, Gorizia, Venezia, and Lombardy. The affable Italians were much impressed by Elizabeth's loveliness, and the atmosphere of the journey was more agreeable than skeptics had anticipated. As a consequence, the emperor decided in 1857 to make a similar trip to Hungary, his second if subordinated corporeal entity.

To the immense relief of Elizabeth, who had come increasingly to detest the ceremonial stiffness that surrounded her imperial life, she delighted in Budapest and even mastered Hungarian, an exceptionally difficult langauge. There she

The theater in the palace at Schonbrunn.

found that all the more magical elements of her Magyar adviser's careful tutelage actually existed: the conjoined cities of Buda, on a bluff above the Danube's right bank, and Pest lazing along the left bank flatlands; the impressive public buildings being constructed; the handsome, vigorous people with flamboyant costumes and a hint of wildness in their cheekbones; the piquant food, strong Bull's Blood wine, haunting gypsy music; the feeling of an omnipresent countryside with its prevalence of horses. Thanks in good part to her sympathy and enthusiasm she was able to prevail upon Franz Josef to moderate his harsh, retributive policy. He pardoned and permitted the return of important exiled rebel leaders. But a personal tragedy supervened: their elder daughter, Sophie, died in the Hungarian capital.

It is difficult to ascertain with any accuracy how important a role the empress played in terms of concrete political influence. She was certainly valuable as a conduit of emotional sympathy from the unquiet masses to their rulers and vice versa. And she was helped by her striking beauty, her splendid figure, and piles of warm, rustling hair above a delicately featured, long face and tender brown eyes.

Immensely active, she knew music well, studied under the famous Franz Liszt, lion of the Danube valley, and was well acquainted with the writings of all the best German, French, and English poets, certain of whose works she actually translated. She was gracefully athletic and horses fascinated her; among her favorite decorations at the vast Habsburg palace of Schönbrunn were dozens of equine paintings and, as the techniques became familiar, early photographs.

She loved walking energetically, rising early with her Spartan husband. She venerated the sea, which to her meant primarily the Adriatic rolling southward from Trieste and Venice; she adored her neo-Greek palace at Corfu. Thanks to these qualities—and also to the fact that she produced a royal heir, Prince Rudolf—her husband, the emperor, increasingly adored her, a most unusual occurrence in the marital annals of the Habsburgs for whom imperialism was essentially a bedtime story of aggrandizement.

On the whole the restless Elizabeth was more of an escapist than an empress, neurotic, infatuated with momentary extravagances, adoring travel to comparatively strange places like Madeira or roaming the countryside on horseback. Yet she had a kind of tender feeling for her rigid, old-fashioned, unimaginative husband who, despite the extravagant pomp of his court ceremonials, which followed the fantastic Spanish formula ever since the era of the greatest Habsburg, Karl (Carlos) V, privately preferred beer to champagne. This symbolized his personal taste for the plain life.

The greatest favor the empress ever did her imperial spouse was to encourage him in a long, sympathetic liaison with a retired actress, the plump, agreeable Katharina von Schratt, who was the sole solace of his later years, after the death of his daughter, the slaughter by a Mexican firing squad of his brother Maximilian, the suicide of his son and heir, the assassination of the succeeding heir, his nephew, and the murder by an anarchist of his lovely wife in 1898.

As this chapter of the Habsburg dynasty began to approach its close, all the agreeable cliché illusions prevailed: the evermore enthusiastically received waltzes of the young Johann Strauss; the new wines and peppery food, the increasingly popular coffeehouses with their whipped creams, pastries, earnest writers, and conversationalists; the famous opera house; the sudden realization that the Danube was an attraction transcending a mere waterway or a militarily defensive position; the plethora of handsome uniforms; and, above all, the ceaseless competition for successful decor and insistence on gaiety in a society that had not yet recognized that it was doomed. But already unmistakable and increasing intimations of mortality shimmered above the Danube's coil and gleam.

The attempt to create a Habsburg empire in Mexico ended in tragedy when Maximilian was slaughtered by a Mexican firing squad. Maximilian is pictured here in his imperial robes, and then in Manet's famous painting of his execution.

IV

ODD MAN IN AND ODD WOMAN OUT

THE ENGLISH GENIUS IS EXTRAORDINARILY VERSATILE, AND one of its most impressive facets is the talent for self-government. In this respect, England led the world in three revolutions. The first was the Cromwellian revolution against egotistical royal rule. The second was the gradual but amazingly flexible development of a parliamentary revolution. Under this, legislators dutifully consulted their sovereigns but, in the end, told them what to do. And the third was the Industrial Revolution.

The Industrial Revolution not only gave Britain the sinews

with which to extend global power but also altered the prevailing social system, building up a newly rich commercial and mercantile class that could assert influence in an evolving political structure. Slowly a brand-new method of national administration matured. Victoria, reigning over the most immense, mighty, and fantastic conglomeration of peoples the nineteenth century knew, was also personally, in theory, the least powerful sovereign. She ruled by popular acceptance, not fear.

It is therefore not surprising that 1848, which marked the century's greatest international upheaval, caused relatively little stir in England. The remarkable and anomalous British political structure, endorsed by a far more homogeneous population than those of continental empires (save for France, which briefly experimented with neo-Bonapartism) should have been a lesson for the vain, grasping, land-hungry Habsburg, Romanov, and Hohenzollern dynasties. Yet they all chose to live by Metternich's dreams of unimpeded royal authority long after Metternich was dead.

In the sense of the eagle-emperors, Victoria, the British lioness, was the odd ruler out. Her sceptered isle had settled down with much-admired equanimity to a system that adjusted to modern conditions not even recognized as important by the pretentious courts of Vienna, St. Petersburg, and Berlin.

Adjustments haphazardly produced after a tortured and bloody seventeenth century permitted the establishment in London of an initially feckless dynasty of German rulers. Their first contributions to England's governance were even marred by inadequate understanding of the local language. Yet the Hanoverians assumed the crown at Westminster by blood connection alone without upsetting the even course of national development.

George I and George II were scarcely notable examples of the concept of majesty, but the idea of veritable autocratic rule had vanished before their arrival on the throne. George

III was a portly, good-natured monarch, not in the same intellectual class as the brilliant statesmen of his day, such men as William Pitt and Charles James Fox. But, even though he had the bad luck to preside over Britain's enormous territorial loss in North America and even though his mind crumbled during his latter years, Parliament's habit of on the whole tolerating even indifferent sovereigns, allowed the state to persevere smoothly through the subsequent debauched and profligate years of George IV.

The British royal Hanoverian house of Saxe-Coburg-Gotha (which changed its name to Windsor during World War I, just as sauerkraut became "liberty cabbage" in the U.S.A.) gained its title to the English crown in 1702. Prior to her coronation the pious and obstinate Queen Anne, then the last direct Stuart heir, yielded her claim to pass on the succession after all her children had died during, or shortly after, birth.

Descended from the undistinguished, unpromising House of Hanover, Queen Victoria, by far the greatest British sovereign after Elizabeth I, represented both Britain and its enormous empire throughout most of the nineteenth century. If not personally brilliant, she was a woman of much sense and considerable sensibility. She is famous for the way she managed to get on with dynamic, shrewd, and competitive prime ministers, to balance her prestige above the changeable whims of politics, to absorb with tranquil pleasure the distant peoples and territories added to her domains, to lead a dignified plain life (unmarred by a discreet and mild affair with a gamekeeper), and to adore her royal consort, Prince Albert of Saxe-Coburg-Gotha, a German prince of far more cultivated and liberal tradition than the Hohenzollerns then ascending history's horizon.

Among other things, Victoria established herself as the matriarch of royal Europe. Eventually her descendants or their close relatives were connected with almost every important ruling house on the Continent. Thus, although Britain was

The portrait of the young Victoria is anonymous. That of Albert of Coburg is by Winterhalter. The queen had no intention of getting married when her uncle, Leopold of the Belgians, proposed Albert as a suitable husband. Victoria invited Albert to come to London, but with no enthusiasm. When she saw him she became a classic victim of love at first sight.

Queen Victoria and the Prince Consort, c. 1858.

the sole constitutional monarchy of major importance (the others existed only in the Low Countries and Scandinavia), and although Victoria was the only major sovereign who did not herself lay down the law, she became the symbol of regal grandeur and stability, titular possessor of an empire upon which the sun never set.

This position, incomprehensible to continental traditionalists who had settled into autocratic, splendiferous post-Napoleonic reaction, was resented by the principal dynasts—except for the second Bonaparte emperor. Napoleon III aspired to broaden his influence and fought beside the British against Russia in the Black Sea campaign. The czar, already irritated by Britain's open sympathy for the Italian rebels against Habsburg rule and enraged by Franco-British invasion of the Crimea, was also deeply, personally hurt by Franz Josef's refusal to send him military help to pay off the 1849 blood-debt of Budapest.

In an atmosphere of dynastic disagreements, Victoria (stimulated by her beloved Albert) began shopping around the Teutonic marriage mart, favorite source of regal spouses, to find a husband for their eldest daughter, Vicky. For Prince Albert this was a personal diplomatic opportunity. As representative of the Coburgs, most widely wedded of the lesser German royalty, he had long cherished a dominating geo-political ambition.

This was to weld together the disparate states of a Germany whose people had still escaped the newly popular idea of nationhood. From the constitutional kingdom he envisioned, Albert hoped to build a single entity under a single ruler who would subsequently be tied by dynastic bonds to Britain's liberal destiny. Fifteen-year-old Vicky, an intelligent girl with soft eyes and a luxurious figure, was the bait.

Albert had long considered the only prince capable of playing the role he imagined was Friedrich Wilhelm of Prussia, son and heir to the ruler of that rising and

The eldest child of Victoria and Albert was not yet fifteen, but it had long been Albert's hope—and, therefore, Victoria's—that she should marry Fritz Wilhelm, the only son of the prince of Prussia and eventual heir to the Prussian throne. These are portraits of the young lovers at the time of their marriage.

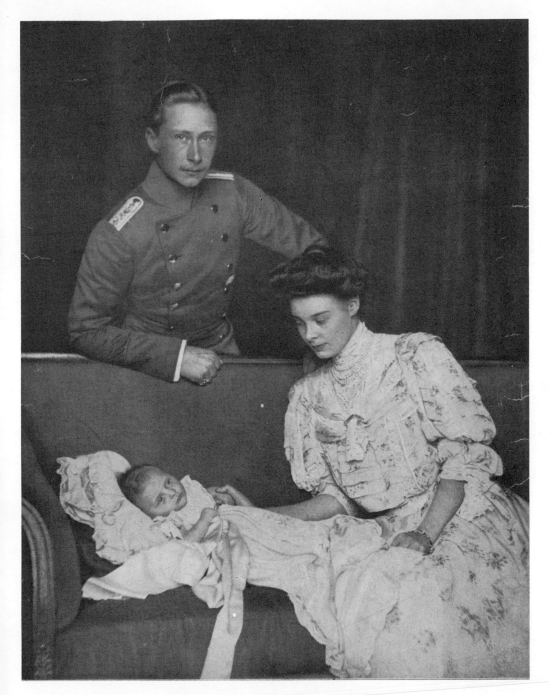

The family of Crown Prince Wilhelm.

dynamic state. Prussia had already established suzerainty over much of Germany, even including part of the Rhineland. Fritz, as the young man (then twenty-four) was generally called, had a liberal-minded mother who shared Albert's views both on German unity and on constitutional government. Moreover, Fritz's father had been a reluctant refugee in England for a short time after the 1848 revolution. While there he had listened politely to a great deal of unsolicited political advice from the parliamentary-minded Albert.

The young Prussian visited Vicky and her parents at Balmoral, the family residence in Aberdeenshire, Scotland, on the banks of the river Dee. After six days of riding together over the heather-studded moorlands, he professed himself enraptured with the princess. Queen Victoria wrote her uncle, King Leopold of Belgium: "*our* wishes on the subject of a future marriage for Vicky have been realized in the *most gratifying* and *satisfactory* manner."

In 1858 the nuptial ceremony was held in England, at the Chapel Royal. The occasion was generally accepted as propitious. A conclave of aristocratic notables participated and the famous Wedding March of the late Felix Mendelssohn, personally known to and much admired by the bride's parents, was played in public for the first time.

Prince Albert's dream was eminently reasonable, but it never worked out according to his logic. Neither principal, the seventeen-year-old bride nor the twenty-six-year-old groom, was in fact well suited to their mutual destiny. Vicky's psychological background and preparation for the heel-clicking, militaristic life of a Prussian court was little better than that of a gentle clavichord player for the atmosphere of a prize ring.

The princess was warm, vital, intelligent, affectionate. She adored her parents and had been well educated. She was familiar with all the better aspects of the erudite and poetic German culture, its literature, and its language. She admired her prince's handsome, blond bearing and was pleased that Queen Victoria, always susceptible, found him a "dear, excellent young man."

But, although he persuaded his new English family that he too was open-minded and liberal, he was not so bright as his wife. Nor was his personality sufficiently strong to bridge the wide cleavage between Vicky's loyal English bias and the stiff, reactionary Prussians, dominated by Junkers whose sole vocation was the army and whose sole avocation was the hunt. "How my eyes have been opened," Vicky wrote to her parents after but a few weeks in Europe's most narrow-minded, boring court. She also wrote: "It is terribly cold here and strange."

The significant contribution to history made by the befuddled English princess and her handsome Prussian prince was joint production of a son who became the Emperor Wilhelm II of united Germany and acquired a simple label, "The Kaiser," from the mass of enemies he made for his nation and himself. Most of these enemies, unhappily (considering who his mother and grandma were), spoke English as their native tongue.

Had poor Princess Vicky been gifted with magic foresight, the destiny of this baby, whose left arm was torn during an arduous birth and never recovered from the wrench, would have scared the unhappy Englishwoman out of her wits. For she was a determined and even pugnacious progressive. She always assured the Prussians that their society was backward as compared with Britain's. It would have been more than even her firm character could have borne to witness the hatred that developed between her ill-spirited, malformed Teutonic son and the liberal English ancestry from which in part he stemmed.

Two years after the boy's birth in 1859, his grandfather finally ascended the Prussian throne as King Wilhelm I. No contemporary could have imagined that this mild, amenable man of sixty-four would launch (if reluctantly) and triumph in three brutally successful wars, that he would be created the first emperor of modern Germany, and that he would rule until his ninety-first year, balanced almost like some meaningless piece of flotsam atop one of modern history's tidal waves.

Wilhelm I was, in fact, a decent, gentlemanly nonentity. He had so much confidence in himself, however, that he decided to disdain what he remembered of his 1848 experience as a refugee in liberal England. Instead he ruled as a virtual despot, backed by a newly invigorated army. Naturally this development epitomized the discomfort already felt by his English daughter-in-law.

He started things off by announcing pompously that "this crown comes to me from God alone." Like Austria's Franz Josef, whose unexceptional talents glittered by comparison, he also chose to sleep in a military cot installed in the palatial bedchamber. He was tough-looking, impeccably polite, honorable, strongly built, and rather stupid. The one profoundly important thing he did was name as chancellor Otto von Bismarck-Schönhausen, certainly the most brilliant, the most versatile, and the most arrogant statesman in German history.

Bismarck and Princess Vicky never got along. During all those years while she passively awaited the death of her husband's aged father amid the discomfort of uncouth royal surroundings, they each recognized in the other an uncompromising opponent. The difference was that the huge, red-faced, hard drinking Junker held the power. And—intelligent, cynical, charming (when he wished to be), and violent (when he permitted himself the luxury)—he knew it.

The princess was a true English liberal of her day, anathema to Bismarck's reactionary chauvinism. His vision was a Europe dominated by a united Germany, as destined by divine justice. He supported this view with the mealymouthed explanation: "I am content when I can see where the Lord wishes me to go and can stumble after Him." He feared the immensity of Russia, distrusted England, hated France, and had no use for parliamentary government. Thus, after dissolving Prussia's Chamber of Deputies, he proclaimed: "The great questions of the day cannot be decided by speeches and majority votes—that was the great mistake of 1848 and 1849—but by iron and blood."

Nevertheless, he was a very human as well as very vigorous person. He worshiped bravery in the peculiar German way of respecting it especially when it had carved tangible signs upon the body; he was a fierce, strong, excellent duelist and acquired saber scars at his university in the approved fashion with much clangor and well-protected features. This was a form of vanity as well as physical courage.

In several ways he resembled another man who was born during his lifetime in a country Bismarck personally respected but also detested. This was a man whom he might well have envied, a man whose career flowered after the Prussian had wilted: Winston Churchill. Much as both would have admired but almost certainly hated each other, they shared an unusual gusto.

Each, among other mutual traits, adored champagne. Bismarck decided, when launched upon that bibulous road, to save the bottles he had personally emptied, having them stored in the dungeon of his *Schloss.* Churchill was more modern. In 1941, aboard the battle cruiser *Prince of Wales* which bore him to the Argentia conference with Roosevelt in Newfoundland, he summoned Professor Lindemann (later Lord Cherwell), his scientific adviser, and asked him to calculate how deeply the vessel's deck would have been covered by the champagne Churchill himself had drunk, reckoning at the rate of a bottle per diem. The "Prof," as he was called, took out his slide rule and made the estimate. It was a matter of scant inches. Churchill was immensely disappointed; his record was surely less impressive than the Junker's heaped monument of glass.

Bismarck was not an evil man, simply an effective practitioner of nineteenth-century statesmanship seeking to create a place in the sun for his hitherto disunited and inadequately organized people. He disliked liberals, distrusted politicians, hated parliaments. *Realpolitik* was his approach. This did not, as he saw it, involve a question of good or evil, of morality. Nevertheless, because of his abrupt directness which had no time for abstract sentiment, he and the unfortunate English Princess Vicky disliked each other intensely and almost from the start.

Poor Vicky, disconsolate after her father's death when she was only twenty-one, frightened by the ominous and belligerent turn of events in her adopted country, sought to use her husband's rather tentative position to hearten the few liberal Germans she knew. She asked Fritz to dissociate himself from Bismarck's attacks on press freedom. Queen Victoria cheered on her spirited daughter, and the dubious Fritz took sides with her despite his devotion to his father, Wilhelm I. But soon the ruthless Iron Chancellor managed to exclude him utterly from political affairs while, at the same time, closing in implacably on Vicky.

He contemptuously referred to her as "The Englishwoman." One after another he placed his trusted personal agents among the princely entourage. Although, by kindly expressed reason and deliberate diplomacy, Bismarck was able to win the crown prince's support on several issues, between the Junker and *die Engländerin* the hostility was total, bleak, and undisguised.

As if this human tension was insufficient to inspire complexes in the emotional young heir, Willy, with his afflicted left arm which he sought to but could not disguise or hide, a wholly political factor heightened the growing differences represented by Vicky, the mother, at one pole, and eventually Wilhelm, her son, at the other.

The sentimental English girl, enormously imbued with matriarchal spirit by her own indomitable mother, was unaware for years of the fact that her lively boy, who seemed properly affectionate and whose handsome appearance was minimally marred by his physical weakness, had the slightest intimation of any familial divisions. She encouraged poor Wilhelm's efforts to cure his enfeebled arm by special exercises, mechanical massages, and electric shocks. She shared his anguish as he sought to manage unruly horses and was forced time and again, in the name of Prussian honor and Prussian courage, to remount steeds that had thrown him.

To Vicky's delight, the boy initially showed affection for his English relatives. He gave pleasure to Queen Victoria who urged his mother to "bring him up simply," although this was by no means meant in the rigid sense of his grandfather, the king, or Franz Josef, the Austrian emperor. After all, as Victoria explained, soldiers were not proper company for a young prince. They were not "free." Yet in the end it was the soldiers who were to conquer Willy. And Vicky's maternal love for her complicated son, who was to develop symptoms of paranoia, faded.

Perhaps it was a case of the Stoic philosophy applying: if a man loses a limb, he also loses an equivalent portion of his soul. No doubt the physical imbalance caused to Wilhelm by his crippled arm produced in him a commensurate psychological imbalance. He became if anything more military in bearing, in predilection, and in thought than a normal, whole boy.

Young Willy's passion for soldiering was encouraged by his grandfather, the king, whom the boy venerated far more than his parents. This delighted Bismarck who never got over his dislike for Vicky, suspected Fritz, and was already preparing with painstaking care to substitute Prussian efficiency for the hapless Habsburgs at the head of the loose Confederation of north German states.

In 1864, when the eventual kaiser was still a five-year-old, the chancellor took the first step, also for the first time ignor-

Otto von Bismarck. Certainly the most brilliant, the most versatile, and the most arrogant statesman in German history.

ing the objections of his sovereign, Wilhelm. He used the flimsy excuse of a litigious argument over the border provinces of Schleswig and Holstein to seize that area from Denmark.

King Wilhelm I. He was a decent, gentlemanly nonentity. He had so much confidence in himself, however, that he disdained what he remembered of his 1848 experience as a refugee in liberal England. Instead he ruled as a virtual despot, backed by a newly invigorated army.

Then, while digesting that plump and pleasing pasture-land, he again employed the issue's ramifications to pick a quarrel with Austria in 1866. Although professing a distaste

Bismarck, although professing a distaste for the "clumsy method" of war, launched the Prussian army under Moltke, in a smashing, swift assault that culminated at the grim Battle of Sadowa where the brand-new, quick-firing needle gun produced impressive casualties. Here the advance of the Prussian army is depicted, with Wilhelm, the crown prince of Prussia, at its head.

for the "clumsy method" of war, he launched the Prussian army, under General Helmuth von Moltke, in a smashing, swift assault that culminated at the grim battle of Sadowa where the brand-new, quick-firing needle gun produced impressive casualties. In that battle alone the Habsburgs lost almost forty-five thousand dead, a figure considered horrifying even as applied to the American civil conflict which had just ended.

Vicky could not mask her distress. She called Bismarck "that clever madman." She acknowledged that: "For me this war will ever be a crime, brought on by the irresponsibility and temerity of one man [Bismarck]." She also observed that her "dearest Papa," the late Prince Albert, "would be shocked and distressed beyond measure" by the holocaust. But this was by no means true for the wholly unsentimental Prussian chancellor.

He had managed in ten days to crush the only empire existing in the Teutonic world. As a consequence, he was able to gather swiftly to Berlin's administrative bosom all the ministates of western Germany lying north of Bavaria and Frankfurt. With much foresight he refrained from seizing any actual Austrian territory and thus avoided the curse of future revindications. This permitted the possibility of later diplomatic understanding with an abashed Vienna.

Having exposed the flabbiness of Habsburg power and having consolidated the prior position of Prussia in the entire area between Russia and the North Sea, but one final obstacle remained before a united, modern German nation could assert itself. This was the eccentric and unfamiliar British empire which, in a fashion vaguely reminiscent of Athens and Carthage, maintained itself by trade, by finance, by large, skillful fleets, and by small, darting, military lodgments which could not easily be destroyed before they vanished and without whose backing France was reckoned incapable of resisting German might.

Carefully, immutably, not even aware that his projects inevitably planned for the ascendance of an arrogant Wilhelm II, Europe's distinctly *odd* man in, who brought down with his excesses the last vestigial columns of the Metternich inheritance, Bismarck also consciously planned for the extrusion of all influence on the Continent of that odd woman *out,* Victorian England. In terms of imperial sex symbolism the latter was correctly represented by two empresses named Victoria, one that British empress, and the other, her daughter, only legally, not spiritually, German.

V

THE HALL
OF MIRRORS

THERE WERE ONLY TWO ALTERNATIVES, AS BISMARCK SAW IT, providing for the attainment of his great goal, a unified German empire, led by Prussia and dominating Europe. The first, of course, could have been development of a soundly based, popularly backed, parliamentary government headed by a monarch similar to the British queen in that such a sovereign would be more content to reign in consultation with designated ministers than to rule by virtual fiat. Even Prince Fritz favored this type of kaiser. But the second alternative, preferred by the chancellor, was to retain the existing autocratic system of what was still the small, if dynamic, Prussian kingdom, a system based on the officer corps.

To pursue that line to its logical goal, Bismarck recognized the necessity of keeping the other royal despotisms, Austria-Hungary and Russia, either allied with him or quiescent. And if he was to assert a continental priority, it was necessary at the same time to smash France so that its mounting friendship with Great Britain would present no danger to his plans.

Bismarck's decision was not based on any emotional dislike of the British. He spoke English perfectly, thanks to his early diplomatic schooling, and his first love affair was with a fresh-faced English girl. His disagreement was purely ideological. He considered democracy, as it was already evolving, to be an ineffective, dangerous illusion, and he detested illusions. Whenever there was a chance of liberalism gathering way in the Germany of his lifetime, he did all in his power to thwart it. He contemptuously called the parliamentary idea "revolution."

As a consequence, every time tired King Wilhelm of Prussia talked of abdicating to Crown Prince Fritz, with his determinedly liberal English wife, the grim chancellor balked. He kept the reluctant old ruler on the throne until his death at almost ninety-one, leading him against his own royal inclination into the three speedily victorious wars that marked his reign. Finally he arranged to have him crowned as German emperor in the Hall of Mirrors at Versailles, a prepossessing reminder of that royal France, Europe's military superpower, which no longer existed.

Bismarck had no use for Queen Victoria and her political theories, vague and pragmatic as these were. He held Prime Minister William Ewart Gladstone in contempt as a useless liberal and referred to him with heavy Teutonic sarcasm as Herr Professor. And he increasingly despised Prussia's Crown Princess Vicky, whom he regarded as responsible for infecting Prince Fritz with dangerously alien and radical ideas which he was determined to frustrate.

THE GERMAN QUESTION

1815-1871

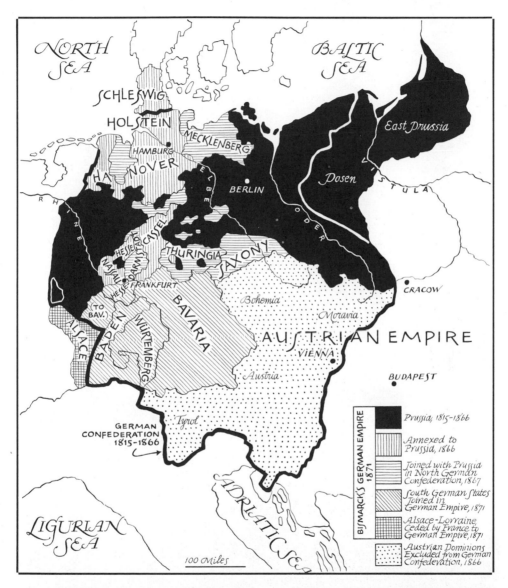

"*The German Question, 1815–1871.*" *From 1815 to 1866 there were thirty-eight states in the Confederation of 1815. At the Frankfurt Assembly in 1848 two groups developed, the Great Germans who adhered to the idea of an all-German union, including the Austrian lands except Hungary; and the Little Germans who were willing to exclude Austria and her empire. Bismarck was a Little German but a Great Prussian. He (1) enlarged Prussia by conquest in 1866, (2) joined Mecklenburg, Saxony, etc., with his enlarged Prussia in a North German Confederation of 1867, (3) combined this in turn with Bavaria, Würtemberg, etc., to form the German Empire of 1871, (4) conquered Alsace-Lorraine from France, and (5) ejected Austria. The boundaries of Bismarckian Germany remained unchanged until 1918.*

Bismarck's great goal, the attainment of a unified German empire, led by Prussia, was to be obtained by supporting the present autocratic system with the Prussian officer corps. The inbreeding of the military caste throughout Hohenzollern domains often tempted caricature.

Vicky, who had no illusions about the course Bismarck was following, wrote that constitutional governing principles "are the only ones which can alone be the saving—not only of Prussia's position in Europe and in Germany—but of the Prussian monarchy." Prussia, however, had already been committed to its iron destiny by its Iron Chancellor.

He took great care, following the war which eliminated Austria from the hegemonic German rivalry, to treat the Habsburgs with a generous civility he did not habitually display. At the same time he saw to it that Franz Josef was continually reminded of the terrible defeat administered by the French and Italians to Austrian forces in Lombardy. First at Magenta and then, when Franz Josef personally took command, at Solferino, Napoleon III and a briefly inspirited neo-Bonapartist army (added to Italian patriots) tore the Habsburg divisions apart in bloody engagements. A red dye discovered at the time was henceforth called magenta.

The recently proclaimed French emperor never realized that by seeking to popularize himself with the masses through giving armed support to the king of Sardinia and Piedmont and to north Italian states revolting against Vienna, he was helping prepare his own doom in France. After Austria was thus weakened it became even easier for Bismarck to smash its remaining military pretensions in a trumped-up war. Then, once the Habsburg empire was truly supine, the chancellor made caressive gestures of admiration and understanding to Vienna, founded upon common dynastic views and sentimental memories of the faded Holy Alliance. Prussia's southern flank was at last wholly safe and Bismarck could prepare his final triumph.

For a statesman in such total control as he there was nothing easier than to find a good excuse for war as soon as his troops were suitably prepared. After all, the intricate and unimportant Schleswig-Holstein question and its ramifications had already well served that purpose in facilitating con-

At the Battle of Solferino, Franz Josef had no allies, and his troops, incompetently led and inadequately provisioned, were driven back and suffered at Magenta a defeat bloody enough to coin a new word for red. Franz Josef took personal command of his soldiers, and on the twenty-fourth of June, 1859, he faced Napoleon III at Solferino, where the opposing sovereigns stood at the head of two vast armies which neither knew how to command. At the end of the day Franz Josef retired, leaving forty thousand Austrians dead and dying.

Following pages:
Napoleon III at Solferino.

flicts with Denmark and with Austria-Hungary.

The French confirmed to his sense of *realpolitik* an absolute necessity of dealing with the new Bonaparte, rendered giddy by his rapid successes, when Paris demanded a territorial adjustment as the price for accepting Prussia's increased power. This adjustment would have included cession of German possessions in the Rhineland or possibly Luxembourg. The latter state, which had been a member of the previous German confederation, was actually neutralized.

At this time, seeking to enlarge the authority symbolized by his sovereign, Bismarck unsuccessfully proposed (as had been done in 1849) that the Prussian king be given the title of Kaiser Wilhelm I, emperor of Germany. The chancellor also suggested that Hohenzollern princes should offer to accept any European thrones that might fall vacant. The latter idea produced more immediate results than the imperial quest and cunningly prepared for the former's advent.

In 1866, the year of Austria-Hungary's defeat by Prussia, Prince Karl of Hohenzollern-Sigmaringen agreed, on Bismarck's advice, to take over the reign of Rumania, a weak Balkan province only beginning to emerge from long Turkish rule. Three years later, his brother, Prince Leopold, was offered the throne of Spain which had been empty for some months following a revolution. Bismarck privately urged Leopold's candidacy on the Spaniards and asked that they act secretly and in a hurry. Thus the whole matter could be a *fait accompli* before France realized it was being ringed by German monarchs.

The news was leaked by mistakes in the ciphering of confidential messages, and souped-up accounts appeared in the press. Napoleon III haughtily demanded Leopold's swift departure. King Wilhelm of Prussia, as so often indecisive and incapable of making up his mind, agreed. At the time, Prussia's sovereign, already a septuagenarian, was taking his usual summer holiday cure, drinking sulfuric waters at the modest,

NATION BUILDING

1859-1867

Formation of Dual Monarchy of Austria-Hungary 1867

AUSTRIA

VIENNA •

• BUDAPEST

HUNGARY

LOMBARDY

VENETIA

TURIN • • MILAN

PIEDMONT

VENICE

PARMA
MODENA

PAPAL
STATES

FLORENCE

KINGDOM
OF
SARDINIA

TUSCANY

ROME

NAPLES

SARDINIA

SICILY

Unification of Italy 1859-1870

200 Miles

"Nation Building": Unification of Italy, 1859–1870; Formation of the Dual Monarchy of Austria-Hungary, 1867. In eight years, from 1859 to 1867, Italy was unified (except for the city of Rome which was annexed in 1870), and the Habsburg government tried to solve its nationalities problem by creating a Dual Monarchy of Austria-Hungary.

A dinner and ball given at the court of Wilhelm I in 1878. The painter, Adolph Menzel, devoted much of his work to the celebration of the Hohenzollern dynasty.

riverside spa of Ems. The French ambassador hurried there to convey in person the urgent news that France had been dangerously upset by the Spanish affair. Since Wilhelm also favored Leopold's departure, there seemed to be no problem. The king sat down on a bench beside the nervous envoy and reassured him that the matter would easily be resolved.

To accomplish this, Wilhelm drafted a conciliatory telegram to Napoleon. He sent it on to Bismarck in Berlin, already the nerve ganglion of an expanding Prussianized Germany, for formal transmission to the French emperor.

Friedrich III. German kaiser, 1831–88. Upon the death of Wilhelm I, Prince Fritz took the throne and held it only ninety-nine days as Emperor Friedrich III. He was already stricken with cancer of the throat and breathing through a tube, a dying man, when he succeeded.

Napoleon III, emperor of the French.

Bismarck, however, deftly altered the message just enough
to change its tone from one of surrender to one of defiance.
The amended text was then forwarded to Paris in Wilhelm's
name. Bismarck had consulted with the army chief of staff,
Field Marshal Helmuth von Moltke, and knew all dispositions
had been made for hostilities. The unfortunate Leopold
abandoned his Spanish pretensions, but Bismarck anyway got
the war he sought with France.

Napoleon reacted precisely as foreseen. One week after
receiving what he termed a provocation, he declared war,

The Battle of Sedan, showing Prussian troops in actual attacking formation.

and the Prussians complained in an injured tone that once again Germany had fallen victim to French aggression. They rallied the south German states to their support.

Even Prince Fritz assumed command of a Württemberg-Bavarian army. Vicky, appalled by what was happening and not in the least suspecting the role of her *bête noire*, the chancellor, called on her own countrymen for assistance in a conflict "we are forced into against our will." On August 4, after a bare fortnight of maneuvering on both sides of the frontier, Moltke and his magnificently organized Prussian army, with

the first efficient logistical support system of modern Europe, invaded France.

Since Russia had political problems of her own and had been well dosed with Bismarck's soothing syrup, the only nation that might conceivably have felt a strategic need to join in was Britain. London deeply mistrusted the growing might of Prussia and also feared for the future of Belgium, and the vital Channel ports, which Bismarck had vaguely suggested might be up for grabs. But the British, with their small number of divisions and preference for avoiding major continental conflicts when possible, also believed (as they would again do in 1939) that France's army, heritage of the first Napoleon, fellow-ally in the Crimea, and victor of Magenta and Solferino, was invincible.

Moltke's tide of infantry in spiked helmets, with sweating cavalry and rumbling caissons of heavy artillery from the efficient foundries of the Ruhr area, poured on to Metz, then trapped and surrounded Napoleon and his principal army at Sedan. There the short-lived second empire collapsed, led by its pretentious emperor. All told, France lost almost a hundred thousand men in a disastrous three-day campaign.

The coronation of Wilhelm at Versailles in 1871. "On me and mine devolves the task of setting our hands in true German fashion to the mighty edifice on principles in conformity with modern times and free from prejudices," said Wilhelm. Bismarck accused him of suffering from "emperor madness." On January 18, in Louis XIV's Hall of Mirrors, he was crowned as German emperor.

Even Bismarck was astonished by the extent of this triumph. He would probably have preferred to act generously toward France, as he had toward Austria. He wished to ensure future French neutrality if not benevolence as his nationalistic dreams progressed. But he no longer controlled the situation. Although they had lost their chief of state and their finest army, although all their frontier defenses had been overrun and the bastion of Metz was isolated and invested, the French grittily sought to continue the war.

This hardly distressed Moltke and his generals. They wanted to annex Alsace and Lorraine, long a contested territory between France and Germany, and had no desire to see soft diplomacy deprive them of their wish. For his part,

Bismarck, perhaps ready to toy with another generous, Austrian-type peace, obviously favored anything that enhanced the prestige and power of the great new Germany for which he strove. Moreover, the chancellor was eager to coddle the rapidly developing spirit of German nationalism and to estrange friendly feelings between liberals of both countries in order to weaken the progressive cause he held to be so dangerous and "revolutionary."

Moltke's troops therefore resumed their westward and southward march. They lumbered up to the gates of Paris and settled down to a siege. All through northeastern France the Prussians were earning a terrifying reputation for brutality as their commanders ordered savage, violent behavior in order to force an early peace.

Prince Fritz, who had been awarded an Iron Cross, confided to his diary: "I am appalled by the behavior of our soldiers and the ruthlessness of our command—particularly Bismarck. He has made us great and powerful, but he has robbed us of our friends, of the sympathy of the world, and of our conscience." Yet, despite his embarrassment, the crown prince was given command of the forces besieging Paris. He acknowledged, "I felt a lump rise in my throat as I thought of the innocent folk who would have to suffer."

King Wilhelm, rather befuddled and certainly amazed by the consequences of his amiable chat with the French ambassador at Ems and the seemingly harmless message he had composed, was installed in glittering Versailles, the world's most famous palace. There he made a symbolic and highly personal war effort by confining himself to bread and hard rations. Around him the Junkers and the military aristocracy complained and conspired while Bismarck, ever faithful to his tastes, consumed huge quantities of champagne.

Although an armistice had been arranged with the shattered Bonaparte regime, when news of this reached Paris the city rioted, spurned the truce together with the defeated

Wilhelm I in a January 7, 1871, caricature in Vanity Fair.

emperor, and a republican government was formed. However, this was politically well to the right of the furiously embittered Parisian mood. It consequently preferred to sit in Versailles, under inferential German protection, rather than risk confrontation with the capital's exacerbated savage population.

Thus in a strange and tragic way the killing continued even after Moltke's armies ceased their cannonade. A new French militia called the National Guard defended the city against the republican forces of seventy-three-year-old President Adolphe Thiers, fighting first in the name of a Central Committee and then in the name of a new organization called the Commune. Although the Germans had clamped their military occupation over all northern France they permitted the Communards to bring food down to Paris and save its citizens from starvation. But finally Thiers, with Bismarck's tacit approval, crushed the insurrection and executed revolutionary leaders. To the satisfaction of the Prussian general staff, an already anemic France was weakened even further by its own bloody civil conflict.

Nevertheless, for so audacious a gambler, Bismarck surprisingly and always sought reinsurance of his policies. Thus, he arranged a highly secret nonaggression pact with Russia to be certain his freedom of action to the west would not be menaced from the rear. And then, not long after the defeat of France, he negotiated a kind of new Holy Alliance called the *Dreikaiserbund.*

This tied together the Hohenzollern, Habsburg, and Romanov sovereigns and afforded what seemed like some diplomatic protection against the day, the chancellor was visionary enough to foresee, when the humiliated French would seek revenge. The pact carefully excluded Britain. Neither its actuality nor its purposes proved enduring and both faded long before 1914 came along and the czar supported France. By then, however, Bismarck had long since been dead, having (as his adversary Gladstone acidly observed) "made Germany great and Germans small."

Even before the Franco-Prussian War wound up, it was clear to the chancellor that his dream of greater glory for the irresolute Wilhelm was capable of being realized in the most impressive circumstances possible. He told the king that the moment had come for him to be crowned emperor, an idea that had flickered on and off in Germany for more than twenty years.

Once again the old monarch hesitated. He saw no reason to aspire to anything more than "the splendid crown of Prussia." Moreover, the various German princes, although united temporarily in war, were by no means unanimously inclined to yield their sovereignty to a superior. Nor would Wilhelm accept unless the imperial rule was voluntarily offered. Bismarck, as usual, prevailed. He bribed King Ludwig of Bavaria, leader of the reluctant states, by offering him a sizable annual income in exchange for agreeing to the election of a kaiser.

The siege of Paris was still on. It was a cold, hard winter and the inhabitants of the City of Light were famished. But in the long Hall of Mirrors at Versailles, Wilhelm shuffled before his assembled vassals, generals, princes, princelings, Junkers, and ambassadors and mounted a brand-new throne, that of the emperor of all Germany. Bismarck said later: "I carried him on my shoulders to the imperial throne." But when the new kaiser descended and slowly left the awed throng, he walked past the Iron Chancellor without a single word and proceeded onward to thank his triumphant generals.

From that date, January 18, 1871, for a brief period the newly created kaiser played a relatively active role. On March 21 he opened an imperial but submissive German Reichstag. In May he was induced to approve a brutal formal treaty the French were forced to sign in Frankfurt, ceding the two bor-

INCENDIE ET DESTRUCTION DE L'HÔTEL DE VILLE DE PARIS
par les Insurgés. (Mai 1871).

Burning of the Paris Hôtel de Ville (City Hall) by the anti-Republican insurgents who solidified into the Paris Commune.

NOUVELLE CARTE D'EUROPE DRESSÉE POUR 1870

War of 1870: new map of Europe in caricature.

ASSASSINAT DE 62 OTAGES RUE HAXO 85 À BELLEVILLE
Le 26 Mai 1871, à 5 heures du Soir.

The assassination of sixty-two hostages in Haxo Road, Belleville, France, by the Communards. This happened during the Civil War of 1871 between the Third Republic and the Paris Commune.

Louis Adolphe Thiers. During the Siege of Paris, the defense of the city had been taken over by a citizens' militia whose leaders formed a central committee to administer the city. The mass of Parisians were already suspicious of France's new bourgeois government and the old antagonisms of 1848 revived when, on March 18, Thiers sent government troops to the city with orders to disarm the National Guard. Thiers' soldiers were thrown out, and from then on an undeclared state of war existed between Paris and the Versailles government.

The troops of the Paris Commune destroy the column in the Place Vendôme.

Vienna. The old Burgtheater on Michaelerplatz. Watercolor by Rudolf Alt, 1883.

Wilhelm I lying in state. Wilhelm died in 1888 in his iron soldier's cot, a mildly popular simpleminded patriarch.

der provinces of Alsace and Lorraine and paying an indemnity of five billion gold francs, a huge sum for the time. Finally, on June 16, he led a victory parade through Berlin, riding heavily astride his great horse. Fritz and the twelve-year-old Willy curvetted along beside him through the heart of what had become Europe's most powerful if not its handsomest capital.

Thereafter Wilhelm left the fate of Germany almost wholly in the hands of Bismarck. Although remaining astonishingly robust despite two subsequent attempts on his life

The short dream ends. The funeral of Emperor Friedrich in solemn procession from the new palace at Potsdam. Friedrich III and the hopes of a liberal Germany were together carried to the grave.

(in one of which he was gravely wounded), he died only in 1888 in his iron soldier's cot, a mildly popular, simple-minded patriarch. Crown Prince Fritz took the throne and held it but ninety-nine days as Emperor Friedrich III. He was already stricken with cancer of the throat and breathing through a tube, a dying man, when he succeeded. Neither he nor, through him, his Empress Victoria, *die Engländerin*, had any chance to influence history along the gentle lines she favored.

VI   THREE OF A KIND

THREE OF A KIND MAKES A FAIR HAND IN POKER, BUT IN
power politics, unless the trio involved have common interests,
it doesn't serve as a valid basis for alliance. Yet much of the
latter nineteenth century was dominated by such an arrangement, the *Dreikaiserbund* under which the Continent's autocratic emperors swore loyalty to one another.

Since none seriously trusted the rest and their countries
had conflicting aims, it was always a frail system. It collapsed
when Austria-Hungary betrayed its partners by signing a
secret treaty with the pro-Vienna king of Serbia, a nasty

trickster named Milan Obrenović. On the whole the wobbly covenant reminds me more than any other of that *Ten Year* Treaty of *Eternal* Friendship signed between Budapest and Belgrade in 1940 and violated within four months when Hungarian troops poured into Yugoslavia, impaling many unfortunate Serbs who happened to get in their way.

The three dynasts, fully aware of the danger of mutual disputes—particularly in the Balkans where restive peoples were rising as Ottoman Turkey retreated—tried to avoid trouble by forming their imperial club, the Three Emperors' League. Its link was as frail as its membership was limited. Yet, for a while, it helped avoid wars when new tension arose between France and Germany and subsequently when South Slav insurrections threatened to embroil the Habsburgs with the Romanovs.

This curiously medieval alliance, in which interests of ruling families were regarded as paramount, prevailed during several nervous years. Bismarck preferred peace in order to organize the new German empire and saw the wisdom of keeping Europe calm. He used the fear of what we call democracy and he called revolution to scare his partners into line.

Therefore, in 1873, the first tripartite pact was initiated. In 1881 it was renewed for another three years, and the undertaking was repeated again in 1884. Bismarck reinsured his scheme by separate bilateral pacts with Austria and Russia. But Vienna, seeking to expand in the Balkans, violated its word by signing the double-crossing Serbian treaty. The *Dreikaiserbund* broke up—for good.

The three empires were in different stages of political and economic development. Each suspected the other—and with considerable reason. Their needs and objectives differed. The Austrians, having been excluded from territorial pretensions in Germany, by Bismarck's war and the subsequent Hohenzollern imperial coup, and having been expelled from many of their Italian domains, were seeking to recover in the Balkans. But the czar felt emotional blood ties to the South Slavic cousins of his own great people. Besides, he always kept one eye peering down the east coast of the Balkan peninsula toward Constantinople, or Czarigrad, traditional locus of Russia's imperial dream. And the Hohenzollerns, which is to say, during the life of the *Bund,* Bismarck, were above all intent on keeping the other two dynasties happy enough not to interfere with the new German empire by ganging up with France or England.

Three emperors is above all not a very good diplomatic hand when each keeps thinking of pulling a trick from his sleeve. Nevertheless, their participating societies and economies were all in a state of evolution and benefited materially from each year of continuing, nervous peace.

Vienna was certainly by far the most agreeable of the imperial capitals. As in St. Petersburg and Berlin, the court was the center of virtually every activity, but an ease of life permeated after years of revolution and warfare. When he came back from his defeat in Lombardy, to lick his wounds, Franz Josef told his domineering mother: "Now we are going to have a little parliamentarianism—but all power stays in my hands."

During the middle of the century the emperor had personally initiated a massive campaign to rebuild the capital on almost the same scale as that similar program launched in Paris by Baron Georges Eugène Haussmann for Napoleon III. This gave rise to vast real estate speculation and Johann Strauss honored (or satirized) the project with his "Demolition Polka." In the name of His Apostolic Majesty the King-Emperor the heart of the old city was rendered more magnificent than ever.

The exceptionally snobbish, distinctly frivolous court society took to swinging through the new centers of amusement: not only the opera, the theaters, the concerts, the court ceremonials, but an endless series of balls in a capital that possibly somehow suspected it was on the road to death but was determined to dance its way along. There was a party of one or another sort almost every night, even embracing the lower tiers of a society with as many layers as a *Dobosch Torte*.

The Viennese sense of display made the best of ostentatious habits acquired with the importation of the Spanish Habsburg ceremonial. The costumes of the higher nobility were magnificent, lavishly bedecked with furs, gold embroidery, silver belt clasps. On somber occasions the remarkably elegant and beautiful ladies appeared in black, set off by the splendid dress uniforms of the men, both military and court officers. The various ancient orders of chivalry like the Teutonic Knights still played their role and, on every suitable occasion, magnificent parades strutted before the emperor in full panoply and behind their impressive bands. The noblest aristocrats amused themselves like spoiled children in this inspiring atmosphere. Visitors to the delightful nineteenth-century hostel, Sacher's, were startled one night to see an archduke bounce out of a private dining room, naked except for his sword belt.

But the aristocracy of talent and that of birth rarely mixed. The novelist Robert Musil later noted of his Vienna that it regarded genius among its citizens, "unless privileged by high birth or State appointment, as ostentation, indeed presumption." However, Musil philosophically added: "A genius was always regarded as a lout but never, as sometimes happened elsewhere, was a mere lout regarded as a genius."

Despite the artificiality of such inhibitions, the reign of Franz Josef (who was born when Andrew Jackson was President of the United States, came to power just after Metternich's dismissal, and lasted into Woodrow Wilson's time) was marked by a considerable display of intellectual and artistic talent. There was not only Strauss but also Arnold Schönberg

The sovereigns of Europe: England, Lower Countries, Russia, Italy, France, Bavaria, Austria, Turkey, Prussia, Portugal, and Spain, 1879. Drawing by Epinal.

and Gustav Mahler, the fathers of modern music; Ernst Mach, the physicist; and Sigmund Freud, the founder of psychiatry; Arthur Schnitzler, Musil, Hugo von Hofmannsthal, and a host of widely known if evanescent writers; also, there was Theodor Herzl, prime mover of Zionism.

How the capital managed to produce such a cultural ferment despite its restrictive prejudices is a mystery. The Viennese thought of themselves as most superior beings and looked down upon all Magyars, Slavs, and Italians as inferiors unless they could prove their status as grandees. Manes Sperber, a writer who was born there but now lives in Paris, says Vienna "was the most anti-Semitic of all the great cities of the world." It was where Adolf Hitler, before World War I, cultivated his passionate hatred for Jews and other lesser creatures such as Slavs. (He fled to Munich before World War I, preferring to serve in a German rather than an Austro-Hungarian army.)

Of Austria it had once been said that it "is not a nation but a system of government." In the same way, Vienna was not the capital of an empire, since one didn't really exist, but of a form of life, based essentially on pleasure. And even for those who were not titled aristocrats or cronies of young bloods, there was the music, the atmosphere of gaiety, the good food, the strong young wine, the lovely girls produced by various racial mixtures, the splendid parks (including The Prater, an imperial gift), and an impression of perpetual motion with black-lacquered fiacres behind merry horses, their tails carefully combed, tapping along the broad new central avenues and the tree-shaded narrow streets, their drivers wearing curled billycock hats. It was a careless, spendthrift city, typified perhaps by one of the early and outstanding Habsburg emperors, Maxmilian, who first established Austria's Spanish connection but who always considered himself above all Viennese. Of him, Machiavelli said that he was "the greatest spendthrift of our time, or any other."

Vienna and its multiracial Habsburg domains were dominated by a single man from the revolution of 1848 right through the nineteenth century and, indeed, into and almost to the end of World War I. Franz Josef, that rather uncomplicated traditionalist who looked the part the people were happy to have him play, was a handsome cynosure and he carried off the scene. The dramatic history of the newly rich and newly puissant other Teutonic capital, Berlin, was far otherwise. There, three kaisers succeeded one another in relatively rapid succession. First there was old Wilhelm I, the reluctant dragon of the great new empire; then unhappy Friedrich III, his son, who ruled just over three months, dying with a tube in his throat, speechless and pain-racked with cancer. And finally Wilhelm II, the slightly paranoid, bright, unwise bully. This arrogant man, known to the later world simply as "The Kaiser," somehow symbolized Berlin itself in all its very worst aspects. As for St. Petersburg, its nineteenth-century destiny lay somewhere in between—although ultimately its ruler lost his life and it lost its role as a capital city.

St. Petersburg was a creation of one czar, the man for whom it was named, who still symbolizes his dominance over his city (now Leningrad) in a huge equestrian statue, *The Bronze Horseman*. However, it was, in fact, far less representative of Russia's despotic rulers than brooding Moscow, with its onion-domed churches, its maze of narrow streets, lined with wooden houses, above which towered an architectural eminence of vast structures erected by earlier czars or feudal chieftains around a central walled fortress, the Kremlin.

St. Petersburg (renamed Petrograd during World War I —when Britain's House of Hanover was becoming "Windsor" —and Leningrad after the death of the Bolshevik Revolution's patron saint) is a beautiful, fairy-tale place. Surely it is on a par in loveliness with those other European jewels, Bruges,

Paris, Bologna, and Prague. As George Kennan has written of it:

> The city is one of the strangest, loveliest, most terrible of the world's great urban centers. . . . The heaven is vast, the skyline remote and extended. . . . Under such a sky, fingers of fate seem to reach in from a great distance, like the beams of the sun, to find and shape the lives and affairs of individuals; events have a tendency to move with dramatic precision to dénouements which no one devised but which everyone recognizes after the fact as inevitable and somehow familiar.

As a dynastic symbol St. Petersburg was just as Romanov as Berlin was Hohenzollern. Czar Peter carved his city from the flat low-lying marshes of the Neva delta, a river along which lay an ancient trade route linking the Baltic to Russia's mysterious hinterland and endless forests. It was built by thousands and thousands of drafted laborers pursuing a pattern of broad squares, avenues, and long, low-lying palaces. From the start it was protected by coastal fortresses. Industries grew up around the early cannon foundries created to support a brand-new northern fleet.

In the late eighteenth century Catherine II supervised a second construction program, employing the finest French and Italian architects to replace the initial baroque layout with classical purity. Gray and pink granite from Finland was hauled up to line the Neva with fine embankments; theaters, concert halls, universities, and palaces sprang up. Catherine furthermore took pains to launch the Hermitage Collection which has grown into one of the earth's richest and most splendid museums.

Almost from its Petrine birth in 1703, St. Petersburg was Russia's most "European" city. Although the old fashion of speaking French in high society, even among the numerous families of baronial Baltic Germany, has vanished with the entire class that practiced this form of snobbery, even today's inhabitants of Leningrad, accustomed to looking through their window on the West, consider themselves more occidental than and superior to the claustrophobic Muscovites. It is a true "Venice of the North" and is at its most perfect in winter when snow lies heavy along the streets, rooftops, and frozen river, giving a clarity of vision to the icy beauty of Peter's marvelous capital.

But, though St. Petersburg was the child of one man and, throughout all but the very end of its life as a capital knew only Romanov rulers, it was not dominated by a single emperor the way Vienna, in the nineteenth century, knew only Franz Josef. During the latter's period of Austro-Hungarian reign St. Petersburg had four czars: Nicholas I, Alexander II, Alexander III, and the ill-fated Nicholas II, all of whom preferred to be known as emperor or imperator as a token of their "Westernism." It was a tragic family. As Dmitri Merezhkovsky, the fine novelist and translator of Greek classics, wrote: "In the house of the Romanovs, as in that of the Atrides, a mysterious curse descends from generation to generation. Murder and adultery, blood and mud. . . . The block, the rope and poison—these are the true emblems of the Russian autocracy." And, one may add, the bomb was the emblem of its numerous enemies.

Although the imperial system rested on a huge military caste under a rigidly controlled officer hierarchy as well as on an immense secret police system known as the *Okhrana,* this foundation was infirm. From the early post-Napoleonic era, starting with idealistic upper-class liberals, proceeding through university student groups who called themselves *Narodniki,* and on to the extremists dubbed Nihilists by Ivan Turgeniev, there was a constant opposition to the dictatorship. Serfdom remained a deep national shame; persecution of dissenters and stifling of independent thought were the habit; and censorship was a national custom. Police agents

Alexander II, Czar of All the Russias. From a photograph made in 1877.

Lenin.

infiltrated everywhere; Yevno Azev, an *Okhrana* man, worked in the heart of the Socialist Revolutionary assassination squads while his employers encouraged the bigoted, violent Black Hundred gangs and organized anti-Semitic pogroms.

Yet, despite such precautions, terrorists managed to blow up Alexander II (after two earlier failures). Some years later (probably with Azev's knowledge) they murdered the latter's employer, Interior Minister Plehve, and Grand Duke Sergei, uncle of the next czar, Alexander III. In 1887 a student was arrested for plotting with a secret group to murder the last Alexander, and was subsequently hanged with four other conspirators in the courtyard of a fortress. His name was Alexander Ulyanov. His younger brother subsequently took the *nom de revolution*, Nikolai Lenin.

Notwithstanding that the Russian center of gravity had removed from lowering Moscow with its medieval Kremlin and its pretensions to being, after Constantinople, the "Third Rome" to the cold, piny Baltic coast, the same Byzantine, Middle Eastern governmental methods were transferred to that brink of Europe. The total administrative surveillance and control of every citizen, from cradle to grave, remained unchanged, save only the nation's face turned to St. Petersburg, not Moscow.

The old system of feudal appanages mixed with a variety of communal hierarchies controlling land tenure and tillage was largely unaffected either by transference of the capital or passage of time. The Orthodox Church, with its magnificent antiphonies, enharmonic scales, and clouds of incense, was not disturbed by relocating the Holy Synod. And, although Peter the Great himself had sought to westernize his nation as well as its capital, personally shaving off the beards of his principal lieutenants, Russia remained a semi-Asiatic barracks-state until the end.

It is almost a miracle that through this grim final period during which the procession of czars moved slowly, grandiosely, and almost unconsciously toward its doom, a literary and musical renaissance still managed to explode, testimonial to the eternal vigor and genius of the Russian people. This, with rare spells of exception, was the period of oppression; and yet it was also the period of Tchaikovsky, the flowering of the great ballet, and, above all, of one of the extraordinary flourishes of writing talent known to history: Pushkin, Tolstoi, Dostoievski, Turgeniev, Aksakov, Nekrassov, and so forth.

The third capital of the emperors' club, Berlin, was spacious and pretentious, but without any genuine claim to beauty. In a sense, one might say it was not dominated by any of the four sovereigns who ruled it during the time-span covered in Vienna by Franz Josef. Until his unceremonious discharge

Berlin: Unter den Linden. In 1871, Berlin, at the conclusion of the Franco-Prussian War, was the most powerful if not the most beautiful city of Europe.

by the last and, in some ways, least emperor, Wilhelm II, it was led by Prince Bismarck who, after all, made Berlin an imperial city and also, incidentally, fathered the *Dreikaiserbund* itself.

Berlin held little importance, despite its link by river to the Hanseatic Baltic ports, until after 1415 when the Hohenzollerns had established themselves as permanent rulers of Brandenburg. Only after it became their residence two hundred fifty years later and was then amalgamated with other small towns and fortified, did it gain even the slightest renown or civic ambition. The rise of Prussia, and finally of the German empire, made Berlin more important than other, far more ancient, more populous, and more cultured cities. And when, prodded by the general staff as well as by commercial interests, an extensive railway system was laid across Germany, Berlin became its hub. Industries, canals, trading centers, palaces, museums, theaters, merged to develop it into a true metropolis. Berlin reached out in all directions to the extensive forests, parklands, and lakes that surrounded it and gave it a notably pleasant atmosphere even with its absence of architectural splendor.

Together with imperial grandeur Berlin assumed a military aspect that had never been important to its earlier, modest, commercial position. Its broad new avenues now became accustomed to lavish parades seeking to restore, in the wake of a French occupation by Napoleon's troops, a nineteenth-century self-confidence bolstered by the triumph of three victorious campaigns against Denmark, Austria, and France. The thump of martial bands and the frightening smack of the peculiar Prussian goose step became familiar to Unter den Linden, the Kurfürstendamm, and the Charlottenburger Chaussee. Moreover, Berlin, as it grew ever larger, wealthier, and more prestigious, developed brand-new claims to cultural eminence that had not existed even during the days when French intellectuals were visiting Frederick the Great at nearby Sans Souci.

Symphonic orchestral and chamber music assumed an importance in Berlin that had hitherto been gained only in Bavaria and the Rhineland. The opera and theater moved grandly into preeminence following Heinrich von Kleist, the

Prussian poet-dramatist, during the latter part of the nine-teenth century. While the pictorial arts were never to reach an apogee of excellence, the writing of both fiction and non-fiction with scholars like Schlegel and Adolf Harnack and romantics like von Arnim, Brentano, and Theodor Fontana settling in Berlin, gave it increasing intellectual weight. The capital's magazines and daily newspapers assumed growing importance; a special brand of satirical wit became its trade-mark. Robert Koch and Hermann von Helmholtz conducted their scientific inquiries there.

By the time the nineteenth century entered its final quarter each of the three imperial eagle dynasties had managed in one or another way to impress its personality upon its chosen capital: Franz Josef by sheer longevity and an ability to lead a dual life of Spartan simplicity and resplendent Spanish court ceremonial; the Romanovs by consolidating in the lovely, snowbound city of their own creation all the trappings of a refulgence marked by traditions of Byzantium and cen-tral Asia; and the Hohenzollerns by an increasingly tragi-comic procession of overbearing but efficient and splendidly attired drum majors.

The eagle dynasties shared several traits in common. All three suffered from tragedies at this time: murders and sui-cides among the Habsburgs; assassinations and attempted assassinations among the Romanovs; cancer and brutality among the Hohenzollerns. All three were unabashedly anti-Semitic, immensely caste-ridden, ceremoniously pompous, and almost ridiculously militaristic. And each was infected by its own variety of plots: the continual war between the *Okhrana* and underground terrorists in Russia; deep-seated spy rings in Austria (featuring the infamous Colonel Redl, who headed Habsburg military intelligence while he was on Russia's payroll); and incessantly scheming military cabals in Germany which laid down aggressive plans that had subsequently to be imposed upon the emperor and his diplomats.

All three pretended to observe some kind of parliamentary method and none of them really honored the implied obligation. ". . . A little parliamentarianism—but all power stays in my hands," said Franz Josef. "Men are like animals—they're contented so long as they're secure and well fed," said Bismarck. "Constitutional liberalism is a heresy as well as a stupid chimera," said Konstantin Pobedonostsev, gray eminence of Alexander III.

VII

FIRST SIGNS
OF DANGER

In the ninth decade of the nineteenth century each of the eagle dynasties was stricken with a catatonic experience. Czar Alexander II, that rare thing among Romanovs, an intelligent man who, although bleakly conservative when compared with the western concept of a liberal, still eliminated serfdom, was assassinated by terrorists in 1881. This brought to the throne Alexander III, an immense and immensely reactionary ruler who snuffed out any flicker of progress.

In 1888 poor Emperor Friedrich III died in Berlin of his

intolerably painful cancer. Wilhelm II succeeded. And in 1889 Crown Prince Rudolf, the intelligent son and heir of Franz Josef, committed suicide in an imperial hunting lodge together with his young mistress. Rudolf had progressive ideas of popular reform, equal rights among different nationalities, and the obligation of a sovereign to his people.

Thus, in a few brief years, the cause of social and political advance in a vast and potentially promising part of that world which called itself civilized was immeasurably set back. Alexander III was so horrified by his father's murder that he reintroduced the dark ages to his gloomy country. The new czar was huge and muscular, in appearance a true descendant of Peter the Great.

In fact, it is at best dubious that, like the first two Alexanders, his veins contained any Romanov blood at all. One may consider it unlikely that Catherine the Great was ever impregnated by her husband, Peter III, before she had him murdered. She herself was a hundred percent German, and her lovers were a mixed lot prior to the birth of Paul, her legal heir. But if not an imperial Slav, one might say, Alexander III seemed an affirmation of Lamarckian genetics, the living proof that acquired characteristics can be inherited. He was overwhelmingly Russian.

Also, he was a political throwback. He cancelled or eviscerated the various reform measures his father had already sponsored, even ordering his censorship to forbid press mention of the very word "constitution." He ordered a brutal and extensive campaign against all revolutionary organizations (which was how Lenin's brother was swept up by the police and hanged just six years later, a deed for which the Romanovs were repaid manifold within three decades). And he selected as his most intimate adviser (and tutor to his unfortunate son, Nicholas II, last of the Romanovs) the cold, cruel Konstantin Pobedonostsev, who repressed anything having to do with the

Professor Konstantin Pobedonostsev, tutor of Alexander III, taught him three things: nationalism, autocracy, and orthodoxy. He was the ascetic embodiment of reaction and, as Procurator of the Holy Synod, the suppressor of everything un-Orthodox— Doukhobors, Stundists (Baptists), and Jews. Because of him, under Alexander III came Russia's first pogroms in Odessa and Kiev.

mind: education, press, jury trial, and even peaceful religious dissent.

The end of Friedrich III after a tragically brief reign was an unmitigated disaster for his nation and for the world. It was not simply a question of a vanished last chance that the lessons of Victoria and Albert, so well learned by their daughter, the German empress, might be given the opportunity to flourish with royal encouragement. Far worse, Friedrich's premature death brought to the throne a conceited psychological unbalanced coxcomb.

Wilhelm II went through life with his mouth open and his ears closed. He believed almost everything he said. In that approved Wagnerian fashion, to be so lugubriously emulated by Hitler one war later, he dreamed of glory and brought only manifest catastrophe. But unlike the intuitive if dreadful genius who finished the gravedigger's job Wilhelm had begun, the last kaiser managed to finish his life tranquilly sawing wood as a comfortable exile in Holland, muttering platitudes about what might have been.

Wilhelm's childhood was not happy. He resented his mother, never admired his father, and probably was jealous of their implied preference for his healthier brothers and sisters. He suffered both pain and embarrassment from his weak arm which never improved despite incessant medical treatments. When Prince Fritz succeeded to the throne at last —and promptly died—Wilhelm ordered an autopsy to prove the cause had been cancer. This was a cruel way of embarrassing his mother who had always denied that medical fact.

Wilhelm's grandfather, the first emperor, seemed to him an infinitely nobler figure than his father. Bismarck sought and managed to exercise a considerable influence over him, even bribing him by allowing the perusal of state papers kept away from Prince Fritz. Nevertheless, Wilhelm's first major decision, when he himself became kaiser, was to discharge that astonishing old statesman who had served the German people so well with his mixture of subtle and brutal efficiency.

In 1881, the year of the czar's assassination, twenty-two-year-old Wilhelm married Princess Augusta Victoria of Schleswig-Holstein-Augustenburg, a pleasant pious girl known to her intimates as "Dona." Already before his accession in 1888, he started to learn something of the complex patterns of dynastic diplomacy. Baron Friedrich von Holstein, a slick diplomat, began filling him in on Bismarck's instructions and told him, among other things, of the *Dreikaiserbund*. But Holstein left little impress. His name is principally known to history by his single culinary contribution, a veal cutlet covered by a fried egg.

When Wilhelm inherited the empire in 1888, Bismarck had been privately warned by the young man's father, the late Kaiser Friedrich, that he was an immature, inexperienced prince much inclined to overvalue his own capacities. Despite extensive briefings from Holstein and even from the Iron Chancellor himself, he really knew little about either internal or external policy when he mounted the throne. The prin-

In 1881, the year of Alexander II's assassination, Wilhelm, at the age of twenty-two, married Princess Augusta Victoria of Schleswig-Holstein-Augustenberg, a large, placid, fertile girl, known in the family as Dona—"the cow from Holstein," Bismarck called her.

Baron Friedrich von Holstein. Before Wilhelm's accession in 1888, he started to learn something of the complex patterns of dynastic diplomacy. Baron Freidrich von Holstein, a slick diplomat, began filling him in on Bismarck's instructions and told him among other things, of the Dreikaiserbund. But Holstein left little impress. His name is principally known to history by his single culinary contribution, a veal cutlet covered by a fried egg.

ciples which governed his reign were belief in a powerful armed force, a strong monarchy, and foreign respect for his empire. Before he had been kaiser a decade he happily boasted: "I trust in God and in my unsheathed sword, and I piss on all resolutions of international conferences."

His egomania was sometimes quite astonishing. He publicly declared that "The king's will is the highest law" and "I regard myself as an instrument of Heaven." In a speech to German marines, departing for China during the Boxer Rebellion, he gave his people the subsequent sobriquet of "Huns" by exhorting the detachment: "Give no quarter. Take no prisoners. Even as a thousand years ago when the Huns under King Attila made such a name for themselves as still resounds in terror, so may the name of Germany resound through Chinese history for a thousand years."

Despite his boasts, he was never truly confident of either his prowess or his judgment so long as Bismarck remained at the helm as chancellor. Although the old man had gone out of his way to flatter Wilhelm even as a young prince (and, incidentally, had helped encourage Willy's distaste for his mother and her political ideas), he astutely and very soon realized that this antidote for the disease of English parliamentarianism was perhaps even worse than the malady itself.

Bismarck had deliberately sought to deflect French dynamism and British interest in European affairs to imperial aspirations overseas, in distant Africa and Asia, leaving Berlin a fair field on the Continent. He was worried by the new kaiser's giddy talk of building an ever-larger battle fleet and seeking colonies for Germany as well. The chancellor even speculated in a letter to his wife that perhaps "I have been the means of making it [the imperial authority] a little too powerful." Vicky, shoved into the background of isolated widowhood, expressed herself more assertively. She foresaw the evil demon in her son the emperor. "It seems," she wrote with sadly accurate clairvoyance, "as if I had seen a fine, noble ship sink at sea, with all the nation's hopes, its freedom, its progress."

The first significant steps taken by the last kaiser were to discard his mother as a heinous influence, to visit St. Petersburg and conclude by intuition that the czar was building up Russian armed strength only to aim it at Germany, and therefore to respond by constructing an even more powerful military machine of his own. His initial proclamation announced: "We belong to each other—I and the army—we were born for each other." And his oddly personal conception of himself as a super-field marshal infected all his policy. His postscript to the kind of democracy toward which his parents had sought to lead the Germans blatantly differed from their ideal. "The people are the troops and I am their commander in chief," he prattled.

An open clash between this inexperienced young sovereign, overwhelmed by his own imagined importance, and Bismarck was not long in coming. Wilhelm blithely ignored an edict that had been decreed in 1850 which forbade the sovereign (then only king of Prussia) from consulting ministers without first advising the chancellor, as head of the governing cabinet. But Wilhelm forgot this obligation, if indeed he really knew about it, and often talked matters of state over with his special cronies, like Baron von Holstein.

When Bismarck objected, the kaiser made an issue of the matter, and when the chancellor pushed it even harder, he was bluntly fired in 1890. Wilhelm confidently boasted: "The duty of watch-keeping officer aboard the ship of state has devolved upon me now. The course remains as it was. Full steam ahead." Even Holstein, a cause of the immutable clash, acknowledged: "His Majesty has dramatic rather than political instincts." The humiliated Bismarck stooped to seeking support from ex-Empress Vicky—to no avail. All Europe wondered what would happen now that the event had finally occurred and, as depicted in *Punch*'s famous cartoon, the pilot had been dropped.

Wilhelm's grandson, Prince Louis Ferdinand of Prussia, has told me the kaiser was convinced Bismarck wanted to seize all power for himself in a German version of the famous Japanese shogunate. While I doubt that the old chancellor had this in mind, the kaiser certainly managed to surround himself increasingly with toadies and an unhelpful coterie of yes-men. Among these, of course, was Holstein, a career diplomat of noble Mecklenburg family, who was initially promoted to high office by Bismarck. After the latter's fall he became known as the "wirepuller in chief" whose influence was everywhere. Although three men succeeded Bismarck as chancellor and there was a like number of foreign ministers, Holstein came in the end to be regarded as the technical master and primary instigator of German policy—always, however, in Wilhelm's name and with his advance approval.

Holstein was a clever, shifty man. Initially he gained influence by spying for Bismarck on Holstein's own associates. Later he turned violently against his former patron, displaying for him an unmitigated hatred. The great aim of his policy was to turn Britain and Russia against each other, but he succeeded only in turning both against Germany.

Holstein, who died in 1909, had already fallen from power at the court three years earlier. This occurred thanks not only to his penchant for schemes but particularly to the machinations of Prince Philip zu Eulenburg-Hertefeld whom he in turn succeeded in destroying. Eulenburg, a sycophantic hanger-on of the kaiser, fancied himself a stylish wit in the manner of Oscar Wilde, with whom, in fact, the only trait he apparently shared was homosexuality, a tendency for which he was subsequently tried. More than a decade older than Wilhelm, he cultivated a languorous, artificial manner that stood out strikingly in the martial society of Berlin. He wrote inferior poetry which he was fond of reciting and sang much-appreciated ballads. He had always been a hypochondriac and was borne on a stretcher into the courtroom where his career was ruined by the trial for what much of Europe already knew as the "Prussian affliction."

Thus a headstrong young kaiser, lacking any resolute, independent-minded, and experienced statesman beside him, was able to run wild whenever he so wished or at least to follow capricious and unsound advice from his counselors. Neither Caprivi, the new chancellor, nor Adolf von Marschall, the foreign minister, had much acquaintance with their responsibilities. This allowed a far freer hand than was desirable to a gray eminence like Holstein or to the emotional and shifting judgments of the unsteady Wilhelm himself.

And it also permitted the military chieftains like Admiral Alfred von Tirpitz, naval minister, and the younger Helmuth von Moltke, nephew of the great architect of Bismarck's victories and chief of staff before and at the outbreak of World War I, to gain a strong hold on the bellicose emperor who thoroughly sympathized with their demands for larger fleets and armies. Moltke, incidentally, was decidedly inferior to his uncle. He was fired in 1914, early in the great conflict, for mishandling the critical initial battles.

Thus the quality of the court and government of Germany had deteriorated. Bismarck had been a genius of the highest order, despite his shortcomings. He was ruthless with his enemies, or anyone who opposed him, like Count Harry von Arnim, whom he sucessfully accused of embezzling state papers, committing treason, insulting the emperor, and libeling Bismarck himself. The last was probably the most serious charge, to the chancellor's mind.

But Bismarck, who was sly, vindictive, and reactionary even for his epoch, was gifted with discerning vision. He saw the earth as a whole and Germany's potential role in it, a role that should be confined to Europe, not diluted by overseas expansion. "I am not a colonial man," he declared. And once he had been forced to resign by an emperor he had made virtually all-powerful, the entire course of German rule veered dangerously. This was not just a question of abandoning a trend toward liberalism as had already occurred in Russia after Alexander II's assassination.

It was a matter of abandoning common sense, a quality Bismarck always possessed and one which was totally absent in Kaiser Wilhelm II, with his overweening confidence in his own judgment, his own choice of subordinates, his wisdom and his intuition, a confidence that was unjustified and foolish in the extreme. As Bismarck sadly wrote of him:

> From Friedrich I he inherited love of display, vanity and an autocratic nature; from Friedrich Wilhelm I only the taste for tall fellows; from Frederick the Great only the love of interfering in his officials' business; from Friedrich Wilhelm II a mystic turn and strong sexual impulses; from Friedrich Wilhelm IV the desire to talk a lot.

In the denouement of events that brought down the old order in Europe by crumbling the eagle dynasties, St. Petersburg had precedence in terms of touching off the debacle by violent regicide. Berlin came next in the calendar of change by producing a second-rate *nouveau-puissant* autocrat just at the moment when German imperial autocracy seemed to have gathered its greatest strength. And Vienna, in that same terrible brief period of history, witnessed an imperial suicide that stifled new and sensible governing ideas within a multinational empire and brought the world a step closer to Sarajevo and the disaster that destroyed Europe.

Austria-Hungary, with its original system of two states guided by one sovereign, seemed to shuffle along uneventfully as an empire under the humorless, dignified Franz Josef. By now all but formal ties between him and Empress Elizabeth had ended. Nevertheless, she kindly facilitated his amorous friendship with Katharina von Schratt to ease his final years, years that endured far longer than anyone could imagine, including the restless Elizabeth. She was stabbed to death by an Italian anarchist in 1898, one more terrible sadness in Franz Josef's implacably tragic life. The emperor, with an unusual outburst (for him), said dismally: "I am a *Pechvogel* [the bird of misfortune]."

Although he was their king, Franz Josef had little special interest in the Hungarians, unlike Elizabeth, who firmly believed their national proverb: "Outside Hungary there is no life; or if there is, it doesn't stand comparison." He was entirely a creature of Vienna, and although earnestly devout and sternly above the gay *Schlamperei* which governed the capital's mood, he understood the Viennese and they him. He was an austere man, except for his discreet love affairs. However, he could appreciate a city whose personality was analyzed accordingly by an English observer:

> Centuries of absolutist government working upon a temperament compounded of Celtic versatility, south German slackness, and Slav sensuousness, have—thanks to the constant effort of the authorities to turn attention away from public affairs and toward amusement—ended by producing a population of *dilettanti* disposed to take nothing seriously except the present pleasure.

Such an outlook—emphasis on "the present pleasure"—seemed to be typified by the imperial heir apparent, Crown Prince Rudolf, a charming, handsome man who adored hunting and was a great success with women. He was very popular, especially in Hungary, for which he, like his mother, had much sympathy. Magyar separatists adopted him as their symbol. The Empress Elizabeth adored him and Franz Josef seemed to feel for him genuine fondness.

But Count Eduard von Taaffe, the only prime minister of Austria with Irish blood, disapproved of his liberal political views. Rudolf was an avowed progressive who had actually written in a study paper, when he was fifteen: "Monarchy is now a mighty ruin which may remain from today till to-

Rudolf, as the crown prince of Austria. An English observer of the times analyzed the Viennese temperament thusly: "Centuries of absolutist government working upon a temperament compounded of Celtic versatility, South German slackness, and Slav sensuousness, have—thanks to the constant effort of the authorities to turn attention away from public affairs and toward amusement—ended by producing a population of dilettants disposed to take nothing seriously except the present pleasure." Such an outlook—emphasis on "the present pleasure"—seemed to be typified by the imperial heir apparent.

morrow but which will ultimately tumble." He disliked the conforming aristocracy and strongly favored reorganizing the administration of non-German minorities like the South Slavs, the Magyars, and the Czechs. While he was above all notably pro-Hungarian, he contended also: "Only by cultivating the Slavs can Russian influence be paralyzed," and hoped the Habsburg empire, with a new system of mutually complimentary autonomies, could gain from the collapse of Turkey's empire in the Balkans.

In 1881 Rudolf was pressed into the usual Habsburg formula of a dynastic marriage—with the homely but Catholic daughter of the Belgian king. The crown prince had already started to display a morbid streak; he drank, took drugs, and

Baroness Marie Vetsera. Rudolf's dynastic formula marriage did not inhibit him from a series of flamboyant affairs. When he met Marie Vetsera, he fell deeply in love, wishing even to annul his marriage.

contracted a case of syphilis which he promptly passed on to his wife, who was thereafter prevented from producing an heir. This did not, however, inhibit him from continuing a flamboyant series of affairs, some sentimental, some merely sexual, until finally he met a young baroness named Marie Vetsera, with whose mother it is said he had slept not long before. Marie, part Greek, part Czech-Austrian, had already been involved in a well-advertised romance that occurred in Egypt. In every respect, physical and psychological, the two were made for each other. They fell deeply, emotionally in love. Rudolf even wished to annul his marriage and wed Marie. Franz Josef, Elizabeth, and Vienna court officials were all distressed by the closeness of their attachment which went far beyond the normal passing *affaire* enjoyed by most ardent Viennese.

On January 30, 1889, Rudolf was enjoying himself with the capital's best-known courtesan when he was abruptly overcome by a passionate desire to see his adoring mistress, Marie. He had himself driven to their place of assignation, the imperial hunting lodge at Mayerling. Nobody knows exactly what then happened. They drank a lot of champagne and brandy. They made love. Then, apparently, he shot her in the head—by agreement under a suicide pact—placed one rose on her naked body, wrote a lugubrious last message, and blew off the top of his head. Servants eventually found them sprawled on a hideous carved bed, flanked by a hideous carved cupboard, a mirror in a hideous carved frame reflecting the scene from the wall above a hideous carved table: in all, suicide included, a triumph of Biedermeier.

Both the palace and Taaffe took stringent steps to keep the matter secret when the corpses were discovered. They sought to obscure the scandal under a great coating of propaganda *Schlag,* the special Viennese whipped cream. However, they did not succeed; so Rudolf's body was taken to Vienna while Marie's was hidden in Mayerling until the following night. The girl's two uncles led by Viktor Baltazzi of a respected Constantinople lineage, with long nose, heavy mustache that seemed glued to his stupid face, sideburns, and ears like flat apricots threatened a public scandal if they could not reclaim their niece for the family. Finally the palace acceded. They dressed her stiff corpse, walked it between them to a carriage as if she were merely ill, drove to the capital after forcing it, rigor mortis and all, into a semblance of sitting posture, and had her secretly buried in a Cistercian abbey.

Rudolf's body was attired in uniform and his head, from the brow upward, swathed in a bandage like a turban. It was announced that he had slain himself in a moment of mental crisis—while alone. All the proprieties, including the

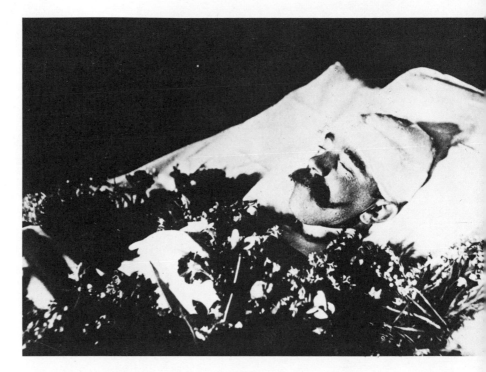

Crown Prince Rudolf after his death.

unhappy, childless widow's existence and the relatively modest origin of Baroness Vetsera, were remembered right up to the grave. But the story—like all love stories in Vienna—soon became known to everyone.

With the crown prince, the last chance vanished for a popular, liberal, direct succession to the throne. Rudolf was mourned even more as an idea than as a man in many progressive corners of Magyar and Slavic discontent with Habsburg administration. There was but one more chance to come in the future, with the designation of the less flamboyantly intelligent, less attractive Prince Franz Ferdinand, as heir apparent.

165 ‡

Franz Ferdinand was Rudolf's first cousin and, while neither so handsome, charming, nor bright, at least had some relatively modern ideas about granting equality of status to the millions of southern and western Slavs in the imperial domain. When he also died, twenty-five years later, of an assassin's bullet in Sarajevo, all empire was doomed. Not just the Habsburg empire; but also the empire of the Romanovs and Hohenzollerns. The process that may be said to have started at Mayerling in 1889, terminating hopes of progress, ended with murder at Sarajevo and exploded World War I.

VIII

AUTOCRACY WITHOUT AN AUTOCRAT

WHAT KILLED THE CHANCES OF NORMAL POLITICAL AND social evolution in the three great continental empires of the nineteer th century was a deliberate stifling of the moderate third force that represented the undoubted aspiration of the majority. This process polarized political choices between the extremes of violent upheaval or bleak reaction.

The former was already being carefully charted by brilliant intellectuals and dauntless revolutionists. They concluded that the death and destruction of the old society, lamely propped up by unimaginative emperors, was the only way to ensure progress, and many among them were clearly pleased when more liberal alternative prospects dimmed.

To be sure, even in remote and semibarbarous Russia, there had been limited efforts to spread the cause of reform without resorting to force. Professor Pavel Miliukov of Moscow University was a widely respected influence among progressive students. But in 1896 he was discharged, banished from Moscow for ten years (internal exile being an old Russian custom), and arrested on and off during his subsequent travels. Nevertheless, with great persistence, he printed and distributed moderate, reformist journals and in 1903 helped found an organization called the Union of Liberation. This represented a rather western type of liberalism but never achieved significant prestige. Eventually he was engulfed by the ultra-leftist tide.

Those who advocated at least mild progress even included a few conservatives. Chief among these was Sergei Witte, who served Alexander III as communications minister and Nicholas II as finance minister, then premier. He tried to budge the successive autocrats from dead center, but he failed. And the total inability of any important political group or individual to influence history by leading Russia down a highway of progress between the poles of total destruction and totalitarian despair, opened the way increasingly to advocates of violence.

Karl Marx, a solemn bearded Protestant from the Prussian Rhineland, whose father was a converted Jew, was the dominant analyst and codifier of the increasingly vigorous movement for change that percolated into Russia. Profoundly influenced by the Stuttgart-born philosopher Georg Wilhelm Friedrich Hegel, Marx developed a novel system of logical synthesis from the Hegelian concept and foresaw that out of it a new kind of communist society might be developed. To this essential, Marx added some formulations and drew upon the dialectical method of another philosopher, Ludwig An-

Friedrich Engels.

Karl Marx.

dreas Feuerbach, especially to support his own strongly anti-religious ideas.

Marx also benefited immensely from a collaboration with Friedrich Engels, another socialist and a brilliant military and political journalist. When, early in 1848, the two published their famous pamphlet, *The Communist Manifesto,* they helped light the fuse from which exploded a revolution that engulfed much of Europe.

It was almost two decades later that Marx, who had spent many years since the 1848 outbreak studying and working in London, issued his equally famous and far more substantial *Das Kapital*. But the first practical test of a proto-communistic system in action came in Paris. There a short-lived revolutionary Commune in 1871 sought to intervene between the death of the Second French Empire and the birth of the conservative Third Republic. It lasted only weeks, but its brief life is still earnestly celebrated in the Soviet Union.

The new Marxist school of political thought and action had good fortune in that from the 1880s on it was opposed in the main theaters of Europe only by impercipient, uncreative, and wholly reactionary governments led by mediocre men in whose hands fate had placed virtually all power. This was true in Vienna where Franz Josef, scarred but unbowed by fate, survived through the final decades of his rule more by dignified momentum than by any sensitivity to the need for change. And it was true in both Berlin and St. Petersburg where two ill-equipped modern Caesars sought both to rule and govern, the kaiser and the czar. But the neo-Caesars of Germany and Russia, who were cousins, possessed beneath pretentious imperial façades qualities more suitable to a third-rate novel had it not led to catastrophe and chaos.

Unlike the posturing Wilhelm, Nicholas II, who succeeded Czar Alexander III, was a meager, unprepossessing little fellow. He was good-looking, with soulful eyes, but he was basically conventional, dutiful, unambitious, unquestioning, and imagined himself a proper, conscientious sovereign. Born only two years before Lenin and in the same vast country, he might have come from another land and inhabited another country. Even Lenin dimly realized this.

Shortly before the 1914 conflict broke out, Lenin wrote to Maxim Gorki: "War between Austria and Russia would be very useful to the cause of the revolution in Western Europe." Not even the brilliant revolutionist could imagine that the doddering old Habsburg and the proper little Romanov, who looked so much like England's George V, would jointly conspire to destroy themselves by sheer stupidity.

Alexander III was a huge and strong man, slow of thought, ponderously authoritarian, and as obstinately and traditionally Russian as a bear.

Before his coronation (as customary in Moscow, the "third Rome," not St. Petersburg) Nicholas did what was expected of a young prince. He was assigned initially to temporary duty with a small regiment. He had a pleasant liaison with the well-known ballerina, Kschessinska, entirely respectable for a young man in his position. He engaged in a certain amount of partying, gambling, and drinking with other officers, pursuits already usual since Pushkin's day.

This agreeable roistering endured until he became engaged to Alexandra of Hesse-Darmstadt, a shy, austerely lovely princess from one of the small German states which in those days specialized in providing Europe with queens. Her sister was already married to Nicholas's uncle, Grand Duke Sergei. Nevertheless, Czar Alexander III was initially cool to the

A souvenir postcard depicting Alexander III, czar of Russia, beside the two-headed imperial eagle.

Grand Duke Sergei, whose marriage to the sister of Hesse-Darmstadt introduced Nicholas to the family of his bride-to-be.

idea of adding Princess Alix to the Romanov roster. However, Nicholas was genuinely in love and Kaiser Wilhelm pressed his cause. He wrongly calculated that the marriage would foster German influence in the St. Petersburg court.

On November 1, 1894, the huge Alexander died of illness. Nicholas became czar and the following morning Alexandra, brought up as a devout Lutheran, abandoned that plain faith for Orthodoxy. One week later they were married. When Nicholas, as was the traditional custom for each new czar, received a formal delegation from the *zemstvos,* local councils that dotted the Russian countryside, he accepted their professions of loyalty with the promise: "I shall preserve the principle of autocracy as firmly and undeviatingly as did my father."

Having seen his grandfather die in agony, eviscerated by a terrorist's bomb, and having watched his father restore the

strictest form of personal dictatorship, Nicholas knew precisely what he meant by "the principle of autocracy." And
the biased, fanatically right-wing Pobedonostsev, his father's
principal adviser and Nicholas's tutor, had prepared him for
the narrow, bigoted role he felt it his historic duty to play.

Moreover, Alexandra, the new czarina, had prepared herself well to abet him. When she gave up her pragmatic
Lutheran concepts, she also erased from her mind the
slightest tinge of what the Germans always called "English"
liberalism. As Leon Trotsky later wrote: "She adopted with
a kind of cold fury all the traditions and nuances of Russian
medievalism, the most meager and crude of all medievalisms,
in that very period when the people were making mighty
efforts to free themselves from it."

It was astonishing to what a degree the czar, his court, his
ministers, managed to avoid direct involvement in a society
and an economy that, even in their broad, distant land, with

The vast cruelties of Ivan the Terrible and Catherine the Great were horrors of the past, but Russia was still a barbarous despotism, almost untouched by European thought. Throughout the whole of the nineteenth century there was no major social advance within the empire except the emancipation of the serfs by Alexander II in 1861. Twenty years later, on the thirteenth of March, 1881, the same czar drafted an imperial decree giving effect to very tentative reforms, and was assassinated on his way to sign it. His son and successor, Alexander III, cancelled the decree.

its terrible communications, could not escape the impact of an industrial revolution which had been under way in Europe to the West for three generations. The new economic and social thrust was being reflected by the growth of small industrialist, mercantile, and proletarian nuclei in Russia.

Even under Alexander III the only one of his ministers who could be called relatively modern, Witte, had promoted the cause of industrialization. He brought in large amounts of foreign development capital (French, British, German) and sought to tie the sprawling imperial domain more closely together by building a more extensive railway system, including the Trans-Siberian line, most famous in the world. Yet this was but a start, and a late start at that. The entire dilapidated state had to be reconstructed in order to adjust to new conditions.

And society, the status of the czar's subjects, did not evolve at all. Under Alexander III it actually regressed; under

Nicholas II it remained lamentably static. Jews were mostly confined in an area known as the Pale, near the western borders, and were habitually persecuted in the most brutal, sordid way. Intellectuals were frowned upon and discouraged, if not actually silenced. Censorship was stifling. Any form of opposition was squashed. And the terrible distribution system abetted frequent local famines. These, in turn, drove hungry peasants into the cities seeking work.

Such was the superficially magnificent but backward, preindustrial system that faced Nicholas when he was eventually crowned in Moscow's Uspensky Cathedral, after one year of solemn mourning for his father. He was proclaimed czar of the following lands: "All the Russias, Moscow, Kiev, Novgorod, Kazan, Astrakhan; of Poland; of Siberia; of Tauric Chersonese; of Georgia," as well as supreme lord, grand duke, or sovereign of countless other fiefdoms in both Europe and Asia.

Nicholas placed the heavy crown upon his own head. Then he and Alexandra sat through five hours of ceremonial, followed by a Kremlin banquet and dance for more than seven thousand guests. Next day (it was May) there was a traditional open-air feast for the poor and simple Muscovites, with plenty of free *kvass* and other drinks.

The frightened crowd got out of hand; thirteen hundred were trampled to death. As a consequence, Nicholas wished to avoid attending a ball arranged in his honor that evening by the French ambassador. However, Grand Duke Sergei, his uncle and brother-in-law, told him he simply must attend, for France, an important ally courted by his father, could not be offended. He went, and the public repercussions were a mixture of distress and horror.

The new czar assumed his responsibilities largely by dodging them. He and Alexandra greatly preferred living outside St. Petersburg, sometimes in the Palace of Gatchina, usually at the more magnificent Czarskoe Selo. As much as possible

Czar Nicholas II. Having seen his grandfather die in agony, eviscerated by a terrorist's bomb, and having watched his father restore the strictest form of personal dictatorship, he knew precisely what he meant by "the principle of autocracy."

they avoided the lovely capital with its administrative problems and municipal inconveniences. Considering their royal origins and their obligations as public figures, they showed a strange preference for the obscure life.

The empress soon entered into the business of motherhood, producing four lovely daughters and, at last, the tainted handsome czarevitch, Alexis. All of the boy's brief life was under continual menace from hemophilia with its incessant danger of massive hemorrhage until that terrible day in 1918 when he, his parents, and his sisters were mown down by Bolshevik gunmen in the cellar of a dreary Siberian villa.

During their early years together, Alexandra knitted, sang lullabies, and listened while Nicholas read aloud, often from English novels. The empress felt uncomfortable in the capital's giddy society. The latter responded by whispering snide remarks about "the German woman," much as Germans a generation or more earlier had called Princess Vicky, eventually the empress, *die Engländerin*.

The imperial family entertained little and then, in a most un-Russian way, preferred small luncheons and dinners on an informal basis. This antisocial, rather middle-class mode of life, placing private sentiment above public obligations to the state and preferring dull friends to intellectual or political stimulus, was a most ineffective way of practicing the highly specialized profession of autocrat. That coldly formal job required much knowledge, wide acquaintance, shrewd intuition, a feeling for international affairs, and a sense of national requirements. Nicholas had none of these.

He attempted to do his routine work regularly, but he was not very competent: simply a delicate, small man, in every respect unimposing although gently handsome. His intelligence was average, his education limited. He had the stubbornness of many weak men, was given to shifting moods, fatalistic, mistrustful, affectionate when possible (which, after his marriage, was only with his family), and a mystical nationalist. The start of his reign coincided with torrential arguments between "westernizers" and "Slavophils" in the gossipy Russian intellectual world. Nicholas was decidedly a Slavophil, Great-Russian to the boot-tops.

He had learned from Pobedonostsev to look down on all his subjects other than the true, Orthodox Slavs. The millions of Jews, Catholics, Protestants, and Moslems subject to his domination rarely figured in his thoughts and then only in a prejudiced, negative way. Despite his soft, indecisive nature, the czar happily approved of anti-Jewish pogroms. These were provoked and conducted by the Black Hundred gangs, egged on by a certain Prince Meshcherski, friend of his late, reactionary father. And, until the disastrous denouement of that policy, he implicitly agreed when his cousin, Kaiser Wilhelm, wrote him in 1895: "The great task of the future for Russia is to cultivate the Asian continent and defend Europe from the inroads of the Great Yellow race."

Such was Russia and such its inept, inefficient, autocratic rule, when the century turned and raced into a calamitous war with Japan and the first (1905) revolution. Even before those twinned cataclysms, while the imperial family lived a pretend-life of bourgeois escapism, the empire itself was already marked by growing signs of political and social discontent.

The peasants were unhappy with bad crops, low prices for them, high taxes, and uncomprehending absentee landlords. The new proletariat in mushrooming cities felt oppressed by an ignorant new class of exploiters. The minority races increasingly resented their Russian overlords. Everyone felt paralyzed by an unwieldy, stupid, unresponsive bureaucracy which had to funnel virtually each decision back and forth to St. Petersburg. Although Nicholas, on Witte's urging, reluctantly granted a tepid constitution after the 1905 insurrections, it was too late. The whole system collapsed in disorder even before the outbreak of World War I. Reaction

179 ‡

returned to the saddle. Ultimately the successive revolutions of 1917 took Russia out of the conflict and extinguished imperial rule.

Witte, who had failed in his own limited efforts to achieve progress in time to be effective, at least recognized why. He wrote of Nicholas II:

> His character is the source of all our misfortunes. . . . His outstanding failure is a lamentable lack of willpower. Though benevolent and not unintelligent, this shortcoming disqualifies him totally as the unlimited autocratic ruler of the Russian people.

Although Witte credited the czar with better intentions and brains than was probably the case, he saw the basic point. An autocracy required an autocrat to work and Russia didn't have one in the twentieth century—until the arrival of Lenin.

Blue enamel box by Fabergé with portrait of Czar Nicholas II.

IX

A SMALL WAR
TO STEM THE TIDE

WHEN IT WAS ALREADY TOO LATE, NICHOLAS TRIED TO
bolster his sagging regime by a toughness he was not personally capable of applying. On the one hand, he appointed
Viacheslav Plehve, a hard right-winger, as his minister of interior in 1902. On the other hand, he allowed himself to be
persuaded that an easy little war with Japan would not only
gain valuable territories for his empire in critical Far Eastern
areas but would divert popular attention from internal
troubles. As was his unfortunate custom, the czar misjudged
each situation and also its proposed remedy.

Plehve was nothing but a high-level cop. He first became director of the state police in 1881 and earned a certain renown by his ruthless investigation of Alexander II's assassination. "Russification" of everything and everyone was his answer to long-range security problems. He specialized in oppressing Poles, Armenians, Finns, Lithuanians, and, above all, Jews. Thoroughly detested, he was ultimately blown up by a terrorist bomb in 1904 shortly before the Russo-Japanese War and the 1905 revolution which followed.

The man almost certainly responsible for the murder was Yevno Azev, most effective member of Plehve's own spy apparatus. In the line of duty, Azev had become chief of the Terrorist Brigade, special assassination squad of the underground Russian Socialist Revolutionary party. To ensure the validity of his own cover, Azev, although working for the *Okhrana*, planned the killings of various high officials, including Plehve and the equally unpopular Grand Duke Sergei. He was surely a double agent, but no one can ever be positive where his final loyalties resided. Azev's pocketbook was replenished with police funds, but it is entirely possible his brain and his heart—if he had one—leaned to the Socialist Revolutionaries.

It was Plehve, the resolute, narrow-minded, and demonstrably cynical spy-master and repressor, who proposed to Nicholas "a small victorious war to stem the tide of revolution." Even Witte, conservative but intelligent, eager for new eastern outlets for his Trans-Siberian railway but aware that military conflicts always contained the possibility of nasty surprises, objected to this idea.

The czar handled this by firing Witte, paying increasing heed to the ideas of Kaiser Wilhelm who counseled that Russia's great mission was to safeguard Europe from encroachments of the Yellow Menace, and cracking down on every known kind of opposition, underground or open, ranging from anarchists to liberals. Nicholas had been sufficiently in-

Count Sergei Witte. Witte as Minister of Finance had a good administrative brain and achieved immense material benefits for his country, including the construction of the Trans-Siberian railway. Yet, despite the czar's admiration for Witte, he ignored Witte's pleas for modernization of Russian society. About Nicholas, Witte said, "His standing failure is a lamentable lack of willpower. Though benevolent and not unintelligent, this shortcoming disqualifies him totally as the unlimited autocratic ruler of the Russian people.

fected by Plehve's prejudices and the bias then normal to Russia's imperial court, to suspect that anyway most of them were Jews.

The kaiser wished to divert Russia from any overweening interest in its German neighbor, now that the *Dreikaiserbund* was dead. Therefore he gave free rein to his pre-Hitlerian, Asia-oriented racial prejudices which seasoned all advice to his cousin "Nicky." Flattering the czar's inflated esteem for his own inexperienced and outmoded navy, Wilhelm put forward the pleasing idea: "I wish you would assume, from now on, the title of Admiral of the Pacific. I shall call myself Admiral of the Atlantic," he added smugly, confident that the huge fleet he was already in the process of building in German yards would soon be capable of ending Britannia's rule of the waves, at any rate in European waters.

Nicholas consequently was prevailed upon by Plehve and cousin Willy to provoke Japan in Korea. In the spring of 1904 Tokyo reacted by smashing the Russian hold on Port Arthur, a naval base in Manchuria that had been occupied by the czar's forces, and swiftly sinking much of Russia's Far Eastern Fleet. Then, with their supply routes fully ensured, the Japanese sent a huge army northward against the main concentration of Russian divisions. St. Petersburg reacted in the way best calculated to please the kaiser.

The czar dispatched his Baltic Fleet, the greatest naval strength of the empire, from its base at Kronstadt slowly around the world to the North China Sea, on a trip marred by continual errors in judgment and lack of organizational skills. Just off a rockbound island near the south Korean coast, the Japanese attacked and wrecked this second armada, killing its admiral aboard the command vessel, *Czarevich*. Just one week earlier the actual czarevitch had been born to Alexandra, her youngest child and only son, the hemophiliac Alexis.

These disastrous consequences to what was to have been a "small, victorious war" produced astounded and enraged reactions in European Russia, above all St. Petersburg. A mass strike was launched by the workers of the Putilov steel plant, largest industrial enterprise in the empire. And each of the various revolutionary or reform groups sought to capitalize on the critical situation. Moreover, the despondency of the masses had been greatly heightened by national humiliation, especially since it was caused by a hitherto disregarded, underestimated nation, not even reckoned among the great world powers.

Broadly speaking, the plotters who sought to guide public despair to their own advantage, divided into Marxist and non-Marxist factions, although on either side of this ideological frontier there were active and also quarrelsome internal splits. The non-Marxists, who turned out to be far less important because they were poorly organized and had but vague programs and goals, included Miliukov's Liberals and the Socialist Revolutionaries. The latter, despite their fanaticism and their savage murder squads, had taken a different ideological road from the Prussian philosopher.

In addition to their terrorist minority they had fairly extensive support among more restrained elements including some intellectuals and many peasants. Indeed, the lawyer and parliamentarian Alexander Kerensky, who led the first 1917 Revolution that overthrew the czar, was an S.R. member and a vigorous opponent of the brilliant Lenin. Strangely enough Kerensky was born in the same central Russian town of Simbirsk as was Lenin. His father was director of education at the school where Lenin's father taught and where the Bolshevik leader received his initial training. Kerensky subsequently wrote, from exile, in much the same analytical pattern as the later Alexander Solzhenitsyn:

> I saw the same limitless horizons from the same high bank of the Volga and I know in my blood and bones that it is only by losing all touch with our native land, only by stamping out all native feeling for it, only so could one do what Lenin did in deliberately and cruelly mutilating Russia.

More than two generations before the 1905 revolution that was touched off by the Russo-Japanese War, Marx himself had calculated that a period of liberal rule, marked by bourgeois ideas of political freedom, would be a natural predecessor to his ultimate aim of a truly socialist system. Marx also had been infected by Hohenzollern prejudices and regarded Slavs—at least the western and southern Slavs—as

Alexander Kerensky was an orator, a passionate humanist, enthusiastic, able, brilliant in debate, theatrical, egotistical, and convinced that Russia's spirit and destiny were linked to his own. He became Lenin's chief opponent in the Revolution.

"ethnic trash." But these ideas were never shared by Marx's greatest disciple, Vladimir Ilyich Ulyanov, known to history as Lenin. He took the sobriquet of the Lena River from his elder brother who had been hanged for plotting to kill the czar.

Already when he was only eighteen, Lenin read *Das Kapital* in Simbirsk (which shows how ineffective the czarist censorship was). Five years later, in St. Petersburg, he had become immersed in revolutionary studies and agitation work. He not only learned revolutionary theory and philosophy but also such techniques of conspiracy as the use of invisible ink, secret codes, organizational cells, and message drops, the falsification of papers, and the continual switch of aliases.

Lenin was highly intelligent, resolute, brave, and single-minded. He was also arrogant and authoritarian. Even today, one can feel the ghost of this dynamic vitality, frozen in death's repose, when regarding him as he lies entombed in the imposing Red Square, preserved by secret Russian mummifying processes.

He was widely read, above all in history, economics, and military science, and he had a most retentive mind. As a young man he spent months personally investigating the harsh condition of Russian workers, ascertaining their political outlook and, from the viewpoint of his own plans, their potential capacities.

When he was twenty-three, he met a plain, serious woman whose affectionate warmth is not conveyed in photographs of a cold, bleak, heavy face. Her name was Nadezhda Krupskaya; she was also a Marxist and in 1898 she became his wife. One might almost say she was the mother of the Bolshevik Revolution because she stayed loyally beside its leader, followed him into Siberian exile and eventually to a difficult, sometimes apparently hopeless, life abroad, in Austrian Galicia, in Munich, in London, in Zurich, and in many conspiratorial meeting places or transient points.

Inessa Armand was an impressive, large, blond woman, who may have been Lenin's mistress while he and Krupskaia were living in London.

Nadezhda Krupskaia. In 1898, when Lenin was twenty-three and she was twenty-two, they were married. One might say that she was the mother of the Bolshevik Revolution because she stayed loyally beside its leader, followed him into Siberian exile, and eventually to a difficult, sometimes apparently hopeless, life abroad, in Austrian Galicia, in Munich, in London, in Zurich, and in many conspiratorial meeting places or transient points.

Here one may interpolate that London played a peculiarly important role in incubating the Russian revolution. Its increasing liberal tradition of tolerance, its libraries and museums, attracted a wide variety of plotters. Not only was it for long the residence of Marx; at various times it welcomed Lenin and Krupskaia (under the names Dr. and Mrs. Richter), Martov, Trotsky, and other early Marxist figures. It served as the editorial base of Lenin's hortatory underground paper, *Iskra,* which was sent clandestinely back to Russia. It harbored the vital 1903 Social Democratic party congress off quintessentially middle-class Tottenham Court Road.

Although a highly willful zealot, Lenin was in some respects a peculiarly normal man. He loved to walk in the country, to skate on frozen ponds; at one time he enjoyed shooting. Also, although he was not afflicted with levity or inconstancy in anything he did, he was not a strict monogamist. In any case, he had a very curious relationship with a French-born Social Democrat who called herself Inessa (her real name was Ines) Armand, formerly a governess in a prosperous St. Petersburg home. She was an impressive, large, blond woman, a few years younger than her colleague (lover?), and Lenin introduced her into his household, creating a strange variety of the usual *ménage à trois,* which Krupskaia seemed quite willing to tolerate. Inessa helped the revolutionary leader as a secretary and also amused him as a musician and, most likely, as a mistress.

The Social Democrats were a Marxist group founded by Engels's friend, Georgi Plekhanov, most orthodox of the German philosopher's Russian exponents, a man who had seceded from the populist *Narodniks* when they turned to terrorism and who thereafter spent most of his adult life as an exile in Geneva. At one time he was very close to Lenin. However, they became bitter enemies when Plekhanov opposed the Bolsheviks both before and after their eventual seizure of power.

The issue that split them was basically one of method. Lenin insisted not only that it was "necessary" to turn away from any truck with liberalism "and go to what is diametrically opposed to the bourgeoisie." He also was adamant in his belief that a small, disciplined minority, serving as "the vanguard of the revolution," must take control of the proposed state. This became what Trotsky (born Lev Davidovitch Bronstein) was to call "a dictatorship *over* the proletariat" and what eventually became the sacred shibboleth of all orthodox communism everywhere, "dictatorship *of* the proletariat." Trotsky's usage was and is more accurate.

The term "Bolshevik" became familiar after the Russian Social Democratic party congress of 1903 in hospitable London where Lenin's dictatorial doctrine triumphed. For "Bolshevik" is a derivation of the Russian word for "majority" and from that date on he had established the ascendancy of his position among the squabbling Marxists.

Nicholas II had already demonstrated his incapacity to face the development of such revolutionary techniques which were (wholly unknown to him) now starting to be shaped by Lenin's fanatical genius with its arsenal of simple, single-minded tenets. Even Kerensky, a far milder man than Lenin, endowed with a sense of tolerance that ultimately vitiated his effectiveness, concluded that the czar's ignorance and weakness were fatal flaws. He wrote that Nicholas's belief in a sublime destiny as autocrat "led me to the inescapable conclusion that for the salvation of Russia and her future the reigning monarch must be removed."

Such a removal, set immutably upon its course by the Japanese disaster, almost occurred in early 1905 after the famous St. Petersburg Bloody Sunday of January 9 (under the old calendar, now January 22). The humiliating Russian defeats by a country hitherto regarded as inferior and weak had a profoundly adverse effect on the imperial prestige. A new wave of strikes and manifestations, mirroring a discontent only briefly interrupted during the initial period of war, began to break out at various points of the empire.

One consequence of this was a huge protest in the capital, formed around a talented rabble-rousing priest named Father Georgi Gapon. Gapon, as was so often the case in that paradoxical time when one of the *Okhrana*'s chief agents, Azev, helped plan the murder of his bosses, was both a genuine sympathizer of the impoverished workers' cause and in the pay of the police. He had been recruited by an *Okhrana* official named Zubatov to organize a carefully supervised labor movement called the Association of Russian Factory and Mill Workers.

It is hard to know what Gapon, a thoroughly confused and Dostoievskian figure, was really thinking when he led an unarmed crowd of protesters by the frozen Neva to the Winter Palace, lowering darkly above the snow-whitened square. The purpose was to petition the czar for peace, civil liberties, an amnesty for political prisoners, and a constituent assembly. It is estimated that more than a hundred thousand men, women, and children participated in this disorganized mass demonstration.

Nicholas was not in St. Petersburg; but his soldiers were. When the procession, bearing the czar's portrait as well as icons and religious flags, arrived before the palace, a company of infantry swung opposite the demonstrators across the square, presented arms, aimed, and fired. The savage job was completed by troops of cossacks who charged the frightened and astonished mob with swinging sabers. Several hundred were killed. A horrified world promptly denounced Nicholas as a mass murderer. The czar wrote meticulously in his personal journal: "a painful day."

Gapon fled. He managed to get to Switzerland where he met Lenin and Trotsky. The priest appeared to be attracted by the latter's more flamboyant theories and joined the Socialist Revolutionaries. He also reensured his personal fate, or so

"Bloody Sunday," when Father Gapon, a thoroughly confused and Dostoievskian figure, and his unarmed followers were faced suddenly by troops. A company of infantry swung opposite the demonstrators, presented arms, aimed, and fired. The savage job was completed by a troop of cossacks who charged, swinging sabers.

"Bloody Sunday."

he thought, by resuming his connection with the *Okhrana* (if, indeed, it had ever wholly been broken). Eventually he was tracked down in Finland by angry S.R. terrorists who slew him.

The "Bloody Sunday" massacre was only a beginning to a time of violence. The next month Grand Duke Sergei was blown into many pieces by an S.R. bomb outside the Kremlin. Preparations for this murder of the czar's detested uncle–brother-in-law, who was then Moscow's military governor, were certainly known by the monstrous Azev. Whether Azev fully informed the government ahead of time or whether he actually sponsored the crime will never truly be known.

One week after this assassination the Japanese overran the principal Russian army in Manchuria. All over Nicholas's empire wrathful peasants began to rise up against their land-lords. Even the reticent Liberals and officially permitted local councils, the *zemstvos,* joined the increasingly urgent insistence on reforms and peace. Social Democrats, Socialist Revolutionaries, the powerful Jewish Bundists, stirred the ferment. Then, in May, the Tsushima naval disaster struck, as soon as the befuddled Baltic Fleet arrived in the China Sea off the tip of the Korean peninsula. This blow provoked a mutiny among the crews of the only remaining Russian fleet afloat, the Black Sea squadron. The mutiny was led by sailors of the battleship *Potemkin* whose action has been commemorated in Sergei Eisenstein's famous movie. Nicholas recognized that he had lost the conflict he had idiotically sought, and even his dim mind perceived that he might also soon lose his crown.

As a result, he summoned Witte back to avail Russia of the diplomatic opportunity provided by the United States president, Theodore Roosevelt, to arrange a Japanese peace at Portsmouth, New Hampshire. While the negotiations were taking place, a crippling general strike began to spread across Russia. It was massive, not at all well organized, and included such varied supporters as the Socialist Revolutionaries, the Liberals, Bundists, embryonic labor syndicates, and even the imperial ballet. A workers' soviet, dominated by Trotsky, seized the governance of St. Petersburg itself, isolating the imperial family in a palace beside the Gulf of Finland. Lenin, who had thought the moment not yet ripe for his return, decided he had wrongly analyzed the situation and headed back.

Witte returned with what were correctly adjudged to be favorable peace terms despite the fact that Russia had to cede a great deal of territory to Japan: southern Sakhalin, all Korea, Manchuria, Kwantung, and Port Arthur. As a reward for his astute diplomacy, Nicholas made Witte his chief minister, although under the rule of an autocrat, this was by no means so important a job as it might sound. The czar reluctantly agreed to permit creation of a wobbly parliament called the State Duma whose members were elected in a partially free balloting system. Trotsky scathingly described this as a "police whip wrapped in the parchment of the constitution." Even the Liberals insisted that the basic structure of the police state had not changed. Therefore, when Witte offered the Liberals ministries in his new cabinet, they spurned the invitation.

This provoked Witte's downfall soon afterward, and another general strike broke out to the counterpoint of another dramatic mutiny, this time by the garrison at Kronstadt, the principal fortification of the capital and Russia's greatest naval base.

The main military forces had by now, however, begun to pour back from the Far Eastern front along Witte's Trans-Siberian railway. Consequently the situation started to change and the advocates of harsh retribution gained ascendancy. Any troops suspected of indiscipline were promptly shot. The Kronstadt insurrection was quelled. Lenin, who had gone to Moscow with Krupskaia to support the fledgling Moscow soviet, discovered that revolutionary enthusiasm was no equal to veteran, trained battalions. The St. Petersburg soviet disintegrated and Trotsky was captured. En route to a new exile in Siberia, he managed to escape. Witte resigned and a new ice age of bleak repression set in. It lasted fewer than a dozen years.

X TO FALL ASLEEP FOREVER ... IN YOUR ARMS

THE EMERGENCE OF KAISER WILHELM AS A PERSONALITY OF eminence in the world was destabilizing. The long-enduring *realpolitik* of such methodical statesmen as Metternich and Bismarck, whatever their shortcomings in human sensitivity, now vanished beneath a cloud of unexamined emotionalism, which fed and then controlled by Berlin's ambitions, came to be the dominant influence on Europe's destiny.

Wilhelm had been genuinely fond of his grandmother, Queen Victoria. He even rushed to England as she lay on her deathbed and forced his way through the somber group beside her so that she actually expired in his arms. At her funeral he comported himself with such dignity and so sympathetic a demeanor that King Edward VII, whom he knew as Uncle Bertie, made him a British field marshal. But this was just a passing courtesy. Neither sovereign trusted the other, and each suspected the other's nation.

The final years of the twentieth century's first decade therefore were marked by dramatic shifts in internal and external attitudes of the great continental empires. Austria-Hungary, already verging on its own as well as its ruler's dotage, became more obsessed than ever with the Balkan Slavic problem. In 1903 a pro-Habsburg ruler of Serbia, King Alexander Obrenović, was murdered together with his queen; and the Karageorgević dynasty, as sympathetic to St. Petersburg as it was unsympathetic to Vienna, returned to the throne. Five years later the Austrians lit the slow-burning fuse that finally exploded the Balkan powder keg in 1908 when they officially annexed the two Slav provinces of Bosnia and Herzegovina, militarily occupied from decaying Ottoman suzerainty thirty years earlier.

During this same approximate period Wilhelm gave free rein to both his political and psychological Anglophobia. He rejected halfhearted advances from London in the name of friendship, announcing his determination to supplement the mighty German army with an equally powerful fleet, and making no secret of his sudden and brand-new desire to obtain colonies in Africa and Asia. These ambitions not only followed immediately after the kaiser's well-advertised support for the Boers during their sad war with Britain—which infuriated all Englishmen—but also directly threatened a basic tenet of British policy. Britain insisted that, to maintain its world empire, the island kingdom must constantly maintain a naval strength equal to the combined sea power of any two other nations.

Edward VII at Balmoral with his grandchildren in 1902. In 1903 Wilhelm's "detested Uncle Bertie" visited Paris and was triumphantly received. His journey helped to inaugurate the Entente Cordiale between France and Britain, which ultimately became the basis for the victorious alliance of World War I.

As a counterpoint to this developing diplomatic strategy, Wilhelm sought (with more than a little success) to keep Russian attentions focused eastward into Asia. He abandoned even vestigial thoughts of re-creating the *Dreikaiserbund,* and substituted Italy's limited dynamism and doubtful loyalty as a partner in what became the Triple Alliance—with Austria-Hungary and Germany. Finally, the bumptious kaiser infuriated France by interfering with its advance into Africa, a process that had been encouraged originally by Bismarck to divert French dynamism from Europe.

When Paris, with British acquiescence, was consolidating its military position in Morocco, Wilhelm broke off a Mediterranean pleasure cruise to land at Tangier, climb on an appropriately placid horse (equitation was never his strongpoint), and proclaim his backing for the Moroccan sultan—who soon responded by knuckling under anyway to the French.

What was most distressing was the case of Russia. Following the cataclysms of Japanese defeat in Asia and a major revolution at home, the czar was in no condition to behave in a rational way. His government had once again come into the hands of outright reactionary elements. And his cousin Willy was busily seeking to entrap him in a succession of intrigues.

First the kaiser had encouraged the "Admiral of the Pacific" to take a crack at Japan in order to safeguard the spotless purity of a white man's Europe. Then he suggested that maybe peace could best be preserved by a Russo-Germanic alliance which would isolate the pro-Japanese British. He also warned him against agreeing to any pact with France, a dangerous republic, because "Heaven has imposed a sacred duty . . . on us Christian kings and emperors to uphold the doctrine of the divine right of kings."

Finally, as if his cup were not yet sufficiently filled with bitterness and confusion, Nicholas (and above all his czarina) came under the hypnotic dominance of a cunning, ambitious, priestly sex maniac named Rasputin who was so vital a personality that all alone he might have proven capable of destroying what was left of the Romanov heritage. And Rasputin was far from alone.

So closely interwoven is this ominous tapestry of the final prewar decade of the Habsburgs, Hohenzollerns, and Romanovs that it is sometimes difficult to follow any individual skein before it disappears into the confused general pattern. This is above all true of events in the Balkans where everything by tradition is both flamboyant and conspiratorial, an intricate and rarely successful mixture.

Since Serbia had emerged from Turkish rule as an independent principality, it had been guided by alternating factions gathered around the rival Karageorgević and Obrenović dynasties and influenced by rival empires, Russia and Austria-Hungary. The first of these empires tried continually to reach farther and farther southward across the Black Sea, in the general direction of Constantinople which itself was never coveted by the Habsburgs. However, it had always been coveted by the rulers of Russia, even before the Romanovs and as far back as Prince Rurik in the Middle Ages. Austria simply sought to digest increasing numbers of Balkan Slavs. As a result of these paired southerly ambitions, Vienna and St. Petersburg were always mistrustfully competing in this area no matter how closely they were bound by intermittent understandings elsewhere.

The first Serbian sovereign, Karageorge, was a squire—a gentleman pig farmer. His name, which means Black George, derived from both his swarthy face and his morose disposition. From him stemmed the main royal line which bobbed in and out of power amid a choppy sea of plots until 1941 when the last king (he ruled his country less than a week), Peter II of Jugoslavia, died an overwhelmed alcoholic refugee in the United States.

The final true sovereign, Prince Paul Karageorgević, regent after the child Peter's father had been murdered, and ruler from 1934 to 1941, was a remarkable terminus of this unusual line: perhaps the most cultivated, open-minded, and intelligent of the European royals during the past century. He was dumped and disgraced in a conspiracy mounted by those he considered his best friends, the British.

The Karageorgevićs were generally considered to be pro-Russian and the Obrenovićs pro-Austrian, and there is more than a little reason to suspect that each was at various times financially supported by its foreign sponsors. In 1903 an Obrenović, King Alexander, was on the throne. For some reason he was snobbishly disliked by his peasant compatriots more for the fact that his wife, Queen Draga, had previously been a lady-in-waiting than for the indication that he was a tool of the unpopular Habsburgs. The latter had been especially detested since 1878 when their troops occupied Bosnia-Herzegovina, a Slavic region and, thereby, barred westward access to the Adriatic by fellow Slavs in Serbia.

Alexander's displacement was a particularly gaudy affair, even for the unrestrained Balkans. The murder was organized by a group of army officers headed by Colonel Dragutin Dimitrijević—who was in the pay of the Russians and rejoiced in the nickname "Apis," because he had a fuzzy yellow bee-like bald spot in the matted hair on his pate—and by several politicians headed by a future premier named Nikola Pašić. I had an elderly friend, during my younger days, who participated in the assassination as a lieutenant. He used to recount with gusto how they burst into the little palace, found the king and queen cowering in a closet (both in silken nightgowns, according to my murderer-friend), stabbed them and chucked them out the window onto garden manure heaps, hacking off Alexander's fingers when he clung desperately to the sill.

Peter Karageorgević, then an elderly exile living a Spartan

life in Geneva with his sons and nephew, Prince Paul, came back to assume the uneasy throne to the unmitigated pleasure of both Pan-Serb expansionists and the Russians, and to the despair of the worried Habsburg court. The Austrians responded by what was known as the Pig War in 1906, a tight embargo on Serbia's main export, pork. The fur-hatted, slippered Serbs nevertheless managed to continue, driving their snorting razor-backed hogs into greedy Austria. The boycott didn't work and served only to exacerbate Habsburg relations with the new Belgrade regime. Two years later Vienna simply grabbed, de jure, the Bosnian-Herzegovinan provinces it already held de facto, although this move flagrantly violated an international treaty. Serbia, with its backward four million population, was helpless to react effectively against the Habsburg empire, more than twelve times larger.

The net result of these actions was a permanently festering situation along the edge of Austria-Hungary. The Serbs were enthusiastically engaged in organizing conspiratorial groups which in turn were supported both by the Orthodox church, traditionally warlike and politically minded, and by various Pan-Slav societies in Russia. Moreover, there is ample reason to suspect that secret funds were transferred by St. Petersburg to a new Serbian guerrilla-training outfit called *Narodna Obrana* and headed by Apis who had also become chief of Belgrade's military intelligence. It was Apis who guided (and Russia which possibly teleguided, certainly helped) the subsequent assassination of the Habsburg heir-apparent in 1914, an event which touched off the Great War.

Meanwhile, as the old Teuton-Slav rivalry warmed up again to the south of Hohenzollern Germany, Kaiser Wilhelm started to poke the ashes in the north. In this endeavor he was suitably aided by the egregious Bernhard, Prince von Bülow, and Holstein, who together dominated policy in the initial post-Bismarck years and helped guide the emperor to his self-sought doom.

Edward VII in Vanity Fair elegance.

Bülow, as chancellor, proved himself a good diplomat and cool man of the world, but he knew little about the realities of politics or policy. An esteemed wit and a fine orator, he was astute enough to realize that the program of a naval race with Britain (planted in the kaiser's eager mind by Admiral von Tirpitz, the ambitious navy minister) would further poison relations with London. Nevertheless, he made no im-

THE "MONTAGNE RUSSE."—A VERY DANGEROUS GAME.

THE CALL OF THE TSAR.

"WHO FOLLOWS ME FOR HOLY RUSSIA'S SAKE?"

England's allegiance to Russia against Germany was prompted more by a common enemy than by enduring political and social admiration. England's refusal to harbor Nicholas II's family after their dethronement, on the grounds that England was no place for a despot, is a telling example of England's ambivalence toward her Russian ally and royal cousin. The two cartoons above illustrate this dichotomous attitude.

pressive effort to dissuade his imperial master. Thus the atmosphere was already beclouded when Joseph Chamberlain explored the prospects of a closer Anglo-Germanic understanding on London's initiative. The idea was wholly scotched when Holstein, as fatuous as he was superficially clever, persuaded the kaiser that the British were seeking only to embroil him with Russia.

In 1903 Wilhelm's detested Uncle Bertie visited Paris and was triumphantly received. His journey helped to inaugurate the Entente Cordiale between France and Britain which ultimately became the basis for the victorious alliance of World War I. Wilhelm responded by a burst of his own personal diplomacy, melodramatic and counterproductive as usual. In July 1905, after that great "Admiral of the Pacific," Nicholas II, had lost his two principal fleets to the "Yellow Menace" of Japan, the kaiser boarded his splendid yacht, *Hohenzollern,* flying his personal pennant with the legend *Gott Mit Uns,* and steamed away over the bright blue Baltic, even lovelier and clearer than the Mediterranean at that season of the year. He anchored in Björkö Bay off Finland. There he was joined by the czar and his family aboard his own imperial yacht, *Stella Polaris.*

Cousin Willy had kept his project secret from all his officials save Bülow. Cousin Nicky didn't tell anyone at all. But Wilhelm prepared his own immodest record of the encounter which he believed would be a dazzling stroke, an example to be remembered in later annals of international intercourse. With all the shrewdness of a small-town huckster, he reminded Nicholas in their initial shipboard chats that the untrustworthy English and the undependable French were cooking up nasty deals aimed at the noble autocrats.

After this come-on he suggested: "How would it be if we were to make a little agreement too?" When the naïve czar nodded agreeably, Wilhelm hauled out of his pocket a draft copy which he happened "by extraordinary chance" to have with him. The czar read this and (according to Wilhelm) commented: "That is quite excellent. I quite agree." The kaiser promptly prevailed on him to sign it then and there. He called the document "a very nice souvenir of our interview."

The "souvenir," known subsequently as the Treaty of Björkö, provided for a defensive alliance to take effect the moment the inevitable Russo-Japanese peace was concluded. Of course the accord was an outright violation of the Russian pact with France negotiated by Alexander III in 1893. But its validity was never tested. The French intelligence service very soon found out something fishy had happened and advised its government. Paris promptly put the heat on St. Petersburg.

When Nicholas was forced to confess to his ministers what he had done, they pointed out the total confusion of his position amid a network of contradictory obligations. He had to write to Cousin Willy lamely begging off. The kaiser complained of the "schoolboy ideologue in St. Petersburg," but even Holstein privately dubbed the unfortunate affair "operetta politics."

All the former sympathy between the imperial cousins evaporated, and in 1907 the Anglo-Russian accord was signed, Nicholas's subconscious motives growing out of his resentment of Wilhelm's Machiavellian bullying. What London considered Wilhelm's excessive ambitions combined with London's uneasiness about the czar's appetite for India to make attractive a pact separating Russia and Germany while pacifying Russia's Indian ambitions. The only tangible outcome of the ridiculous Björkö affair was the emergence of Germany as a dangerously egotistical bogeyman for all of Europe, west and east. Wilhelm had made himself clearly eligible for Uncle Bertie's comment that he was "the most brilliant failure in history."

Björkö marked a significant juncture on the complex road

to imperial suicide. In June 1908 Edward VII, more put out than ever by his Hohenzollern nephew and now firmly bound to France, by the Entente Cordiale, boarded his own regal yacht, *Victoria and Albert,* for a far more businesslike voyage of exploration. He was accompanied by a group of competent officials, and they hove to off Tallinn, the port-capital of Russian Estonia, where Nicholas II, his family, and an equally professional entourage, were waiting aboard the Romanov yachts, *Standart* and *Polaris.*

Peter Stolypin and his foreign minister, Count Alexander Izvolsky, joined their British colleagues in drafting an initial accord with Britain that complemented the understanding each nation had with France. Subsequently this developed into the Triple Entente that ultimately fought and defeated the Central Powers, Germany and Austria-Hungary.

That same September Izvolsky met his Austrian peer, Alois von Aehrenthal at Buchlau, a castle in Moravia owned by the former Viennese envoy to St. Petersburg. There, at a weekend house party, the two ministers agreed to turn a blind eye to each other's ambitions in the direction of the collapsing Ottoman Empire. Russia accepted Austria's annexation of Bosnia-Herzegovina. Austria acknowledged that it would not interfere if Russia wished to press for freedom of the Turkish straits.

Nevertheless, the rambunctious Serbs, now under the pro-Russian Karageorgevićs, had not been informed of this secret understanding. They begged for St. Petersburg's assistance in ousting the Habsburgs from the seized Slavic provinces. Stolypin, however, was too cautious to use the occasion to move against the Dardanelles unless the other European capitals approved.

The opportunity to act dramatically was too much for Wilhelm. He announced his determination to stand beside Franz Josef at this critical moment. Von Moltke (the younger), who had become chief of the German General

Nicholas II with the Empress Alexandra aboard the Royal Yacht Standart.

Staff two years before, assured his Austrian opposite, General Franz Conrad von Hötzendorf: "The moment Russia mobilizes, Germany . . . will unquestionably mobilize her whole army."

Russia, bewildered by the whole affair and unwilling to risk war because of what was starting to look like a Viennese betrayal, backed down. The Serbs were furious, disappointed, helpless. And Nicholas II, once again recalling his earlier humiliation at Björkö, wrote: "German action toward us has been simply brutal. We won't forget it."

The kaiser was now driven even more feverishly to push ahead in the naval-building race urged by Tirpitz and condemned to continue by his own folly. Moreover, he was pressed by a tight Prussian military clique to get ready for a new war. The jingoes argued that this was necessary following a whole generation of peace. They secretly called the kaiser a coward, which must have come to his ears. At any rate, he responded with an endless spate of provocative speeches filled with inane references to shining armor, the victorious German sword, Neptune's trident, and the whole Wagnerian trumpery of the *Nibelungen*.

With his usual deft touch, Wilhelm then chose to advertise what he described as his "Anglophile views" by granting an interview to the *London Daily Telegraph* in October 1908. In this interview he sought to restore affable relations and British affection for Germany by saying with delicate tact: "You English are like mad bulls; you see red everywhere. What on earth has come over you, that you should heap on us such suspicion? What can I do more?"

When the resulting storm subsided, the kaiser passed the buck. He fired Bülow (who pretended—probably lying—that he knew nothing of the incident) and replaced him as chancellor with the mediocre Theobald von Bethmann-Hollweg who had the dubious honor of presiding over the cabinet that led Germany into World War I. He could also boast the dubious distinction of having told the British ambassador that Berlin's guarantee of Belgian neutrality was nothing but a "scrap of paper." Bülow had not been a genius, but Wilhelm had considered him a friend—a trust he did not confer on Bethmann-Hollweg.

Meanwhile the general dilapidation of the Romanov family which had been proceeding apace since the Petrine throwback, Alexander III, gained momentum. Having been duped by his own vanity and misjudgment of Cousin Willy's propaganda and by Plehve's counsel that a swift, cheap military success in Asia would ease internal problems in Europe, Nicholas found himself being eaten up by two ravenous dogs he had personally unleashed, war and revolution. This traumatic experience was succeeded by the unpleasant discovery that he had been duped by that untrustworthy diplomatic rube, the kaiser.

Nevertheless, by one of history's strange paradoxes, the first decade of the twentieth century had certain amazingly positive effects in socially and economically underdeveloped Russia. Science, technical competence, industry, agriculture, and the national economy strangely enough spurted forward despite the diversion of war and the chaos of revolution. And even though the Duma (imposed by popular demand for a legislature) had virtually no real power, the mere fact that a form of parliament existed encouraged the struggling forces of progress.

The need to repress the 1905 revolution and the wave of strikes and manifestations rippling across the land threw Nicholas straight back into the hands of reactionary elements, a situation he undoubtably regarded as suitable to a divinely anointed autocrat. It was his good fortune, however, to discover among the leaders of this faction a remarkably efficient, honest if conservative man, Peter Stolypin, who became prime minister in November 1906.

Stolypin at least put the basic economic and social system

Peter Stolypin, was a large bearlike man of stolid courage and vigorous patriotism. When Witte fell, he was made Minister of the Interior and then president of the Council of Ministers. After a year of parliamentary chaos he emerged as the strong man of Russia. "The more I see of that man," Nicholas declared, "the more I like him."

in order. He encouraged the growth of an independent farmer class, the *muzhiks,* and the more prosperous *kulaks,* who were hard-working, staunchly loyal to the empire, and eager to advance, until they were wiped out some years afterward by a man named Stalin, more successfully autocratic than Nicholas ever dreamed of being. Stolypin remained in office until 1911 when, as was becoming commonplace, he was shot to death in Kiev by a terrorist who was probably an *Okhrana* agent, at least by avocation.

It is significant that in Kiev at that moment, exiled from St. Petersburg by Stolypin's personal order, was an unkempt, shaggy priest who shouted as the prime minister's carriage

Rasputin.

drove through the city a day before his assignation with doom: "Death is after him! Death is driving behind him!" The name of this extraordinary clairvoyant was Grigori Efimovitch Rasputin. And the effect of his personal influence upon the last chapter of the Romanovs was in some ways even more dangerous and more doleful than that of Kaiser Wilhelm.

Rasputin was a man of fascinating vitality, incredible sexual capacity and endurance, an unquestionable hypnotic power and, with what developed into an enormous appeal for society ladies, an appeal apparently enhanced by his personal filthiness and animal magnetism. An Orthodox quasi-monk, descended from poor Siberian peasants, he was virtually illiterate. He lived in his village until the age of thirty-three together with his wife and three children (a normal privilege of monastics from the Eastern creed, although Rasputin wasn't even officially ordained). He adopted the philosophy (if not proven membership) of a sect called Khlysty whose foremost idea was that salvation could be attained only by total repentance and that this became far more achievable for one who had truly transgressed. "Sin in order that you may obtain forgiveness" was the practical rule of the Khlysty. Rasputin followed this instruction with commendable and lavish thoroughness.

The impressive fashion in which the *starets,* or holy man, carried out his credo early earned for him the surname (at that time, like many peasants, he had none) of Rasputin which means approximately "the dissolute." His fantastic sexuality was famous even among the lusty and primitive folk of his native Tobolsk province, who had little amusement apart from procreation. Once he had established himself in St. Petersburg and set to work sinning with wholesale determination among the gossipy female upper crust, this prowess almost came to be regarded as a national asset to be shared among the capital's penitent set.

The hairy, stinking *starets* with his uncombed mane and beard and burning eyes was initially taken up in St. Petersburg by Bishop Hermogen of Saratov and Heliodor, a well-known clerical mystic. Hermogen had entrée to many fashionable salons as was then customary in devout Orthodox, upperclass Russian circles. He first came to the attention of the imperial family through Grand Duchess Militsa. Within a very short time queues of society women, interspersed with prostitutes, the wives and daughters of millionaires, and actresses and ballerinas, were forming at his modest lodgings craving the benefit of his saintly attentions. Rumor spread that he had correctly prophesied the birth of a male heir, the czarevitch, shortly before the poor hemophiliac arrived on earth. Shortly thereafter Militsa persuaded the Grand Duke Nicholas to introduce Rasputin to the czar and czarina.

The latter soon fell enthusiastically under Rasputin's sway, especially once she became convinced the monk's mesmeric talent was able to stop Alexis's incessant hemorrhages. Even the czar came under the spell of this Dostoievskian personality. He consulted the weird, uneducated charlatan on abstract matters like foreign policy. Rasputin, who clearly had developed an insatiable lust for power as well as for its trappings, was shrewd enough to reassure Nicholas by always telling him what he most wished to hear. Thus he affirmed the divine inspiration of the czar's terrestrial autocracy.

In the unquestionable decadence of the last Romanov rule Rasputin became a figure of real political importance. Those in search of appointments or promotion for themselves or for their favorites sought his approval in advance. They bribed him with everything from cases of Madeira wine to the availability of their bodies, or those of their daughters or wives.

In between his endless bouts in bed he caroused around the capital, staggering from bar to cabaret to orgy. On the order of those charged with protecting the imperial family, his person was safeguarded and his privacy guaranteed by the police, thus, on occasion, frustrating the rage of deceived husbands and lovers. Meanwhile, always indefatigable, he spent his days alternating between prayer and ceremonial religiosity on the one hand and peddling influence, jobs, and information with the coterie of male toadies that formed around him, hoping to profit from his extraordinary prestige.

A principal messenger and tout for the *starets* was a dumpy, unattractive friend of the czarina named Anna Vyrubova. She was the daughter of a court bureaucrat and therefore had access to the highest ranks of officialdom. Her main role, however, was to serve as a personal liaison between Rasputin and the empress. It thus became possible for Alexandra to send or receive messages directly and also to meet the monk whenever she so desired. Although she could not dare to visit his apartment, the czarina often saw him in Anna's house.

Whether Alexandra ever allowed herself the religious joy of embracing Rasputin in order subsequently to repent, there is no doubt that in her eccentric way she loved him and was spellbound by him. She wrote to the monk in 1909: "I kiss your hands and I lean my head on your beloved shoulders. . . . I only wish one thing: to fall asleep, to fall asleep forever, on your shoulders and in your arms."

Empress Alexandra with her daughters, Olga, Marie, Anastasia, and Tatiana, about 1910.

XI   AND FIRED
THE SHOT HEARD
ROUND THE WORLD

Sᴀʀᴀᴊᴇᴠᴏ, ᴛʜᴇ ᴄᴀᴘɪᴛᴀʟ ᴏꜰ Bᴏꜱɴɪᴀ, ᴡᴀꜱ ᴀ ᴍᴏᴅᴇꜱᴛ ʀɪᴠᴇʀꜱɪᴅᴇ town in 1914, set among wooded hills and featured by slender minarets reaching skyward from the numerous mosques. The bazaars were noted throughout Islam and metal-smiths hammered, carpenters sawed furniture, veiled women wove at their treadle-looms, merchants gathered daily for their pilaff and *razniči,* broiled nuggets of mutton. The Bosniaks were largely Moslem in that region, but all save a few Albanians were Slavic. Their ancestors had been forcibly converted by Turkish conquerors and overlords since they preferred a switch in gods to the agony of impalement.

Storks customarily nested on Sarajevo rooftops during their seasonal flights. Beadles from Mecca came for prolonged visits each year to arrange, for cash, surrogate pilgrimages by prosperous, devout but lazy or unhealthy Moslems or, if the customer had already died, prayers at the Kaaba for the departed souls, in exchange for payments by affectionate relatives. While awaiting custom, they sat around quaffing saffron-flavored drinks and puffing hubble-bubble pipes through their long stems, their glittering bird-of-prey eyes and hooked noses marking them as Arabs. Through Sarajevo rilled the shallow Miljačka River, tumbling down from the surrounding low mountains.

In June 1914 the sclerotic old emperor, Franz Josef, decided to send his nephew and heir, Archduke Franz Ferdinand, on a visit to this delightful place in order to demonstrate to the world and especially to all Slavs the finality of Bosnia-Herzegovina's inclusion in the Habsburg domain. Perhaps he also wished to hint that this was but a foretaste of further aggrandizement yet to come. There had been Austrian military maneuvers near Bosnia's Serbian border and the archduke was inspector general of the army. As a special concession, Franz Josef permitted his nephew, whom he didn't in the least bit care for, to take with him on the official journey his morganatic wife, Sophie Chotek, duchess of Hohenberg, whom the emperor both disapproved of and detested.

At fifty-one, Franz Ferdinand, had he worn a white apron instead of a bemedaled uniform, would have looked like the local butcher. He was heavy-set, thick-necked, had a bovine gaze, and sported a thick, upturned mustache. No one ever accused him of having a sense of humor or a subtle touch. Yet, withal, he was an honorable, decent man of considerable political vision, loyal to his poor if blue-blooded Czech wife (who had been a lady-in-waiting at court), and fond of his three children who had been banned from any succession rights by the rigidly snobbish emperor. Franz Josef had been legally forced to name his nephew heir after Rudolf's suicide, but he never felt that was reason enough to like him.

The prince dutifully did the jobs expected of his position, although these were limited. His uncle managed his best to keep him uninformed and far removed from matters of state. Nevertheless, since the emperor was by then eighty-four years old, the army (which meant the officers corps) had slowly swung behind Franz Ferdinand. He had a quiet but growing military influence. Moreover, he had formed a private "kitchen cabinet" of political counselors. Whenever he could do so, he preferred to get away from the baroque discomfort of his palace in Vienna and relax with his family at the lovely Villa d'Este in Austrian Venezia.

Rightly or wrongly—and the arguments on this subject have never been settled except by prejudice—Franz Ferdinand is widely regarded as the symbol of what might have been ethnic modernization in the Habsburg empire. To him was attributed a desire to lift the status of all Slavs under Vienna's rule to a condition equal to that of the Austrian-Germans and the Hungarians, forming a triune kingdom like the two-headed Ausgleich of 1867. Under that settlement Franz Josef remained emperor of Austria, on the one hand, but became king of Hungary, a largely autonomous state, on the other. The concept of this settlement was to attribute to Franz Josef's heir the rule of a similar kind of Slavic nation, which might someday spread from the frontiers of Montenegro into Poland.

Franz Ferdinand was a good friend of Wilhelm II who heartily endorsed the formula of a Habsburg-ruled Slavdom. That should have been enough to warn off the archduke; but it didn't. The kaiser, favoring his special genius for clothing small thoughts in striking phrases, assured Franz Ferdinand that Russia wouldn't dare oppose such a move since its cowed mood by then resembled "the spirit of a sick tomcat."

But, whatever Russia's open attitude, it clearly didn't like the idea. The Hungarians also didn't like it because it would promote to an equality with them such of their own special subject peoples as the Croats and the Slovaks. However, Franz Ferdinand was known for hearty contempt of the Magyars. For their part, the violent Serbs openly hated the concept. They regarded it as a trick designed to tie the ethnic Slavs of eastern and southeastern Europe even more tightly to Vienna. What Belgrade wanted was to center a union of all Balkan Slavs, including those of Bosnia-Herzegovina, the Slovenes of Austria, and the Croats of Hungary, under its own ambitious rule.

Belgrade is an ugly city, even though placed upon an imposing site where Romans, Turks, and Slavs have all in their turn erected fortified positions to dominate the demilune of plain extended about it, over willowed, grain-sown, river flatlands. Never having benefited from any architectural genius, singularly lacking in a sense of style or order, noisy, raucous, colorful, Belgrade possesses nevertheless a special magic of its own, like the taste of hot pepper or the sight of bright colors. It is a very old and persuasive magic.

In June 1914 the sclerotic old emperor Franz Josef decided to send his nephew and heir, Archduke Franz Ferdinand, to delightful Sarajevo in order to demonstrate to the world and especially to all Slavs the finality of Bosnia-Heregovina's inclusion in the Habsburg domain.

Three years after Vienna annexed Bosnia-Herzegovina, so coveted by the Serbs, Apis Dimitrijević, by now chief of military intelligence, reorganized his terrorist affiliate under the new name *Ujedinjenje ili Smrt* (Union or Death). Almost immediately the group's supposedly secret existence became known and it was popularly referred to as the Black Hand. The same military conspirators who had planned and carried out the assassination of King Alexander and Queen Draga controlled this political murder gang. Its aim was blazingly clear, as incorporated in its written credo: to unify "all the Serbs." This was a most loosely interpreted definition and meant a broad band of people then living in Bosnia-Herzegovina or elsewhere under the Hapsburgs as well as the inhabitants of Turkish or Bulgarian Macedonia who, according to themselves, are not "Serbian" at all. This fact was emphasized in the two Balkan wars just before World War I from which the Serbs emerged triumphant over their Bulgarian neighbors and cousins.

King Peter Karageorgević felt a genuine bond of friendship with Russia and was opposed to Austria not only because it had favored the rival Obrenović family but also because it seemed deliberately to pursue a policy of hemming in the Serbs with the implied objective of ultimately crushing them. Aehrenthal, Franz Josef's foreign minister (whom Kaiser Wilhelm snobbishly referred to as "that Jew"), had thought he could dissipate Belgrade's Pan-Serb dreams by a policy of wooing Bulgaria, the traditional enemy on Serbia's rear. Even the czar, who was influenced by Witte's cautious analysis of the Izvolsky-Aehrenthal Balkans deal at Buchlau, had to warn Vienna against the risk of war with the headstrong Serbs. "To maintain peace," he said, "I would have to choose between my own conscience and the unleashed passions of my people."

These, then, were the increasingly tense circumstances which were the background to the Sarajevo journey of Franz Ferdinand and Duchess Sophie. For years already, helped with Russian secret funds ladled out by the czar's military attaché in Belgrade, the Black Hand had been training Serbian youths and irredentists in the arts of war. They were instructed on how to use handguns, knives, rifles, grenades, and various types of bombs. Nobody can say that they were not apt learners. And any hard-working diplomat or spy could easily have been aware of this deadly postgraduate instructional course. The Habsburgs, however, dwelling amid the dilapidated grandeur of their own illusions, which they so helplessly mistook for facts, were quite innocent of impending danger.

Shortly before the Germans and Italians attacked Jugoslavia (swollen successor state of Serbia) in World War II, I came

Sophie Chotek came from an aristocratic but poor Czech family. Emperor Franz Josef disapproved and Franz Ferdinand was forced to marry her morganatically; their children were barred from the imperial succession.

to know a group of youthful Serbs learning how to be Partisans. Among them was a thin, handsome young man named Slobodan Princip. Slobodan was particularly admired because he was the nephew of Gavrilo Princip, to whom the Serbs (French being their favored foreign language) used to refer as *le principe de la guerre,* "Princip" and *"principe"* being pronounced exactly the same way in French. What they meant by this was that Gavrilo Princip had started World War I, which was a fact. His nephew, my friend Slobodan (meaning "freedom"), became a colonel in Tito's guerrilla army and died before a firing squad of Italians who had captured him—possibly he was thinking of Uncle Gavrilo in his final moments.

Apis had armed a volunteer squad of selected assassins and

The Sarajevo conspirators in a Belgrade park, May 1914. Left to right: Trifke Grabezh, Djure Sarac, and Gavrilo Princip.

helped them across the Austrian frontier into Bosnia. By the time Franz Ferdinand, Sophie, and their entourage were making their official tour of Sarajevo on June 28, 1914, the Union or Death agents were in place at selected positions along the imperial route. The more immediate result of their activities that Sunday morning was death. But the ultimate result was indeed union. All the Bosnians, Herzegovinans, Croats, Slavonians, and Slovenes of the Habsburg empire (save an unimportant small minority), as well as most of the Slavic Macedonians, soon came under Belgrade's rule.

June 28 is the Feast of St. Vitus, or *Vidovdan,* the most sacred patriotic day on the Serbian calendar. It recalls the defeat at Kossovo, the Field of Blackbirds, in 1389, when a mighty Turkish army destroyed the flourishing medieval kingdom of the Serbs and enslaved the survivors. For any Serb the word "Vidovdan" or "Kossovo" is equivalent to the Old Testament admonishment to Jews: "O Jerusalem, if I forget thee. . . ." All the Balkan peoples have the habit of commemorating their defeats, like the Dalmatians with their black-banded caps; but most of all the Serbs.

Six young men took part in the actual assassination plot. Five were Bosnian Serbs (Orthodox Christians) who had

Franz Ferdinand and his wife in Sarajevo about an hour before their assassination. For Sophie, who had been excluded by Franz Josef from the royal processions, her visit of state with Franz Ferdinand was an unusual honor.

been trained by Apis's men and the sixth a Bosniak (Moslem). Princip, who was only nineteen, commanded the operation. It was also Princip who fired the fatal shots that killed Franz Ferdinand and Sophie, after two of the conspirators had muffed bombing opportunities.

At his trial Princip defended himself with an argument that is fascinatingly similar to those used later in the century by other, less famous political killers. "I am not a criminal for I have suppressed a harmful man," he protested at his trial. "My aim is the union of all South Slavs, under whatever political regime, and their freedom from Austria."

"By what means did you think to accomplish that?" inquired the judge.

"By terrorism."

The young assassin escaped the death sentence because of his age but expired of tuberculosis and a fungus growth in April 1918, in the dank dungeon of Theresienstadt, Bohemia, a prison that became a concentration camp under the Nazis in World War II. Apropos of this grim fate, it is interesting to recall what Adolf Hitler himself wrote in *Mein Kampf*

225 ‡

"A Chain of Friendship": "If Austria attacks Serbia, Russia will fall upon Austria, Germany upon Russia, and France and England upon Germany."

of Princip's deed: "I was filled with muffled dread at this vengeance of an inscrutable destiny. The greatest friend of the Slavs [sic] had fallen under the bullets of Slav fanatics."

The reactions of other people at the time more important than the paranoiac young Austrian, who was to become brief ruler of all Europe, have a certain acerb interest today. Franz Josef could not restrain his pleasure at the thought that now, when he was summoned to other duties in an imperial paradise, his throne would be inherited by young Archduke Karl, a nephew of the slain Franz Ferdinand, and not by the latter ungracious prince who had so little sense of Habsburg proprieties that he had married a lady-in-waiting. "A Higher Power," he said sententiously, "has restored that order which I myself was unable to maintain."

The kaiser first confided to friends: "I cannot imagine the old gentleman in Schönbrunn [Franz Josef] will go to war, and certainly not if it is a war over Archduke Franz Ferdinand." But shortly afterward he invited the Austrian ambassador to lunch and that envoy reported to his government: "He quite understood that His Imperial and Royal Apostolic Majesty with his well-known love of peace, would find it hard to march into Serbia, but if we really recognized the necessity of military measures against Serbia, he would deplore our not taking advantage of the present moment, which is so favorable to us."

Nicholas II and the Prince of Wales (later George V), at Cowes, 1909.

When Nicholas received a patently deceitful message from Cousin Willy, the famous Admiral of the Atlantic, suggesting he refrain from mobilization, he interpreted this as an effort "to shake my resolution, disconcert me and inspire me to some absurd and dishonorable step. . . . I felt that all was over forever between me and Wilhelm." He was certainly right and the two were never to see each other again. But the czar had been a long time getting there. Already in 1908, after Germany had made him look as foolish as he was, he was muttering: "We won't forget it." But the "Willy-Nicky" correspondence between the two emperors, one of history's silliest and most mawkish, continued until the brink of Armageddon.

As for Rasputin, with his weirdly intuitive sense, he telegraphed through an intermediary to his good friend, Czarina Alexandra, warning her about her husband: "Let Papa not plan war, for with the war will come the end of Russia and yourselves and you will lose to the last man."

King George V of England wrote in his diary: "Terrible shock for the dear old Emperor." And the Russian ambassador in Vienna sent word home: "The tragic end of Archduke Franz Ferdinand found little response here and on the stock exchange, this index of the mood in business circles. The value of government stocks did not change which is explained here by confidence in the continuation of peace."

And even Nicholas, when confronted with his worried and incompetent war minister, General Sukhomlinov, left the latter with this tranquil impression: "To judge by the calmness, or more exactly the equanimity, with which the Czar listened to my report of current business, one might have come to the conclusion that there was nothing that might affect in any way the peaceful life of Russia. I was amazed at His Majesty's impassiveness and the slightness of his interest in what I had to say."

XII

PRECISELY
HOW THE LAMPS
WENT OUT

EACH OF THE THREE DYNASTS HAD, BY THE EVE OF WORLD War I, become decreasingly interested in his statesmen and increasingly interested in his generals. Therefore, all three allowed themselves to be bundled off willy-nilly into a conflict which, in fact, only the generals really wanted. Moreover the emperors personally paid an initial price in boredom for this lethargic lack of interest. The generals quite rightly thought they could do better without their theoretical bosses who, although technically commanders-in-chief, were rank and inexperienced amateurs. The ultimate price the emperors paid was loss of their crowns.

The blind and foolish danger of such a martial trend had long been envisaged. Time and again Wilhelm's unhappy mother, Princess (and briefly Empress) Vicky, had spoken of the "dreadful militarism" rising ever more darkly on Germany's horizon. And the percipient Bismarck, before the last kaiser dropped him, had warned Austria: "We must both take care that the privilege of giving political advice to our monarchs does not in fact slip out of our hands and pass over to the General Staffs." Yet this is precisely what occurred —in Vienna, in Berlin, and in St. Petersburg.

During the nineteenth century a particularly stupid philosophy of militarism was developed by Prussia's stiff crop of generals. From them it spread into all the principal military academies and general staffs. The first and greater Helmuth von Moltke, victor of the Franco-Prussian War, expressed this in a letter written on December 11, 1880, in which he said:

> War is an element of the world order established by God. It fosters the noblest virtues of man, courage, self-denial, obedience to duty, and the spirit of sacrifice; the soldier gives his life. Without war the world would stagnate and sink into materialism.

The fact that this is cant did nothing to lessen its effect. He pontificated (with Heinrich von Treitschke, another bellicose pseudo-philosopher) that war was simply one price paid for continuing vitality and a nation would falter without occasional excursions to the battlefield. Indeed, Moltke insisted that the moment a country began to mobilize, politicians should become quite silent and should not resume their normal function until the military gave its assent. The widespread influence of such inhibiting ideas, especially among the professional officer corps of Germany, Russia, and Austria-Hungary, had a detectable paralyzing effect on the national

Kaiser Wilhelm II and General von Moltke at the front, October 1914. General von Moltke was the nephew of the great Prussian field marshall, who was the greatest strategist of the later half of the nineteenth century. General von Moltke's strategy, partially bequeathed him by his mentor von Schlieffen, was devised to meet the problem of a war on two fronts. His vitiation of the boldness of the Schlieffen Plan is thought to have caused the German defeat at the Battle of the Marne.

Wilhelm II, Alfred von Tirpitz, and Honning von Holtzendorf.

thinking processes which, under more normal circumstances, might still have rescued the world from disaster's brink.

In Vienna, General Franz Conrad von Hötzendorf, the chief of staff and an outright hawk, did little to disguise from the emperor his taste for war and ultimate territorial expansion. Conrad had at one time been a protégé of the inadvertent cause of it all, Franz Ferdinand. However, the latter broke with him when he authorized high Austrian officers to order Colonel Redl, the former intelligence chief, to take his own life after it was demonstrably proven he was on the Russian payroll. Franz Ferdinand, as a conventional Roman Catholic, was appalled to see his government become a prime mover in what he believed to be the religious crime of suicide.

General Conrad was overconfident of Habsburg military strength. Furthermore, he was rendered giddy with the support of his friend, the lesser Moltke, who as his opposite number in Kaiser Wilhelm's impressive military apparatus, was spoiling for a chance to show off. Moltke placed absolute confidence in the combination of Krupp's new massive weaponry and the extraordinary German transportation and logistical system which made it possible to shift entire army corps swiftly from the hills of Alsace to the forested plains of Poland.

Moltke (and therefore Conrad) was aware also of the kaiser's efforts to outflank Russia from the south, by direct dealings with the Turkish sultan. He had even been party to the dispatch of General Liman von Sanders, a courteous, polite professional, to reorganize the hopelessly messed-up Ottoman army. For these reasons, plus faith in the famous Schlieffen Plan which was to dominate German strategy and aimed at swift victory, Conrad was ready to take a chance. "It is a sheer gamble," he admitted, but he thought, if it was not accepted, the empire might collapse.

To this argument Franz Josef replied wearily: "If the monarchy is doomed to perish, let it at least go down decorously." Such sentiments were agreeable drumbeats in the ears of Conrad. He persuaded his sovereign to write to Wilhelm: "The policy of peace which all European monarchs have pursued will be jeopardized as long as this gang of criminal agitators in Belgrade goes unpunished."

This view coincided precisely with that of the younger Moltke in Berlin. He correctly believed Russia was not yet in shape to fight a serious war, having not recovered from the agonies of the Japanese defeat and its contrapuntal revolution. Therefore, Moltke reckoned, the quicker Austria slapped down Serbian insolence the better and the less dangerous the Slavic menace would be. And Wilhelm himself, partly outraged that his friend, Franz Ferdinand, had been the Sarajevo victim, was eager for a speedy showdown. He reckoned, wrongly as usual, that the community of imperial interests would inhibit the czar from seeking to protect the murderers of a Habsburg prince by Balkan bandits. The salient fact ignored by the kaiser in his calculations was that his Cousin Nicky was personally too weak to make any such decision alone or even substantially to influence it.

Wilhelm was initially enraged by the Sarajevo murder because, as stated, the victim had been his friend and also because he was an imperial heir. Therefore it was a blow against the whole principle of sovereignty by divine right. From the start he urged violent riposte on Vienna and echoed the already bellicose intentions of his generals. Curiously, however, by the time the world was irretrievably falling into war's burning pit, he suddenly reversed himself and sought to avoid disaster when that was no longer possible. He privately noted that Belgrade's reply to the final Vienna ultimatum was acceptable.

There were no genuine German interests involved in the quarrel between Austria-Hungary and the Serbs. Notwithstanding, the Berlin bureaucracy, so heavily influenced by the military caste system dominating Germany, had fuzzily concluded that war was not only inevitable but, as the elder Moltke had argued, good. It was thought necessary to strengthen the rotting Habsburg empire by helping it defeat the insolent southern Slavs. Furthermore, according to the habits of the time, it was the correct moment for a conflict. The grain harvest had been reaped; there had been an excellent crop, and both the armies and civilians would have ample food.

What is more, there was one overriding fundamental which actually made it quite impossible to avoid a major European war once the second Moltke had virtually given his commitment to General Conrad that Berlin would back up Vienna. That fundamental was the famous Schlieffen Plan. The plan had originally been drafted in 1899 by Count Alfred von Schlieffen when he was chief of the German General Staff. During subsequent years it was continually redrafted and modified.

Schlieffen assumed that Germany would be threatened in the rear by any future war. Therefore he calculated it must prepare what much later came to be called a *Blitzkrieg* strategy. This envisioned a lightning victory over France in the west before the slow-moving Russians in the east could complete the difficult process of mobilizing troops and deploying them for action.

As early as Bismarck's time, once the German empire had been created, there had been a constant fear of simultaneous engagement on two widely separated fronts. After the Triple Entente had been formed in 1907, this fear became almost paranoiac. It dominated all of Germany's military discussions or planning.

The kaiser himself wrote in 1912 that, under Berlin's own alliance with Austria-Hungary, a Russian attack against the Vienna government

> entails mobilization and war on two fronts for Germany, i.e.,
> in order to march against Moscow, Paris must first be taken.

Paris would undoubtedly be supported by London. That would mean Germany having to fight for her existence against three Great Powers with everything at stake and possibly in the end succumb.

To apply the theory that "Paris must first be taken," the Schlieffen Plan foresaw a thrust by the major German army groups through Belgium, outflanking the principal fortified French strongpoints and plunging southward to Paris, thus knocking France swiftly out of the conflict before Russia could move at all effectively. Then, using Germany's marvelous network of railroads, sufficient elements of this conquering force would be transferred speedily eastward to defeat the czar.

Despite its subsequent (and initially minor) alterations, the Schlieffen Plan committed German statesmen to take precisely the back-seat position foreseen for them by the first Moltke, once mobilization started. The emphasis was so emphatically on military speed and military efficiency that once the kaiser pushed the General Staff's mobilization button any meaningful negotiations became impossible. Nothing, it was accepted, should be allowed to interfere with the execution of the immutable armed triumph so carefully blueprinted in advance for a knockout in the west prior to a victory on slow-moving Russia's second front. Diplomacy was finished. And since Belgium was the scheduled highway for the first great invasion of France, the fatuous Bethmann-Hollweg was being cynically but accurately correct when he told Sir Edward Goschen, British ambassador in Berlin, that the guarantee of Belgian neutrality was meaningless.

The logic of Germany's military leaders was implacable, and Wilhelm's eventual wavering attitude didn't dent it more than a feather duster would dent a granite wall. In early July Berlin encouraged the Austrians to draft an ultimatum to Belgrade that could never be accepted by the Serbs. Once the document had been prepared it was trickily held back a few days in order to give an impression to St. Petersburg that tension was easing, thus confusing Russia's strategic resolution. But when the ultimatum was at last presented, despite the fact that Belgrade agreed to virtually all its principal points, Vienna refused the exceptions. It declared war, and on July 29 the guns of General Franz Conrad von Hötzendorf —a reactionary, tough, talented, and unlucky soldier—started to shell Belgrade.

That Russia would promptly involve its enormous if slow-moving army in the resultant conflict was both inevitable and obvious. It was not only a question of political alliances. Emotional Pan-Slavic popular opinion would have damaged the czar's already weak political position had he done nothing to protect the dauntless if foolish and provocative Serbs.

But *realpolitik* also underlay sentimental blood ties. Sergei Sazonov, Nicholas's foreign minister, observed: "Russia cannot allow Austria to crush Serbia and become the predominant power in the Balkans." Already, on February 21, 1914, before the crunch of the Sarajevo crisis, an imperial crown council had agreed in St. Petersburg that only European war would enable Russia to attain its traditional objectives by seizing control of the Turkish straits and Constantinople. But the Russian generals, headed by the commander-in-chief, Grand Duke Nicholas (uncle of the czar), a huge, handsome, conscientious man who was much admired by his own officer corps, and also General Ludendorff, were fully aware their army was not yet ready for a showdown with the Germans. They reckoned this condition would not arise until approximately 1917.

As a result, there was less urgent military pressure, compared with Berlin, to dive over the cliff and be done with it. The London-Paris-St. Petersburg Triple Entente was gaining strength and there was no pell-mell hurry among its partners to test it prematurely. British warships had been visiting Kron-

*Grand Duke Nicholas,
uncle of the czar, a
huge, handsome,
conscientious man who
was much admired by
his own officer corps as
well as his German
opposite number,
General Ludendorff.*

Erich von Ludendorff.

stadt, and French President Jules Henri Poincaré, aboard a battleship, was actually at the capital when the Austrians and Germans were stirring the cauldron. It was the presence in St. Petersburg of France's chief of state that impelled the Austrians to delay presentation of their ultimatum to the Serbs. Only when Poincaré's battleship was steaming eastward into the Baltic on July 24 was the unacceptable challenge laid down.

Even so the irresolute Nicholas, for once wiser than members of his government who were being pressed by Russia's military lobby not to yield in the Balkans, sought to avoid the catastrophe. Naturally he knew nothing of the Schlieffen Plan and its need for prompt war once the General Staff button had been pushed. So the czar had at least a remote hope that he could prevent a conflict which loomed larger each day. On July 29, he even threw his generals into confusion by cancelling a general mobilization order and wiring to Wilhelm. He suggested that the dispute between Austria and Serbia be submitted to the Hague International Court. Indicating both how desperate and how confused he was, he signed the message "Your loving Nicky."

Indeed, on August 2, 1914, the Russian emperor sent a telegram to King George V of England whose text was made available to me by Princess Olga, a Romanov descendant, and which said in part:

> I would gladly have accepted your kind proposal had not the German Ambassador this afternoon presented a note to my government declaring war. Ever since the presentation of the [Austrian] ultimatum at Belgrade, Russia has devoted all her efforts to some pacific solution of the question raised by Austria's action. The object of that action was to crush Servia [Serbia] and make her a vassal of Austria. The effect of this would have been to upset the balance of power in the Balkans which is of such a vital interest to my Empire as well as to those Powers who desire to maintain the balance of power in Europe. Every proposal put forward, including that of your government, was rejected by Germany and Austria and it was only when the favorable moment for bringing pressure to bear on Austria had passed that Germany showed any disposition to mediate. Even then she did not put forward any precise proposal. . . .
>
> In this solemn hour I wish to assure you once more that I have done all in my power to avert war. Now that it has been forced on me I trust that your country will not fail to support France and Russia in fighting to maintain the balance of power in Europe.
>
> God bless and protect you.
>
> *Nicky*

It is puzzling in our own era of instant communications and instant weaponry to look back upon the way the leaders of the most influential powers, and those most directly involved, greeted the onset of a holocaust which ultimately produced about forty million military casualties, substantially more than half of all armed forces mobilized and approximately equivalent to France's population at the time. Wilhelm and Nicholas were both on yachting trips when the trouble erupted. Poincaré, as mentioned above, was also at sea, although it is fair to say there was more than a little political motive for his nautical voyage. Poincaré, as an irredentist, naturally had always to contemplate that his policy might wind up in armed conflict. He wished to reaffirm the Franco-Russian alliance at this dangerous moment.

While high-level to-ing and fro-ing continued in the glorious Baltic, the architects of Armageddon pursued their task. General Conrad's best friend in the Vienna government, Count Leopold von Berchtold, carefully ensured against any possibility that old Emperor Franz Josef might hold back at the last moment. He faked a report to him about a Serbian armed attack which had, in fact, never taken place.

Earl Grey of Fallodon, the wise and careful British foreign secretary, summoned Prince Karl Lichnowsky, Germany's ambassador, and asked Berlin to try to persuade the Austrians to seek a settlement with Serbia by negotiation. But Bethmann-Hollweg, in communicating to Vienna the Grey suggestion (as passed on faithfully by Lichnowsky), deliberately omitted part of it, thus distorting its overall meaning. This deliberate sabotage would have been (if, indeed, it had not already been) approved both by Moltke (the younger) and by Conrad.

The jingo fever rapidly swept over Europe once the guns began to sound at Belgrade which, in those days, was situated only a few hundred yards from the Hapsburg empire's frontier. In hardly any time Austria-Hungary, Serbia, Germany, Russia, Belgium, France, England, were involved. It was only afterward that Turkey, Bulgaria, Rumania, Portugal, and ultimately the United States, Japan, and other distant nations joined the dreadful game. Italy came in a year late—against its former allies of the Central Powers.

In Russia, which was to pay the heaviest price of all, the short-lived Duma endorsed the government's war policy and then decided on its own dissolution. Perhaps it dimly perceived the role envisioned by the older Moltke for politicians, so many years earlier. Almost all Socialists voted in the French and German parliaments to support the war.

Maurice Paléologue, the French ambassador to St. Petersburg, was present at the Winter Palace when the court and the principal officers of the capital's garrison gathered to hear Nicholas II proclaim a state of war. The czar stood straight beneath the most saintly icon of the Virgin of Kazan, brought before him especially for the occasion. Paléologue reported:

> The Emperor approaches the altar and raises his right hand toward the Bible which is presented to him. . . . In slow, short tones, stressing each word, he proclaims: "Officers of my Guard here present, I salute in you the whole army and I bless it. Solemnly I swear that I shall not conclude peace so long as a single enemy remains on the soil of the fatherland."

That was the precise vow of Czar Alexander I in 1812 when Napoleon invaded Russia and started a famous march that ended inside Moscow. Alexander was able to keep his word. He actually sent his own troops as far as Paris where they left a permanent memory in the word "bistro," which is a French version of the Russian for "hurry up" or "make it snappy." By that time Alexander's soldiers were impatient for their drinks. Nicholas never had a chance to keep his promise. He was deposed in February 1917 and shot by the Bolsheviks before the war had ended.

And poor Lord Grey, looking out of his windows as the evening gathered over London, murmured sadly: "The lamps are going out all over Europe. We shall not see them lit again in our time."

XIII

WE OWED
THIS SACRIFICE
TO FRANCE

The German knack for warfare had been brilliantly developed, if on a rather small scale, by Frederick the Great's tough little army. Military impulse and tradition had therefore been firmly implanted in the Prussian mind long before Bismarck managed to unite all the Teutonic peoples (save for those of Austria and Switzerland) into one mighty empire. And the army that plunged into the 1914 furnace had been tempered throughout the nineteenth century. It was initially tutored by Gneisenau and Scharnhorst, then given a philosophical doctrine by Clausewitz, perfected by the elder Moltke and by Roon, and finally presented with a magnificent plan for victory by Count Alfred von Schlieffen, chief of the General Staff between 1891 and 1905.

The extraordinarily effective war machine in which Kaiser Wilhelm rightly placed such confidence was far larger than its enemies suspected, better trained and disciplined, equipped with surprise weapons, and commanded with ruthless intelligence. Every healthy German male was available as a conscript for up to three years if the state so wished. After this there followed five years regular reserve service, then twelve years in the *Landwehr,* and further inscription on *Landsturm* rosters through the age of forty-five. All in all this provided an immense, experienced manpower pool for the high command. It was consequently able to blueprint the use of one reserve corps as a backing for each first-line corps, hopelessly upsetting French calculations of German striking power.

Moreover, a magnificently taught leadership cadre system had welded together an officer corps and general staff professionally unmatched by any other army of the time. Germany's industrial infrastructure—the driving motor of the Central Powers' coalition—was adjusted to the needs of a conflict reckoned by the high command to be inevitable. A splendid system of railways had been developed, far more capable than its foreign rivals of transporting troops and supplies across the country on instant notice.

The Ruhr factories had turned out enormous heavy howitzers which belched death with a noise that sounded like Krupp, their manufacturer's name, and whose potential had not been appreciated by the French. And, far earlier than their enemies, the Germans learned the value of mass grouping of machine guns. With reason, the kaiser's subjects, who had less aversion to discipline than most people, were immensely proud of this force despite the hardships and severities of service life.

Franz Josef's armies, while modeled along similar lines, were of inferior quality. The French, for their part, suffered both from the fact that their population (fewer than forty million) was unequal to Germany's (sixty-five million) and from their failure to qualify their own reservist training system up to German standards, thereby further emphasizing the manpower disadvantage. Paris's General Staff was not on a par with Berlin's. France's single great weapon, the quick-firing seventy-five-millimeter field piece, was insufficient by itself to rectify the balance.

Russia had vast potential strength because of its seemingly limitless human resources and the well-known bravery and hardiness of its peasant soldiery. But its industry lagged far behind that of the West; its leadership was backward and incompetent; its transportation system wholly inadequate to distribute either military material or civilian supplies; and its national morale was sapped by corruption in high places. Britain had an impressive manufacturing capacity and, despite the kaiser's challenge, a distinct naval edge (although it had not recognized in time the vital importance of submarines). However, the British army was small, experienced only in colonial battlefields, and its officers were unused to directing large formations.

These were the basic factors when the powers first hurled themselves upon one another in 1914. And on each side there were serious conceptual mistakes. The Germans knew they were condemned by their position as a sandwich-filler between Franco-British and Russian armies to strike speedily, first at the French, destroying them, while merely seeking to contain Russia's contingents. The reason they had to move initially against France instead of Russia was that the latter's geographical spaces were so immense and the speed of its mobilization therefore so slow that a lightning offensive directed eastward wouldn't manage to achieve any fundamental results. At the start of a conflict German forces would have to penetrate too deeply into Russia before finding armies large enough to be worth destroying.

The Krupp Essen steel foundry, 1873.

In analyzing the probable situation that would confront them, the French made avoidable miscalculations. Although they considered an attack through neutral Belgium a likelihood, given the pitiless amorality of Berlin's General Staff, they did not reckon that the sweep that would thereby be launched against France from north and west could be nearly so extensive as indeed it was. The reason for such an error was that the French command estimated that Germany's western army could not exceed a maximum of sixty-eight infantry divisions; in fact, Moltke deployed more than eighty-three.

Schlieffen had planned this entire audacious maneuver— a massive drive across Belgium, then wheeling down like some great iron-winged condor clanging suddenly out of the storm. But it was bad luck that the younger Moltke was chief of the General Staff when the time for action came, and not his renowned uncle, already in the grave for years. The lesser Moltke was not a sufficiently resolute gambler to play the game so carefully devised.

Schlieffen had reckoned six times as many divisions would be used in the right wing of his planned offensive as those to be deployed along the left wing holding the defensive front along the Rhine and down to Switzerland. What is more, Schlieffen wished to keep but ten divisions stationed on the Russian front in the east during the six weeks period he allowed to crush France. Then he intended to transport his victorious forces eastward against the czar. He was determined to bet everything on this viciously unbalanced maneuver. Indeed, the story is that as he died in 1905 his final words were "Keep my right flank strong."

But Moltke didn't have the grit to stick it out. He allotted eight of the nine new divisions that became available between the time of Schlieffen's death and 1914 to the left wing; only one to the right. And at the height of operations in the west, during August, he reinforced the Russian front with two entire corps. This was largely to please his friend, the Habsburg commander, General Conrad, who was anxious to disrupt Grand Duke Nicholas's mobilization by an immediate offensive. The concept failed because Moltke didn't send enough new troops to accomplish that aim. But he did withdraw too many from the west to demolish French resistance when it verged on collapse.

The first serious fighting of the 1914–18 conflict started August 4 when German troops crossed into Belgium. This invasion forced England (as Belgium's guarantor) to declare a state of war that same midnight. The fact of British entry, which indeed had seemed inevitable, proved to be an overpowering strategic loss to Berlin. Moltke had so diluted the potential effectiveness of Schlieffen's plan that immolation of a little neutral country succeeded only in outraging the world and rallying more immediate opposition to the kaiser's forces. At the same time it failed in its primary objective, the swift destruction of France.

The French hit back by moving into German-occupied Alsace and Lorraine. This kind of counterthrust had been reckoned with by Schlieffen, and tactically his ghost seemed to be prevailing when the attack through Belgium rolled on. The German supply system, however, started to falter. The French were able to fall back intact, and they held the slightly weakened invaders successfully in the first battle of the Marne, August 1914. Moltke abandoned what was left of his original intention to mount a wide sweep around to the west of Paris. The British landed in Belgium to keep Antwerp and the Channel ports out of enemy hands; they held at Ypres, despite enormous losses; and by the year's end they had replaced their originally small professional force with a "people's army" of almost a million men, eventually supported by a like contribution from the overseas empire.

That September Moltke, who had so bungled the critical moment of opportunity, was replaced by Erich von Falken-

*Erich von Falkenhayn
replaced Moltke, who had
failed to employ the
Schlieffen Plan properly.*

hayn. By November 1914 Germany inferentially admitted its strategic defeat by switching from the Schlieffen intention of speedily collapsing France to a holding operation in the west. Instead, it now assumed the offensive against slow-moving Russia, already assembling ponderous strength in its sleep-walk to destruction.

Although the czar's commander, Grand Duke Nicholas, was surprisingly ignorant of the importance of logistics and his supply system was a shambles, he had managed rather more rapidly than expected to mobilize almost a million and

DEUTSCHLANDS STOLZ!

Wilhelm II with Paul von Hindenburg. Along with Erik von Ludendorff, Hindenburg, over Wilhelm's objections, decided to open unrestricted U-boat warfare, thus bringing the United States into the war. They also decided to foment revolution in Russia, and, indeed provided a special train, which transported Lenin, among other Bolsheviks, to the Finland Station and into Russia.

a half men. Their martial capacities were widely esteemed for toughness and courage. Moreover they were backed by reserves of twice their number.

By mid-August, when the full danger of Germany's western thrust first became fully apparent, Paris requested an immediate Russian attack to ease the pressure applied by German forces pouring down from Belgium. Grand Duke Nicholas responded with a drive into East Prussia. The Germans called Field Marshal Paul von Hindenburg, a veteran of Bismarck's wars, out of retirement and made him commander in the east. Although already too old for regular service, Hindenburg lived to be succeeded thirty years later by a 1914 corporal named Hitler. As his chief of staff Hindenburg was given Erich Ludendorff (subsequently adorned with a "von"), an officer whose talents had facilitated the passage between the difficult Belgian forts near Liège.

In September the effective Hindenburg-Ludendorff tandem successively destroyed the Second Russian Army at Tannenberg and the First Russian Army at the Masurian lakes. "We owed this sacrifice to France," said Sergei Sazonov, the czar's foreign minister, when he heard the terrible news.

The deadlock on the western front, the collapse of Schlieffen's *Blitzkrieg* plan because of Moltke's maladministration, and Falkenhayn's decision to shift to a defensive stand against the French, combined to bring a new intensification of pressure against Russia not long after it started to recover from Tannenberg and the Masurian lakes. The grand duke had formed a massive phalanx of seven armies and a widely heralded "steamroller" began to rumble out of the east.

But, outmaneuvered, as inevitable in clumsy Russia, it ran short of ammunition and ground to a halt. So Falkenhayn urged yet further efforts to bring Turkey into the war on the Central Powers' side. This would bar the Black Sea door through which the Allies tried to supply the czar. Turkey's intervention was not offset when Italy abandoned its alliance with Berlin and Italian troops joined the Allies in the hopes of picking up *terra irredenta*.

Falkenhayn's eastward shift of emphasis produced four new events. In the west, British ingenuity sought to break the stalemate in Flanders by introducing a new weapon called the tank. It only succeeded in provoking the Germans to respond not long afterward with massive use of poison gas. Neither novelty was decisive. The British also sought to force a passage through the Turkish Dardanelles and were defeated. Finally, they and the French landed an army in Greek Salonika, to back up the Serbs, but they were too late to stave off that dauntless land's collapse. Meanwhile London started to raise the discontented Arabs against the Ottoman sultan and began its romantic if secondary campaign northward through the Levant.

In a peculiar way the war settled down into a schizophrenic strategic argument between the epoch's two leading German military practitioners. Ludendorff endorsed the idea of a strategy of decision in the east. Falkenhayn, thwarted in both directions, turned back westward again to apply a brand-new strategy of attrition. This aimed at producing meat-grinder battles that would immutably bleed the battered French to death. Verdun, the famous fortress and bone-mill on the Meuse, was chosen as the site to apply this gruesome plan. Falkenhayn personally named it *Operation Gericht*—Operation Judgment. He selected Crown Prince Wilhelm, the kaiser's son, to command the experiment. If it succeeded, the heir could claim the credit. If it failed, another general would be assigned the blame.

The result was a dreadful holocaust in 1916 whose least cruel casualty was Falkenhayn himself. The kaiser replaced him with Hindenburg (as always, aided by Ludendorff at his right hand). Meanwhile, the incredibly brave Russians, who had already lost numberless lives and prisoners, once again came to the rescue, causing a diversion of German

The kaiser with the younger von Moltke.

Field mass for Russian troops in Russian Poland.

efforts. By the end of the year a nearly exhausted French army had recovered all the Verdun area initially lost. The total of killed, wounded, or missing Germans, French, and British at Verdun and the related battle of the Somme alone came to an appalling 1,750,000.

The Somme campaign was for Britain the cruelest and most costly, devouring the better part of its new generation of young men as grunting, clangorous, slow tanks and waves of dauntless infantry imperturbably struggled across the dank and stinking moonscape between rows of zigzag trenches, unaware of the machine-gun bullets that mowed down humans and spattered off the sides of their deliberate vehicles. Greasy clouds of dark, smoky gas, emitted from containers of special shells, spread their poison among friend and foe alike, depending on an uncarefully predicted wind. And amid this horror, the hopeful youths who might somehow have helped to order the peace for which they were then fighting disappeared in the mud.

The human results of the 1916 meat grinder were predictable. In 1917 several divisions of the French army mutinied on the Champagne sector and turned southward to march on Paris. They were halted by hastily commandeered units, and to restore morale, courts-martial handed down two hundred fifty-three death sentences. This checked the dry rot. Nevertheless, revolutionary defeatism infiltrated the armed forces of several nations, including those of Austria-Hungary and Germany, as well as the political systems of corroded societies.

Such tangible war-weariness was given new impetus by development of political warfare techniques. Jozef Pilsudski aspired to reconstitute partitioned Poland; Tomáš Masaryk and Eduard Beneš, the Czechoslovakian minority leaders, developed great talents for this subtle art, and thanks largely to their efforts, considerable numbers of Slavic conscripts began to desert the Hapsburg armies.

One consequence of this debilitation was a secret Habsburg effort to contact Allied leaders in the hope of arranging peace after Franz Josef died in late 1916. The new emperor, Karl I, had married Princess Zita of Bourbon-Parma whose two brothers were French citizens serving as medical aides in the Belgian army. Prodded by the Vatican, Karl persuaded the pair, Prince Sixtus and Prince Xavier, to make the attempt, and they cleared it with France's president and prime minister. Karl wrote privately to Poincaré and offered to try to persuade the Germans to yield Alsace-Lorraine to Paris, also to evacuate Belgium. But all the attempt produced was contempt from the still overconfident Kaiser Wilhelm and the idea vanished into history—eventually to be followed by Karl and Wilhelm.

The attrition campaigns on both sides wrecked the reputations of the principal commanders, Falkenhayn and the French commander in chief Joffre, who were both replaced. Failure, from the German viewpoint, provoked the desperate decision to launch a new phase of sea warfare, the unrestricted sinking of *all* merchant ships within specified strategic zones by packs of U-boats, in a determined effort to cut inter-Allied maritime supply links and isolate Britain from its food sources.

In April 1917 the Allies lost nearly a million tons of shipping, but the price paid for this German gain was fatal: an infuriated United States entered the war as a belligerent. Although Berlin correctly reckoned it would be many months before American fighting power could be brought to bear in any decisive way, ultimately that power, with its fresh reservoir of healthy young men and the potential strength of its ordnance and machinery, had no perceptible limit.

In the final flailing about of the Central Powers' military machine, all kinds of flamboyant if by no means crucial events supervened. The airplane joined the tank and submarine as a key weapon of the twentieth century. Campaigns extended far afield into Africa, west Asia, and the Pacific. And arising from the immense drain on lives and national wealth in dispirited Russia, the specter of revolution loomed, ousting its first great continental dynasty, the Romanovs.

Diabolically instigated by a German General Staff which saw that the initially democratic new Russia would continue the war, Berlin decided to help guide the revolt along more extremist lines. It secretly shipped Lenin from Switzerland back home. However, once undammed, the tide of revolution and mutiny infected the other armies and, for a time, much of Europe.

Ludendorff launched one final offensive in France, which again got as far as the Marne before petering out at the end of May, 1918. On August 8 the Allies struck back viciously. Ludendorff acknowledged: "August 8 was the black day of the German Army in the history of the war. . . . The war must be ended."

Bulgaria, Turkey, eventually Austria-Hungary collapsed. The German navy refused to continue fighting. Prince Max of Baden was summoned to become chancellor and negotiate a peace. But as revolution spread through Germany, he yielded to a socialist, Friedrich Ebert, who headed the republic created when the man who might have avoided the entire cataclysm, Kaiser Wilhelm, fled.

During the first phase of World War I the professional soldiers ran things in every domain for the Central Powers whose politicians were excluded; the statesmen were muted; and the emperors themselves were politely put out to pasture.

Franz Josef didn't mind, a sad old man, battered by time, prepared (if unenthusiastically) to let Conrad von Hötzendorf move around his troops. The Habsburg ruler behaved like some dignified retired drillmaster silently watching his disciples carry on. But Wilhelm resented the fact that he was not allowed to take over direct supreme command. He was relegated to the role of passive onlooker, figuring for the most part only in official photographs with his generals. He

Few men can have inherited such a spectacularly bankrupt estate as Emperor Karl of Austria-Hungary. He is pictured here with his Italian wife Zita in their coronation robes. While the elegant routines of the great Schonbrunn palace in Vienna continued undisturbed, the empire fell apart.

did not at all like leaving decisions in the campaign against Cousin Nicky to Hindenburg and Ludendorff. He had been reluctant even to name them to their new positions. The sole appreciable influence Wilhelm exerted was restraining the use of the new battle fleet of which he was so proud. And this provoked harsh denunciations from Tirpitz.

Only later in the conflict was there one area in which an emperor, much against the advice of his wiser counselors, assumed a personal and heavy share of responsibility. This was on the eastern front where Czar Nicholas, by associating his prestige directly with ceaseless bloodletting and the bleak absence of victory, reensured the ultimate disappearance of the Romanovs, their dynasty, and their concept of political divinity.

The czar was envious of the popularity of Grand Duke Nicholas, so widely respected as an honorable professional. The grand duke, as commander in chief, had already replied tersely to a suggestion from Rasputin that the *starets* should visit headquarters: "Come and I'll hang you." That sealed the fate of Russia's top soldier. The *starets* in a rage told Empress Alexandra and she egged on the czar, playing on his jealousy by telling him he was overshadowed in public esteem by his military uncle. Consequently, in September 1915 the czar relieved the grand duke of his responsibilities, moved to general headquarters (called *Stavka*) at Moghilev, and started to play soldier on a massive, incompetent scale.

The sovereign, in fact, never achieved the role he sought, army control being exercised by General Mikhail Alexeiev, an uninspired professional. However, by replacing the grand duke he removed one of the few highly regarded symbols of both the government and the military establishment, to say nothing of the imperial family itself. And he thereby attracted to his own person all the contumely that normally comes to losing commanders.

Within a year, after the offensive of General Brussilov, designed to help beleaguered French forces at Verdun, the Russian army was truly broken. Although the nation had displayed formidable loyalty to its Alliance obligations and to the successive needs of its partners in the west, it was probably overexploited by them. By 1917, when the first phase of revolution exploded, Russia had suffered almost nine million casualties.

Winston Churchill wrote in *The World Crisis:*

> The struggle upon the Eastern Front is incomparably the greatest war in history. In its scale, in its slaughter, in the exertions of the combatants, in its military kaleidoscope, it far surpasses in magnitude and intensity all similar human episodes. It is also the most mournful conflict of which there is record. All three empires, both sides, victim and vanquished, were ruined.

Russian troops at the time of the "October Revolution" taking the oath of allegiance to Czar Nicholas II.

XIV

THE
SELF-FULFILLING
PROPHECY OF DOOM

I KNOW THAT HISTORY IS OFTEN WRITTEN BY PREJUDICED memorialists, seeking to argue their case, or given particular sentimental twists by the survivors of its events. With this in mind it is conceivable that one may exaggerate in recounting the influence upon the twentieth century of a paranoid Russian priest. Yet I doubt it.

Grigori Efimovitch Rasputin would certainly have never understood that, had he not existed, it is at least theoretically arguable communism might not have come to power in Russia and, from there, spread widely across the world. He didn't put down his own innermost thoughts or write his personal story. But then, after all, he was nearly illiterate. Also, he was murdered.

Rasputin was an astonishing man possessed of a feral animality with all its extrasensory and abnormal perception. Among other strange phenomena with which he was endowed by nature was his previously mentioned, and occasionally astounding, gift of prophecy, sometimes in the form of second sight, sometimes as prevision, as when he saw death riding behind the carriage of Stolypin in Kiev like one of Albrecht Dürer's destructive horsemen, a day before the prime minister was murdered by a terrorist. Through Empress Alexandra, Rasputin warned the czar: "With war will come the end of Russia and yourselves and you will lose to the last man."

This was a remarkable peek into the future since, when Rasputin sent his message, the conflict had not even yet begun. Nevertheless, one may legitimately stress that his was not simply an accurate foretelling. It was also to a terrible degree a self-fulfilling prophecy. For, without the rise to dreadful eminence of the weird Siberian *starets*, the self-proclaimed holy man with a twisted moral sense and no apparent philosophy at all, one can conceive that Russia, disorganized, badly led, but endowed with enormous vitality, strength, and recuperative powers, might have managed to survive the war and thereby avoid revolution.

If the unordained priest had not so persistently and so successfully sought to intervene in state affairs, to use his appalling influence in shifting his cronies and lackeys about the seats of government, today's world might be another. He burrowed for secrets which, when he learned them, he drunkenly echoed throughout the capital so that they became known to (among others) German agents. Through the czarina, who was wholly under his sway, he even exercised

Rasputin surrounded by his court. He used his appalling influence in shifting his cronies and lackeys about the seats of government. He burrowed for secrets which, when he learned them, he drunkenly echoed throughout the capital so that they became known to (among others) German agents. Through the empress, who was totally under his sway, he even exercised a role in strategic matters of which he knew nothing whatsoever.

a role in strategic matters of which he knew nothing whatsoever.

Had there been no such baneful mockery of the administrative system of even a badly run nation, it is conceivable the czar might not have insisted on becoming titular commander in chief of the forces, leaving that domain to his professionally competent uncle. It is also possible, if far from likely, that the central governance in St. Petersburg (or Petrograd, as it was chauvinistically renamed to de-Germanize it) would not have rotted so rapidly into corruption and that therefore Holy Russia might have survived and stumbled into the postwar world.

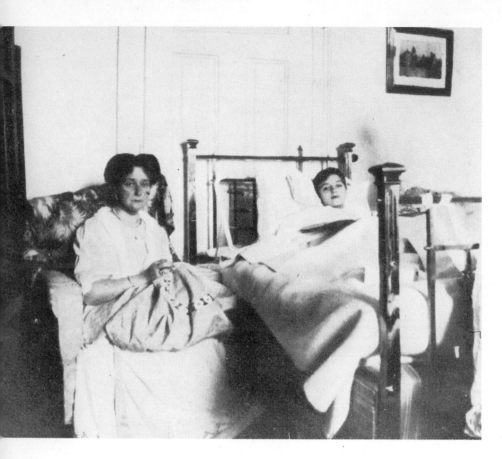

The empress by the bedside of Alexis during his grave crisis of hemophili at Spala in the autumn of 1912.

Walter Duranty, the famous, stylish, but distinctly inaccurate Moscow correspondent of the New York *Times* after World War I, sought to explain the odd relationship between Rasputin and the czarina which was the final source of all the grotesque monk's authority. Alexandra was never a popular figure, but she became heartily detested as the influence of the *starets* grew. According to Duranty, he was told the following tale in 1921 by a Muscovite woman who said she had heard it from her sister, previously a servant at the imperial court.

Twice already Rasputin's hypnotic healing powers had saved the czarevitch from serious hemorrhages. Then, when young Alexis was visiting his father at *Stavka*, the general headquarters, he developed a serious boil that was poisoning his system yet could not be lanced for fear the hemophiliac boy might bleed to death. The czarina, five hundred miles away in the capital, was consoled by Rasputin who told her:

> Daughter, all night I have striven with God, as once the Prophet Jacob strove with Him, for the life of your son. I strove and I prevailed.
>
> God told me, "The child will live," but He told me something else, that your life and the life of your son and your husband and your daughters is tied and enwrapped with mine, that so long as I live, you too will live and flourish, but when I die you will not long survive me.

Rasputin was murdered on December 30, 1916; the czar, czarina, and all their children were shot to death by a Cheka squad July 17, 1918, fewer than nineteen months later. Thus, true or not, the story fits in with the priest's known record of prophetic talents.

Even before he obtained his extraordinary hold on Alexandra and, through her, Nicholas, Rasputin had become both famous and infamous in St. Petersburg (soon to be Petrograd). The very filthiness of his habits, his malodorous body, his sweaty vestments, his hands and beard reeking, seemed to attract the more refined elements of the capital's female society.

And, of course, his legendary sexual exploits were recounted everywhere. One Duma president wrote: "I had in my possession scores of letters from mothers whose daughters had been dishonored by this insolent rake." The *starets* himself acknowledged a preference for the wealthy, aristocratic bed-partners he now acquired, when he compared them with the peasant girls of his native Tobolsk village, Pokrovskoe. The former "smelled better," he admitted, with relish and obvious truth.

Rasputin was immensely strong, although only of middle height, and when he was sober his steel-gray eyes were not only piercing but also exceedingly perceptive. Thus, for example, once he came to know the czar he said that he "lacked insides," or what one now calls "guts." Notwithstanding, when Nicholas himself first met him in 1905 he noted in his plain, unadorned diary: "We have come to know a man of God, Grigori, from the Tobolsk province."

At that time the *starets* had not yet insinuated himself into the imperial circle, since the ailing czarevitch was still little more than a year old; but he had already started to figure on police files as a redoubtable rake. "He arrived with the Princess D. at the Hotel Astoria" ran one entry. "Rasputin came home with Princess Sh.," went another, "very drunk," and a third, "Vararova, the actress, slept at Rasputin's."

He certainly seduced the czarevitch's nurse once Alexandra had started to employ his qualities as a healer; and although it is unlikely, no one will ever know whether he moved higher on the ladder of seduction to the czarina herself. Nevertheless, she wrote to him on one occasion: "Will you soon be again close to me? Come quickly, I am waiting for you and I am tormenting myself for you. I am asking for your holy blessing and I am kissing your blessed hands. I love you forever." Whether it was in a mood of innocence, sarcasm, or jealousy, she protested in writing to her imperial husband: "They accuse Rasputin of kissing women. Read the apostles; they kissed everybody as a form of greeting."

But although he became the favorite of the czar's family and also was widely venerated by the Russian peasant masses, who marveled at the ability of an impoverished, ignorant Siberian to climb to the top layer of success, he was hated by those in between these caste extremes. His original patron, Heliodor, whose own career had been shattered by Rasputin's machinations, personally blessed an organization of women and girls, most of whom had been taken and cast off by the lusty *starets,* whose sole aim was to castrate him. Heliodor even gave a special knife to a former prostitute who had joined this grim society and told her: "With this knife, kill Grishka."

From 1915 on Rasputin had to be reckoned with as perhaps the strongest individual force in the politics of a degenerate Russian government. When he recounted to Alexandra the answer of Grand Duke Nicholas to his request to visit his headquarters—an offer to hang him if he came—the czarina kept nagging at her husband until he had replaced the commander in chief, packed him off to a subsidiary command, and taken the supreme job for himself.

When Polivanov, then minister of war, made plain his dislike and distrust of the *starets,* Alexandra was told and promptly wrote to the czar: "Get rid of Polivanov." The next important victim was Foreign Minister Sergei Sazonov, Stolypin's brother-in-law. In September 1916 Alexandra dutifully complied with Rasputin's wish and wrote the czar: "Grigori earnestly begs you to name Protopopov" as minister of the interior, a half-baked, mediocre politician who had already dabbled in efforts to negotiate a separate peace with Germany, behind his allies' backs.

Quite obviously Alexandra enjoyed this meddling and her own position, as agent between the Supreme (if spineless) Autocrat and the lusty, overconfident priest. "Be the boss," she wrote to Nicholas at Stavka, adding with apparent innocence of the paradox: "Obey your firm little wife and Our Friend [Rasputin]." She would pass on the ignorant Siberian villager's tactical advice: "Our Friend finds better one should not advance too obstinately as the losses will be too great."

Just why the priest should have been so personally concerned with purely military matters isn't known. There has even been some speculation over the years that he was put up to it by German agents who played upon his vanity. In any case, one sees from Alexandra's correspondence with Nicholas that Rasputin showed an increasing interest in the most secret Stavka plans. "Our Friend is so anxious to know," the czarina explained to her husband. And, in other letters, she passed on precise logistical and tactical counsel from this amazing source:

"He says [to feed the cities] you must give the order that only wagons with flour, butter and sugar should be allowed to pass: there are to be no other trains for three days." Or Rasputin, allegedly because of a vision "he saw in the night," requested a Russian offensive on the Latvian sector. "He begs you to order that one should advance near Riga." Once, in a rather threatening phrase, she warned the czar: "He says we must always do what He says." Another time the czarina wrote: "Our Friend hopes we won't climb over the Carpathians."

That Alexandra herself was malleable material for this kind of insane transmission belt of godly advice to a divinely appointed autocrat can be understood from these epistolary observations addressed to doubting, irresolute Nicholas: "Russia likes to feel the whip. . . . Be the Emperor, be Peter the Great, Ivan the Terrible, the Emperor Paul—crush them all under you."

Rasputin was feverishly hated and eventually murdered. This comes as a surprise to no one nowadays, decades after the bizarre event occurred; nor, indeed, does it even seem to have surprised the Russian people of the time. He was without doubt a remarkable man but eminently detestable: by deceived husbands and lovers; by jealous and resentful cast-off mistresses; by honest, high-minded patriots who saw in him a wicked influence; by political leaders, bureaucrats and generals ejected from authority by his machinations; by those in high position who feared his blackmailing capacity; and by those who resented his failure to help them; quite apart from sincerely religious-minded prelates and their congregations who regarded him as evil incarnate. Beyond that, he was viewed as a genuine danger to Mother Russia in a time of terrible war.

Leon Trotsky, in his account, noted with much judgment that Rasputin's actual killing "was carried out in the manner of a moving picture scenario designed for people of bad taste." It was an appalling, frightening, and cheap crime, quite understandably perpetrated by a group of high-minded, well-placed society figures all of whom were ardent czarists. The principal plotter was Prince Felix Yussupov, the czar's nephew by marriage, a well-educated young man of enormous wealth and great privilege, a spoiled eccentric, and occasional transvestite.

His accomplices were Grand Duke Dimitri, the czar's cousin and in the line of succession to the throne, a conservative member of the Duma, Vladimir Purishkevich, a captain named Sukhotin, and Dr. Stanislas Lazovert, a military doctor. All of them, including others who assisted in the preparations but not in the actual bloodshed, were members of the capital's most snobbish social set. And the fact that they were in the end able to succeed in their attempt is quite astonishing because, inexperienced as they all were, they gossiped foolishly about their intentions, and it seems improbable that the ubiquitous police, who had been charged by the imperial family with protecting its protégé, should not have been acquainted with the plot in ample time to halt it, had they so wished.

The most careful account of this gaudy affair is that of Sir Bernard Pares, the distinguished English historian. According to him Rasputin's intuition plus widespread Petrograd chatter gave him advance warnings of danger, but, despite such intimations, he accepted an invitation to midnight supper at the Yussupovs because he apparently was anxious to meet the latter's wife, lovely Princess Irina, Nicholas's niece, and the prince had indicated she would be there because, he said, she was receiving friends. On the evening of December 29, 1916, after the conspirators had made careful plans, Yussupov called for the priest at his modest apartment on Gorokhovoy Street. As usual at that season, the capital was covered with snow, the Neva was frozen, and a black, starless sky hung overhead.

The cellar of Yussupov's palace had been specially readied for the slaughter. A heavy white bearskin rug was cast atop a Persian carpet, muffling the granite floor and useful in case of need to deaden sound. Cakes, chocolate, and sweet Madeira wine (which especially appealed to Rasputin's gluttony) had been placed on low tables. And there was also, as suitable to a *starets,* a sixteenth-century crystal crucifix resting atop an inlaid ebony cabinet.

Yussupov, with a furtive slouch and the nervousness of a novice criminal, led his guest directly to the cellar where a samovar of hot tea bubbled amid a tempting selection of cakes. A log fire burned in the hearth. The other conspirators gathered in the room above and, for some peculiar reason, soothed their anxiety by playing "Yankee Doodle" over and over again on a rather primitive, large-horned phonograph, softly, hoping the victim would imagine it to be the party of Princess Irina, who was actually in the Crimea.

Rasputin was rakishly got up for the occasion. Yussupov recalled later:

> He was dressed in a white silk blouse embroidered with corn-flowers and girded with a thick raspberry-colored cord with large tassels, wide trousers of black velvet, and long boots, brand new. Even his hair and beard were carefully combed and smoothed. As he drew nearer to me I felt a strong smell of cheap soap. He had obviously paid special attention to his toilet that day; certainly I had never before seen him so clean and tidy.

At the beginning the *starets* seemed unusually shy, which was not at all his custom, but as time passed and the two men talked, he gradually warmed up and accepted a glass of his favored Madeira and two cakes from his host. Yussupov neglected to inform him that both were well seasoned with potassium cyanide. Any normal man would have keeled over almost immediately after swallowing the dose.

Rasputin simply gobbled, gulped, and asked for more. He then began to drink seriously and heavily. Yussupov later wrote with recollected amazement: "My head reeled." Rasputin asked the prince to play the guitar for him and sat, hunched over, listening, demanding one song after another, while the fascinated assassin strummed and sang and his colleagues crowded eagerly together upstairs waiting for word that the deed had been accomplished and, in the meantime, listening interminably to "Yankee Doodle."

When nothing at all occurred after two and a half hours, Yussupov excused himself, rushed up to his friends and explained in despair that the victim appeared to be immune to poison. Midnight had long since passed. Grand Duke Dimitri was so stunned by the apparent failure of their scheme that he suggested everything be halted. However, the rest nervously resolved to push the matter to its conclusion and Purishkevich gave Dimitri's Browning revolver to the prince.

Yussupov rejoined Rasputin, holding the gun behind him. The priest was having some difficulty breathing but revived after being handed another glass of deadly wine. He even proposed with a drunken leer that the two of them should go off on a tour of gypsy brothels. Yussupov suggested instead that the *starets* should pray before the crucifix in order, as he later confessed, to "subdue the devil" in him. Then he shot him in the heart. Rasputin keeled over backward on the bearskin.

The rest of the morbid party rushed helter-skelter down after they heard the shot, and when they saw what appeared to be a motionless corpse, they returned upstairs to decide what should next be done. Sukhotin and Dimitri went off into the night to arrange for disposal of the body. However, when the prince went to the cellar again to confirm that the

Yussupov Palace on the Meika, where Rasputin was murdered.

evil priest was indeed dead, he noticed an eye twitching. Paralyzed by fear, he saw Rasputin climb to his feet and felt himself grabbed by the shoulder. One epaulette was torn from his uniform. Once again the *starets* fell backward, but when Yussupov turned and ran back to Purishkevich, Rasputin crawled rapidly after him on all fours.

He managed to summon enough strength to batter down a locked door and emerged in the snow-filled court screaming with rage. Purishkevich fired four shots at the priest, hitting him twice, and then kicked him hard in the temple when he fell sprawling on the snow. Appalled by what he had just done, he ran out into the street and shouted at two soldiers in front of the Yussupov palace: "I have killed Grishka Rasputin, the enemy of Russia and the czar."

To the absolute horror of the plotters, the body began to twitch again as they started to drag it inside, and one baleful eye opened wide. Yussupov vomited, then grabbed a heavy, loaded stick and began to hammer the still-moving corpse with it. Finally the prince passed out. Under the direction of Purishkevich, who took charge of the final stages, Rasputin was wrapped up in a heavy curtain and driven by automobile to a bridge spanning the Neva. There they stopped just long enough to heave their ghastly burden into a hole of unfrozen water. Not until January 1, 1917, after one of the victim's boots had washed up on the ice, did divers descend into the river to recover the remains.

Without doubt Rasputin was a man of nearly unquenchable vitality. It is said that a postmortem examination showed he had not even been dead when cast into the Neva filled with cyanide and three bullet holes, his head badly battered; and that his lungs had a good deal of water in them, indicating he finally expired from drowning. An unlikely story circulated that the *starets* had actually managed to untie the rope bound about his body before he died, aged forty-four.

On the same day it was recovered, the corpse was taken to

a veterans' home near Czarskoe Selo, laid out in a chapel, honored by the imperial family, and finally buried in the imperial park. The czarina kneeled in prayer before her Friend and the czar abandoned *Stavka* and his pretended management of the war to hurry to her solace.

The murder did not seem to have achieved any startling results, although for days it was the only subject of conversation in Petrograd and, indeed, throughout Russia. There were no significant changes in the government or in the political atmosphere. The killers were simply banished. But the priest's uncanny gift of prevision had not ended.

According to Rasputin's secretary, a Jew named Aaron Simanovich who had influenced his employer to oppose Jewish persecution, the *starets* sent an astonishing prophecy to the czar in late December 1916, shortly before his death. This said in part:

> I write and leave behind me this letter at St. Petersburg. I feel that I shall leave life before January 1. I wish to make known to the Russian people, to Papa [Nicholas], to the Russian Mother [Alexandra], and to the Children, to the land of Russia, what they must understand. If I am killed by common assassins, and especially by my brothers the Russian peasants, you, Czar of Russia, have nothing to fear. Remain on your throne and govern, and you, Russian Czar, will have nothing to fear for your children; they will reign for hundreds of years in Russia.
>
> But if I am murdered by *boyars,* nobles, and if they shed my blood, their hands will remain soiled with my blood; for twenty-five years they will not wash my blood from their hands. They will leave Russia. Brothers will kill brothers, and they will kill each other and hate each other, and for twenty-five years there will be no nobles in the country.
>
> Czar of the land of Russia, if you hear the sound of the bell which will tell you that Grigori has been killed, you must know this: if it was your relations who have wrought my death, then no one of your family, that is to say none

of your children or relations, will remain alive for more than two years. They will be killed by the Russian people.

This prophesy was verified by time. As Alexander Blok, a great revolutionary poet, subsequently wrote: "The bullet which killed him reached the very heart of the ruling dynasty." In 1917, only days after the first (pre-Bolshevik) revolution had seized the government, angry soldiers burst into the cemetery, levered the rotting remnants of Rasputin from their coffin, flung them on a pyre of gasoline-soaked logs and burned them.

On March 15, 1917, Czar Nicholas was forced by the first revolution to abdicate to its provisional government. That autumn the second revolution, led by Lenin's Bolsheviks, seized all power. Late during the night of July 16–17, 1918, Nicholas, his wife, and all their children were slaughtered (probably by Lenin's personal order—or, if not, with his advance knowledge) in the cellar of a modest house in Ekaterinburg where they had been held prisoner by the Cheka or security police. The next night five grand dukes and two grand duchesses were slain in a nearby town. Ekaterinburg was soon renamed Sverdlovsk in honor of Yakov Sverdlov, who arranged the administrative details for the massacre.

Looking back on this entire melodramatic and gruesome incident of Russian history, one is struck by the extraordinary gift of foresight possessed by Rasputin and other uncanny aspects of his distorted and hypnotic character. But it is impossible not to conclude that the disasters he forecast, if Russia should enter the war or if he himself should be slain by the nobles who detested him so fanatically, might not have occurred had he not managed to ascend the structure of personal power and assert so overwhelming and so evil an influence on the governance of his beleaguered nation. When a possessed priest becomes the autocrat of an autocrat, the system is immutably condemned and it requires no mad genius to discern as much.

XV

DELETED FROM THE NATION'S THOUGHTS

ONCE THE WESTERN FRONT HAD BOGGED DOWN IN THE dreadful paralysis of trench warfare, so costly in human life and strategically so pointless, the German General Staff abandoned the last vestiges of Schlieffen's battle plan and began to ponder attempts to knock Russia out of the war. Thus, for the first time in 1915, consideration was given to political as well as military action in the east in order to facilitate this objective. A memorandum was submitted to Berlin in which it was suggested that saboteurs should destroy bridges, that propagandists should spread defeatist rumors, that minorities should be incited against the domination of Great Russians, and that financial assistance should be given to the "majority group of the Russian Social Democrats" who were soon to become world famous as the Bolsheviks.

The author of this proposal was Israel Lazarevich Parvus, better known to history as Alexander Helphand, his conspiratorial alias. He was a curious, highly intelligent revolutionary from Odessa who had been a principal aide to Trotsky when the latter dominated the St. Petersburg soviet during the abortive 1905 revolution. An enormous, corpulent genius, Parvus subsequently became a friend of Lenin and at the same time concentrated on making a personal fortune. He explained to all his acquaintances that this was solely for the purpose of financing an upheaval in Russia. He had close contacts with the Germans and was the key to arranging Lenin's 1917 return to Russia; but he was ultimately spurned by the Bolsheviks. Parvus ended his days as an opulent exile at Schwanenwerder, Germany. One can never be sure how much opportunism existed in his politically schizophrenic mind and whether it was as strong a factor as his socialist credo after 1905. Much more will be heard of him later.

But in 1915 Falkenhayn, who had succeeded as the kaiser's staff chief following the failure of Moltke, junior, was still far more interested in applying military power than in toying with crackpot ideas of political conspiracy. In coordination with Franz Josef's polyglot forces he pressed hard against the Russians. The Russians fell back eastward. Their supply system, always bad, became worse. Units were forced time and again to fight without artillery shells or food. Replacements frequently arrived in the lines lacking rifles, merely awaiting the chance to equip themselves from the dead.

Although Grand Duke Nicholas had two good army commanders, Alexeiev and Brussilov, and although the troops fought with their accustomed Russian bravery, thereby preventing any major strategic German gain, by midsummer

1915 the czar had suffered four million casualties. His indecisive mind was therefore ripe for the pressures of Rasputin
and Alexandra to get rid of the grand duke and he modestly
resolved to assume military charge himself. He was probably
not qualified to command much more than a regiment of
horse cavalry. And by abandoning Petrograd for Stavka he
ceded the shadow role of autocrat to a collection of ministers
in the capital, many of whom were decidedly inferior and
some of whom had been intruded into the government for
no other reason than the favor of Rasputin and his ever-
willing friend, the empress.

In January 1916, Mikhail Vladimirovitch Rodzianko, the
Duma president and a constitutional monarchist (who would
have been considered a liberal conservative elsewhere), was
received by Nicholas. He warned the czar his country was in
a restive mood. Rodzianko himself wrote in his memoirs
that he said: "Your Majesty, for twenty-two years you followed a wrong course." He asked for a responsible government to unify the nation and sought to isolate the unpopular
czarina who, for her part, viewed the earnest if pompous
politician as a dangerous radical.

Before the year was over, however, some easement seemed
to appear in the enemy camp. The Austrian prime minister
was assassinated. Shortly afterward Franz Josef finally died,
acknowledging on his deathbed: "I took over the throne under
the most difficult conditions and I am leaving it under even
worse ones." Meanwhile the kaiser showed dissatisfaction
with his own army's failure to bring Russia to its feet. He
fired Falkenhayn and appointed Hindenburg, the old retired
veteran, as chief of staff, as always with Ludendorff beside
him, this time as quartermaster general.

It was the determination of that resolute pair of warriors
which finally brought about Germany's greatest military coup,
the intrusion of Lenin into Russia to take over revolutionary
leadership and bring peace in the east, and Germany's greatest

military debacle, the proclamation of unrestricted submarine warfare, which brought about United States entry into the conflict and disaster in the west.

By the time of this change in the German high command the czar had lost far more than the cream of his initially mobilized huge army; virtually the entire first generation of officers up to field grade had been wiped out. And they had represented a first-line defense of the regime against the increasingly obvious current of discontent and possible revolution that was running through the battered, weary, disconsolate, and badly equipped forces. In addition, as more and more peasant boys were conscripted to fill up manpower gaps in the lines, often accompanied by requisitioned horses, the farmers became surly; agricultural production fell.

Currents of pro-German sentiment, or at least a belief that peace at any price was better than continuation of the hopeless conflict, began to emerge. Even Rasputin was thought by many to oppose the war. The empress's nickname of "the German" was by now supplemented often with scurrilous adjectives. Her close adviser, Alexander Protopopov, an advanced syphilitic, was named minister of interior because as mentioned earlier the *starets* had let it be known through Alexandra that he wished it. The new minister had actually preceded the appointment with almost treasonable secret efforts in Stockholm to negotiate a separate peace with Germany.

By the start of 1917 it was evident to the government, to the capital's intellectuals, to all the various groups of eager revolutionists, to most generals, and to virtually the entire population of Petrograd that trouble was in the offing. The czar had come back to Czarskoe Selo for the annual New Year celebrations. On January 12 he received Sir George Buchanan, the British ambassador, who boldly told him: "Your Majesty must remember that the people and the army are but one, and that in the event of revolution only a small

portion of the army can be counted on to defend the dynasty."
Two days later, at the imperial reception for the New Year
(old-style calendar), Rodzianko added his own potion of
gloom:

> Your Majesty . . . I consider the state of the country to
> have become more crucial and menacing than ever. The
> spirit of the people is such that the gravest upheavals may
> be expected. Parties exist no longer, and all Russia is unani-
> mous in claiming a change in government and the appoint-
> ment of a responsible premier invested with the confidence
> of the nation. . . . To our shame, chaos reigns everywhere.
> There is no government and no system, neither is there, up
> to the present, any coordination between the front and the
> rear.

Neither Buchanan nor Rodzianko possessed quite the gall
to remind the czar that General Krymov, a respected officer,
had told Duma members:

> The spirit of the army is such that the news of a coup
> d'état would be welcomed with joy. A revolution is immi-
> nent, and we at the front feel it to be so. If you decide on
> such an extreme step, we will support you. Clearly there is
> no other way. You, as well as numbers of others, have tried
> everything, but the emperor attaches more weight to his
> wife's pernicious influence than to all honest words of
> warning.

The weak-minded czar, who had never really been an
autocrat in more than his own fuzzy mind, was incapable of
understanding the situation that faced his nation and his
own dynasty. He was even unable to distinguish a true revolutionary from a sincere but loyal opponent, although the revolutionists, in any organized sense, still constituted a very
small and very divided fraction of Russia's immense, angry
and disheartened population.

Alexander Kerensky, guiding spirit of the first, pre-Bolshevik, uprising, himself reckoned that at the start of 1917, the watershed year of modern Russia, there were only thirty-five thousand members of the Socialist Revolutionary and Social Democratic parties and that the maximum strength of the Bolshevik faction was fifteen thousand. Certainly the majority of this amorphous left were relative moderates.

Georgi Valentinovitch Plekhanov, the first important Russian Marxist, was abroad and returned to his country only a few days before Lenin. Plekhanov urged patriotism. He saw victory in the war as the first necessary task. Trotsky, still a Menshevik himself, was in America and by no means convinced that the conflict would directly affect the political balance. Even Kerensky, whom the *Okhrana* particularly feared because of his oratorical brilliance in the Duma, said later: "No party of the left and no revolutionary organization had made any plan for revolution."

But discontent was swelling. The Petrograd garrison of 170,000, mostly untrained draftees, was unenthusiastic about the prospect of becoming cannon fodder. They longed for the peace and bread already being stressed as goals by underground Bolshevik propaganda being smuggled into the country. Moreover, because of the absence of rifles with which to drill, they had an unexpectedly large amount of free time to attend political meetings.

On February 27 Kerensky told the Duma:

> To prevent catastrophe the czar himself must be removed —by terrorist methods if there is no other way. If you will not listen to the voice of warning, you will find yourselves face to face with facts, not warnings. Look up at the distant flashes that are lighting the skies of Russia.

Processions began to crunch through the Petrograd snows chanting, "Give us bread." All public transportation in the capital gradually ceased. Red banners appeared and there were shouts against the government, always to the counter-point of "Down with the war."

On March 9 Buchanan reported to London: "Some disorders occurred today but nothing serious." However, a labor argument at the Putilov steel mills had brought about the lockout of more than thirty thousand workers. This added to the tension produced in Petrograd by a lack of bread, in part occasioned by blizzards which blocked trains coming in from the countryside. The various leftist organizations proclaimed special coordinating committees and announced a three-day strike. Some of their top leaders were arrested, but this had no discernible restraining effect.

The czar was back at Stavka once again playing soldier. When the foolish Protopopov, now prime minister, telephoned him at headquarters on March 10, Nicholas replied by a telegram with which it was impossible to conform, instructing General Khabalov, military governor of Petrograd: "I command that the disorders in the capital, intolerable during these difficult times of war with Germany and Austria, be ended tomorrow." Khabalov placarded the city with posters repeating these instructions. Nobody paid the least attention to them.

By late afternoon of March 11 there was shooting on the loveliest thoroughfare, the Nevsky Prospect, and before midnight approximately two hundred had been killed, although army units fired against civilians with notable reluctance. One company loosed its volleys deliberately into the air; another shot its commander. Rodzianko wired the czar: "There is anarchy in the capital. The government is paralyzed."

March 12 marked the historical frontier, although it was then barely perceptible. In the morning the czar's government remained theoretically in charge, if wholly helpless. But all day long the military garrison chipped off in mass desertions. They seized the powerful fortress of St. Peter and St. Paul, a military barracks as well as a cathedral, in the early afternoon.

By nightfall, almost seventy thousand soldiers and sailors had thrown their lot in with the revolution, a revolution that had not yet consciously taken place.

As the czar's cabinet disintegrated in despair, the Duma named a temporary government with Rodzianko as chairman. It took over one wing of the Tauride Palace while, ominously, a Petrograd Soviet of Workers' and Soldiers' Deputies, already far to the left of the new regime, took over the other. By the morning of the thirteenth, the only organized force remaining loyal to the czar was a unit of fifteen hundred troops under the unfortunate Khabalov. That very day Nicholas left *Stavka* for the last time, heading for the capital aboard his special train.

Meanwhile, there was a fevered scramble to join the revolution. The czar's own imperial guard officially swung behind it, marching past the Tauride Palace bearing its icon-covered regimental standard amid a cluster of red flags. Then came the regular Czarskoe Selo garrison in a procession witnessed by the French ambassador: "At the head were the Cossacks of the escort, those magnificent horsemen. . . . Following was His Majesty's Regiment, the sacred legion." After them marched the marine guard, led by their commander, Grand Duke Kyril, himself a Romanov, who pledged allegiance to the Duma and thus broke his oath to the czar. Wild celebrations encompassed the bewildered city. In Kronstadt sailors slaughtered officers. The capital's prisons were opened; policemen in uniform were torn to pieces. Kerensky observed: "The revolution came of its own accord, born in the chaos of the collapse of czarism."

On March 11, Alexandra had telegraphed Nicholas shortly before he quit *Stavka,* "All is calm in the city." Therefore he was undoubtedly amazed when, on the thirteenth, a message reached him aboard his train advising him that the Winter Palace had fallen to a rebel horde. That night his escort was informed revolutionary soldiers were blocking the track ahead and the train was diverted to Pskov where he learned that the entire Petrograd and Czarskoe Selo garrisons had gone over to the temporary government.

General Alexeiev, meanwhile, told Rodzianko that abdication was immediately needed if there was to be any chance of pacifying the situation and that the generals commanding the different military fronts shared this view. On the fourteenth similar demands poured in from other quarters. The admiral of the Baltic Fleet admitted: "It is only with the greatest difficulty that I keep the troops and fleet under my command in check." Grand Duke Nicholas, the patriotic former commander in chief, begged for abdication.

That same day, while fighting and riots swirled through Petrograd, a packet of documents was handed to Kerensky, who was growing in stature and oratorical skill with each hour of his new eminence. "Those are our secret treaties with the Powers," he announced after a brief study. "Hide them." And shortly afterward the acting government issued its famous Army Order Number One, originally intended for the capital's garrison only but used, in no time, to disrupt and crumble Russia's entire military organization. This placed the forces politically in the charge of the Petrograd soviet or of soldiers' committees, then mushrooming everywhere, and gave to company and battalion committees the charge of all arms.

On March 15 Nicholas signed an abdication document that had been drawn up under General Alexeiev's supervision. It passed on the emperor's titles and authority to the twelve-year-old, hemophiliac czarevitch who thus became, for an instant, His Imperial Majesty Czar Alexis II. However, the same evening, after consulting the boy's doctor and learning how grave was the risk of his unpredictable health, Nicholas changed his mind, explaining:

I have decided to renounce my throne. Until three o'clock

The former czarevitch, Alexis, to whom the former Czar Nicholas II in abdicating did not leave the succession, because he did not want to be separated from his son and his wife, Alexandra.

today I thought I would abdicate in favor of my son, Alexis. But now I have altered my decision in favor of my brother, Mikhail. I trust you will understand the feelings of a father.

He formalized this in an official proclamation, which said:

> The cruel enemy is gathering his last forces, and already the hour is near when our gallant army, together with our glorious allies, will be able finally to crush the enemy. . . .
>
> Not wishing to part with our dear son, we hand over our inheritance to our brother, the Grand Duke Mikhail Alexandrovitch, and give him our blessing to mount the throne of the Russian State. We bequeath it to our brother to direct the forces of the State in full and inviolable union with the representatives of the people in the legislative institutions, on those principles which will by them be established. . . .

No great concession, that—retiring to democratic constitutional monarchy when he no longer had the power to bequeath anything at all. He confided to his private diary: "Left Pskov at one in the morning. All around me I see treason, cowardice and deceit."

Mikhail received the news by imperial telegram at Gatchina, among pine forests along the Izhora River to the north. The message said in part: "To His Majesty the Emperor Mikhail: Recent events have forced me to decide irrevocably to take this extreme step. Forgive me if it grieves you and also for no warning—there was no time. Fervently pray God to help you and our country. Nicky."

But the soviet in Petrograd would have no truck with monarchy at all, under any conditions. Both Rodzianko and Kerensky warned of the violence that would follow Mikhail's accession. Rodzianko was to write: "He asked me point-blank whether I would vouch for his life if he accepted the crown and I was compelled to answer in the negative because there was no armed force I could rely upon." Mikhail thought this over for five minutes and then announced: "I have decided to abdicate." Kerensky was delighted. "Monseigneur, you are the noblest of men," he said. A second abdication was typed out on the desk of his children's schoolroom and Mikhail signed. He was the last czar: theoretical and brief.

The Duma's temporary regime had been transformed, by itself, into a provisional government on that same March 15. Prince Georgi Evgenievitch Lvov, a member of the great nobility but also an old-time member of the *zemstvos* and a Constitutional Democrat, was named the first prime minister. Strangely enough, this blue-blooded inheritor of a revolution played a role vaguely similar to that of another high aristocrat, Prince Maximilian of Baden, who presided over the liquidation of the Hohenzollern dynasty of Germany.

But although Prince Lvov was premier and Pavel Miliukov, a well-known Liberal, was foreign minister, Kerensky, as minister of justice, dominated the new regime. Kerensky was an intelligent man, a generous and ardent lawyer who had defended many people persecuted for their political opinions. He was probably the best Russian public speaker of this century—until Leon Trotsky arrived back on the scene. He was also a brave man who had protected disgraced czarists from menacing crowds, personally escorting the last interior minister, Protopopov, through a savage pack of enemies and warning those who threatened him: "Don't dare touch that man. The Imperial Duma does not shed blood."

Kerensky sought to create a democratic, constitutional form of socialism and at the same time to establish the habit of justice, something that had never really existed in Russia in any widespread, durable sense. He outlawed capital punishment, and although he interrogated the czar and czarina, having personally ordered their arrest, he showed himself merciful and gentle and finally concluded there had been nothing treasonable in the behavior of either. He told a meeting of would-be regicides at the soviet that he refused "to

Kerensky as Minister of War, reviewing the troops in 1917.

The first demonstration in Petrograd, in front of the monument to Alexander II, in March 1917. Already red flags and revolutionary inscriptions can be seen.

play the role of a Russian Marat." It was Marat who insisted on the execution of France's King Louis XVI. Kerensky merely concluded: "Nicholas, as a monarch, was deleted from the nation's thoughts."

In Moghilev, from where Czar Nicholas was taken to Petrograd, he was allowed on March 21 to send a final message to his armies:

> For the last time I address you, the troops which I so fervently love. Since my abdication, for myself and for my son, from the throne of Russia, the power has passed to the

Provisional Government, which has risen on the initiative of the Imperial Duma. May God help it to lead Russia along the road of glory and prosperity. May God help you too, gallant troops, to defend our country from the cruel enemy.

From its beginning the Provisional Government wished to get the czar and his family to safety. Kerensky declared afterward: "The former emperor and the imperial family were no longer enemies but simply human beings who had come under our protection. We regarded any display of revengefulness as unworthy of Free Russia." He hoped a haven could be found for them in England, and tentative arrangements were made to send a British warship to Murmansk, whither Kerensky personally offered to conduct them. The Germans pledged that the vessel could proceed in safety together with its royal passengers. However, the Petrograd soviet objected to this plan. British Liberal and Labor politicians also protested.

The Imperial Manifesto, granting rights and liberties to the Russian people, is read out at the University of St. Petersburg on October 31, 1917.

Consequently, London was forced with some embarrassment to withdraw its hospitable proposal.

At first the Romanovs remained in Czarskoe Selo, leading a secluded life under the constant eye of rough soldiers who had replaced the former elegant imperial guard. The palace was a fine building erected in splendid grounds by Catherine II. It was beautifully furnished and contained many works of art. The rooms of the great empress faced south, overlooking an "English garden" and had not been touched since her death in 1796.

Nicholas behaved with a simple dignity that earned the respect of both the new garrison and occasional officials whom he saw. The entire family worked hard, almost as if it had become a commune. A school was organized, largely under Alexis's Swiss tutor, Pierre Gilliard, and the czar served as history professor. But the czarina, who had aged perceptibly, was remote and subdued.

In August, four months after the return to Russia of the extremist Bolshevik leaders, Kerensky (who succeeded Lvov) decided for their own safety to transfer the Romanovs to Tobolsk in western Siberia, near Rasputin's native village. They lived in a pleasant, simple house and were well treated by sympathetic townspeople. Kerensky, who had just become prime minister August 6, personally instructed a detachment of the ex-czar's guard to behave impeccably. There the imperial Romanovs remained, but their condition deteriorated rapidly after the Bolsheviks took control of Russia. In April 1918 the prisoners were transferred on orders from the Cheka, which had replaced the czarist *Okhrana,* to Ekaterinburg (now Sverdlovsk). That is where they were eventually murdered during the night of July 16–17, 1918.

What killed all chances of survival for the Provisional Government and for the short-lived subsequent Kerensky republic was its determination to keep fighting beside the Allies. Although the Germans had refrained from any initia-

Red guards in Petrograd, 1917.

The czar and his family at Tobolsk where they were interned from September through April 1918.

tive on the eastern front since the first revolution started in 1917, hoping the new regime would ask for peace, it responded to Western pressure by agreeing to continue the war. When former U.S. Secretary of State Elihu Root visited Russia in June 1917, he said bluntly on President Wilson's instructions: "No fight, no loans." He demanded a new Russian offensive. Kerensky agreed.

Even the best army commanders knew this was a fatal mistake. General Alexei Alexeivitch Brussilov, one of the czar's two best generals who later became commander in chief for Prince Lvov's Provisional Government and still later fought for the Bolsheviks, wrote: "The soldiers did not want to fight any more." Indeed, Kerensky's order to resume the conflict was the equivalent of political suicide. The door was opened wide to the ruthless, determined, intellectually brilliant Lenin, with his fundamental slogan, bread, peace, and land. For years he had aspired to power and had planned how to seize it. Once that power was gained, he also knew what to do with it.

XVI

THE
MOST GRISLY
OF ALL WEAPONS

IN REVOLUTIONS THE LEFT, OR EXTREME, FACTION ALMOST
inevitably gains eventual control over the new regime, although it is common that once it is established, reaction sets
in. This was true for the regicides of Cromwell's seventeenth-
century insurrection; for those who insisted on breaking all
ties with Britain and seeking independence instead of a fairer
role for the American colonies in the eighteenth century; and
for the Jacobins, a few years later in France, who slaughtered
the royal family and leading aristocrats until Napoleon took
over and soon assumed the imperial purple.

And it almost surely would have been true of the 1917 Russian revolution even if the Germans had not deliberately shipped Lenin and his principal Bolsheviks to Petrograd. The Hohenzollerns, in effect, used Lenin to overthrow what was left among the ashes of the Romanov legacy and to kill the Romanovs themselves. History, however, has its own grim sense of humor. The revolutionary dragon's teeth sown by Germany in Russia were to grow so mightily that the German army was weakened by the same infection in 1918 and the German state was dismantled and poisoned by it twenty-seven years later.

The greatest single act of political warfare in military annals was unquestionably the decision of the kaiser's General Staff to send Lenin and his Bolshevik companions in a sealed railway coach across warring Germany through Sweden and ultimately to the Finland Station in Petrograd where they arrived April 16, 1917. In a striking and frequently quoted phrase, Winston Churchill was to write: "The German leaders turned upon Russia the most grisly of all weapons. They transported Lenin in a sealed truck like a plague bacillus from Switzerland into Russia."

The consequences of this act, which was designed to collapse the eastern front, were to enable a disciplined, purposeful body of extremists under the brilliant Lenin to seize control of an amorphous, confused revolution, take Russia out of the war, kill the imperial family, and sign a brutal peace dictated by the Germans. The Bolsheviks scarcely liked the terms, indeed they were revolted by them, but they knew how to bide their time.

That in the long run, over a generation later, this action would turn into a form of suicide for the Central Powers, first reducing the Reich and later carving up its successor, while at the same time disintegrating what was left of the former Habsburg domains, establishing a new European political frontier zigzagging southward from Rostock on the

Baltic to Valona on the Adriatic, could be foreseen by no one. Or that a Russia atomized by the combined impact of civil war, German invasion, and Allied intervention, would someday be the only superpower in Europe. Like so many audacious German staff plans this one initially succeeded beyond all expectation. But the final price paid to destiny proved more than exorbitant.

Lenin was the complete negation of Marxism-Leninism because he demonstrated in his own self the vital impact of an outstanding personage on the turbulent forces of history. His ideology diminishes the role of the individual personality and submerges it beneath the tide of timeless dialectics. Yet no such tide would have existed—or could have been produced—in Russia without Lenin's own indomitable revolutionary genius.

Compared to Lenin, Robespierre was an amateur and the Paris Communards were foolhardy. The Bolshevik schemer was also a decisive man of action and he swept before him the gallimaufry of Liberals and Liberal revolutionists, led by Kerensky. As Trotsky said with that lucid sarcasm which was his special literary gift: "Kerensky was not a revolutionary; he merely hung around revolutions."

Yet it is odd to see the link that intertwined the lives of Lenin and Kerensky. The former, born Vladimir Ilyich Ulyanov in 1870, was brought up in Simbirsk where his father, a teacher who had been promoted to the civil service ranks of lower nobility, although he was a serf's son, became director of schools. Lenin himself was educated at an institution whose headmaster was Kerensky's father. Although Kerensky was born eleven years after the man who was to oust him, the two had similar boyhoods in the central Volga countryside and knew the same simple charms of Russian rural life.

Lenin was introduced to revolutionary politics early. His older brother Alexander, as mentioned earlier, was implicated

Lenin addresses a crowd.

in a conspiracy to murder Czar Alexander III and was hanged, an event that left a deep psychological scar on Vladimir. Nevertheless, headmaster Kerensky wrote of him (after the execution) that he

> was first in all his subjects and upon completing his studies received a gold medal as the most deserving pupil with regard to his ability, progress and behavior. . . . Religion and discipline were the basis of this upbringing. . . . Looking more closely at Ulyanov's [Lenin's] character and private life, I have had occasion to note a somewhat excessive tendency toward isolation and reserve.

Because Lenin's father had died, Fyodor Kerensky, the school principal, was temporarily assigned by a court to supervise young Vladimir's affairs. He studied law at home, passed his bar examinations as first among those tested, and then began to devour the works of Karl Marx. In 1893 he went to St. Petersburg, sporting a top hat. There he joined a Marxist study group and met the pudgy, potato-nosed schoolteacher named Nadezhda Krupskaia whom he eventually married. During the next few years he became increasingly involved with revolutionary doctrine, journeyed to Geneva where he met the noted Russian proto-Marxist, Plekhanov, returned, was arrested and sent to prison for a year, then exiled for three more years to Siberia. This form of internal exile was, and is, an old Russian custom.

It was not then, however, the kind of painful existence it was to become in Stalinist days. Lenin fished, hunted, corresponded freely with fellow Marxists, and worked on a study of the development of Russian capitalism. At the end of his first year Krupskaia, arrested for fomenting a strike, joined him. They were married in 1898, at least as much for political as for personal compatibility. They worked steadily together on a translation of *The Theory and Practise of Trade Unionism* by the British socialists, Sidney and Beatrice Webb.

Ultimately they were released separately and met again abroad. Lenin began to draw up his program for the Social Democratic Party in Munich, London, Switzerland, and Austrian Galicia, also at various Marxist conferences in Europe. He wrote articles for *Iskra,* a revolutionary publication printed in other lands in order to be smuggled into Russia. Finally, at a 1903 meeting of Social Democratic delegates in London, Lenin's faction split with that of the more famous Plekhanov on the question of party organization. When the matter was put to a vote, Lenin gained a small majority. The party divided into two wings, Bolshevik (majority) and Menshevik (minority).

The Mensheviks were regarded as relative moderates and they were prepared to work with other parties. But Lenin did not believe largely illiterate Russia could be won for Marxism except under the leadership of a small, well-trained, closely knit group that would be ready to move swiftly and efficiently when the time came to strike. He was percipient enough in his Marxism to believe a great war must inevitably arise from the capitalist struggle for markets and that this might well sweep into the dustbin all existing governmental systems.

Churchill, who detested every form of socialism but especially the Bolshevik system devised by Lenin and is therefore not in the least bit unbiased, wrote:

> Lenin was also Vengeance. Child of the bureaucracy, by birth a petty noble, reared by a locally much respected Government School Inspector, his early ideas turned by not unusual contradictions through pity to revolt extinguishing pity. Lenin had an unimpeachable father and a rebellious older brother. This dearly loved companion meddled in assassination. He was hanged when Lenin was . . . at the age to feel.
>
> His mind was a remarkable instrument. When its light shone it revealed the whole world, its history, its sorrows, its

stupidities, its shams, and above all its wrongs. It revealed all facts in its focus—the most unwelcome, the most inspiring—with an equal ray. The intellect was capacious and in some phases superb. It was capable of universal comprehension in a degree rarely reached among men. The execution of the elder brother deflected this broad white light through a prism: and the prism was red.

But the mind of Lenin was used and driven by a will not less exceptional. The body tough, square and vigorous in spite of disease was well fitted to harbor till middle age these incandescent agencies. Before they burnt it out his work was done, and a thousand years will not forget it. . . . Lenin has left his mark. He has won his place. And in the cutting off of the lives of men and women no Asiatic conquerer, not Tamerlane, not Jenghiz Khan, can match his fame.

Implacable vengeance, rising from a frozen pity in a tranquil, sensible, matter-of-fact, good-humored integument. His weapon logic; his mood opportunist. His sympathies cold and wide as the Arctic Ocean; his hatreds tight as the hangman's noose. His purpose to save the world: his method to blow it up. Absolute principles, but readiness to change them. Apt at once to kill or learn: dooms and afterthoughts: ruffianism and philanthropy: But a good husband; a gentle guest; happy, his biographers assure us, to wash up dishes or dandle the baby; as mildly amused to stalk a capercailzie as to butcher an Emperor. The quality of Lenin's revenge was impersonal. . . .

Lenin was the Grand Repudiator. He repudiated everything. He repudiated God, King, Country, morals, treaties, debts, rents, interest, the laws and customs of centuries, all contracts written or implied, the whole structure—such as it is—of human society. In the end he repudiated himself. He repudiated the Communist system.

Nowadays, more than fifty years after his death, it is still a moving experience to visit the dull maroon marble mau-

THE FALL OF EAGLES

soleum in Moscow's Red Square, following along in a precisely formed queue, organized with a discipline that he
would greatly have admired, and see Lenin's carefully dressed
corpse, laid out beneath glass by Russia's neo-Egyptology. The
little beard on the stubborn chin protrudes obstinately; there
is an impertinent lift to the nose and the slightly Asiatic cheekbones; and the great dome of forehead testifies to the dynamic
intelligence it once housed. Lenin, as even Churchill, perhaps
his worst enemy, acknowledged, was an extraordinary personage.

Full details of the German decision to return Lenin to
Russia in order to destabilize it were not known until U.S.
Army intelligence specialists came upon the secret storage
place of Berlin Foreign Ministry files and started a thorough
study of them after Hitler's collapse in 1945. One memorandum of particular value to historians was dated March 9, 1915
and outlined a program for German political warfare against
the Russians in World War I.

Among the various suggestions listed, the first urged "Financial support for the majority [Bolshevik] group of the
Russian Social Democrats, which is fighting the Czarist government with all the means at its disposal." It forecast:

> Thus the armies of the Central Powers and the revolution-
> ary movement [of Russia] will shatter the colossal political
> centralization which is the embodiment of the Czarist Em-
> pire and which will be a danger to world peace as long as it is
> allowed to survive, and will conquer the stronghold of politi-
> cal reaction in Europe.

This was of course nonsensical, for "the stronghold of
political reaction in Europe" lay in many respects within the
Hohenzollern and Habsburg empires quite as much as within
the purlieu of the Romanovs, and the German General Staff
which ultimately acted on the proposal was scarcely famed
for its visions of peace or liberal tolerance.

Nevertheless, despite the airily couched language, the military purpose of the idea as seen by the generals was disruption of the enormous Russian empire and its armies. The idea was not acted on quickly, when it might have helped Falkenhayn in his efforts to shatter the eastern front. However, after the first 1917 revolution, when the Germans saw that the Provisional Government which had replaced the czar intended to carry on the fight beside the Allies, they reconsidered the project and finally resolved to send back Lenin. They were confident in his determination to destroy the vestigial system left behind after Nicholas's abdication and to agree to peace at any price in order to make this possible.

The author of the original 1915 memorandum was Parvus, already mentioned earlier, a Russian Jew from Odessa who had studied in Germany and joined the German Social Democratic party, moving to the left wing dominated by Rosa Luxemburg. Parvus was a close friend of Trotsky and worked with him in St. Petersburg during the abortive 1905 revolution. Later, when he had decided to make money in order (as he always claimed) to finance future uprisings, he came to know Lenin in Switzerland while at the same time building up extensive secret contacts with German officials, especially from the Wilhelmstrasse.

Israel Lazarevitch Parvus (known as Alexander Helphand) had been the first publisher of *Iskra* when the Social Democratic paper was printed in Leipzig and then smuggled into Russia to encourage revolutionaries. He had also been a successful German left-wing journalist. In 1905 he was the effective leader of the short-lived St. Petersburg soviet. He had then, in line with his search for wealth and his natural economic genius, become financial adviser to the Bulgarian and Turkish governments when they entered hostilities beside the Germans in 1915. From February 1915 on he negotiated sporadically but persistently with the Wilhelmstrasse seeking acceptance for his plan, formalized on March 9.

He persuaded the Germans to send funds to Russian revolutionaries—and after the first (February) revolution of 1917, exclusively to the Bolsheviks. And Parvus devised the intricate, indeed paradoxical, formula that because Germany was fighting harder than anyone against czarist imperialism, the revolutionary movement among the Germans must be put off for a while until class conflict followed the Great War. In this sense, he argued, the victory of Germany represented the triumph of socialism. Simultaneously, he persuaded the Germans that nationalist rebellions in the czar's domains—in Finland, Poland, the Baltic, Georgia, and Armenia—would explode when the real Russian revolution started. He developed this theory at great length to his principal German contact, Berlin's ambassador in Copenhagen, Count Brockdorff-Rantzau, who even assured the Wilhelmstrasse that Parvus had fixed a firm date for the uprising originally projected—January 9, 1916.

Once the czar had abdicated before the thrust of the February 1917 revolution and the Provisional Government had been established, the last German reluctance to accept the plan vanished. Parvus had talked the idea over at great length with Lenin in Zurich where the Bolshevik leader was then living with Krupskaia and Inessa Armand. A list of Bolsheviks was drawn up who would agree to be transported across Germany if Berlin accepted Lenin's precise demands, most of which dealt with the party's security and the secrecy of the project. Among the records discovered by the Americans in 1945 were the following coded messages:

(From Baron Romberg, ambassador in Bern, to Foreign Ministry, March 23, 1917) "Prominent revolutionaries here wish to return to Russia via Germany since they are afraid to go via France because of U-boats."

(Zimmermann, secretary of state, Foreign Ministry, to Staff of Supreme High Command, March 23, 1917) "Since it is in our interests that the influence of the radical wing of revolutionaries should prevail in Russia, it seems appropriate to authorize transit."

(Staff of Supreme High Command to Foreign Ministry, March 25, 1917) "No objections to transit of Russian revolutionaries traveling as a group and reliably escorted."

On March 31 Romberg in Bern was instructed to advise Lenin, in Zurich, that the trip had been approved and the Bolshevik travelers would be accorded extraterritorial privileges en route. Two days later Parvus's friend, Brockdorff-Rantzau, cautioned the Foreign Ministry:

> We must now definitely try to create the utmost chaos in Russia. To this end we must avoid any discernible interference in the course of the Russian revolution. But we must secretly do all we can to aggravate the contradictions between the moderate and the extreme parties, since we are extremely interested in the victory of the latter, for another upheaval will then be inevitable and will take forms which will shake the Russian state to its foundations.

Lenin, Krupskaia, Inessa Armand, Zinoviev, and fifteen Bolshevik followers (plus, one month later, Trotsky, still a Menshevik and coming from America) reached Petrograd April 16 via Germany and, at Berlin's request, Sweden. Both the Bolshevik and Menshevik branches of the Social Democratic party welcomed them noisily at the Finland Station and Lenin was cheered, scrutinized by soldiers sprawling atop armored cars or behind searchlight batteries, hailed with flapping red banners and handed bouquets. He regarded this performance with impassive disdain and then made a cold, incisive speech linking the Paris Commune of 1871, the St. Petersburg Soviet of 1905, and the 1917 Petrograd Soviet of Workers' and Soldiers' Deputies, which he described as "the germ cell of a workers' government." It must have struck some of the better-educated revolutionists that the 1871 and 1905 insurrectional governments had lasted but a very short time indeed.

The revolutionary chief took over Bolshevik headquarters in the already-expropriated house of Mathilde Kschessinska, the famous ballerina and former mistress of Czar Nicholas. From its balcony he began a series of public speeches stressing the need for bread and peace, urging fraternization at the front and preparation for class warfare. On July 2, in response to Allied pressure (especially from the United States), Kerensky went to the front to witness a new Russian offensive.

After a few days of uneasy success, this offensive was hurled back by the Germans and turned into utter debacle. With Kerensky away, the Bolsheviks attempted to seize power by a coup, called the July uprising, and failed by a hairsbreadth. The right wing of remaining army elements reacted in its turn against the provisional government, winning the support of General L. G. Kornilov, newly appointed commander in chief, who was soon arrested.

When Leon Trotsky had returned a month after Lenin, he was, as reported above, still a Menshevik. He now proved his mettle as Lenin's most expert henchman. He collaborated with the great Bolshevik from the moment he got back to Petrograd and actually became an outright member of the Bolshevik faction in July. A brilliant man, a magnificent speaker, personally brave and with a native military knack, the thirty-eight-year-old conspirator masterminded the final and successful October Revolution, so-called because, although it occurred on November 7 under the modern system of dating, it was still October under the old calendar.

The Provisional Government, finally headed by Kerensky, was threatened from both left and right after Kornilov's turnabout, and it was beginning to lose all semblance of control. On November 6 the military committee of the revolution, created by the Bolsheviks in Petrograd, decided the

Civil War in Russia. Leninists besieged the Duma, fighting against the Provisional Government. A group of wounded Georgian officers intervened and general disorder ensued.

time had come for a successful *putsch*. Guided by Trotsky, now president of the capital's soviet, the committee mustered armored cars, artillery, infantry, and the crew of the cruiser *Aurora,* lying at the mouth of the Neva, and when the Winter Palace was attacked it was defended only briefly and, at that, by a few hundred women soldiers. The provisional ministers, discovered when the Winter Palace fell, were thrown into the prison-fortress of St. Peter and St. Paul, joining some of their czarist predecessors. A Bolshevik government was promptly formed with Lenin serving as Chairman of the Council of People's Commissars and Trotsky as Commissar for Foreign Affairs.

The Constituent Assembly was dissolved shortly afterward and its quarters occupied by Red Guard militiamen. The final brief flicker of democracy vanished. Lenin announced: "The dissolution of the Constituent Assembly means the complete and open repudiation of the democratic idea in favor of the dictatorship concept." He did not even bother to pretend that it was a "dictatorship of the proletariat."

Within forty-eight hours all land was nationalized. Moscow was also seized swiftly, and by November 20 a wire was sent to the last regular commander in chief, General Dukhonin, instructing him to start negotiations for a separate peace. When he refused, a band of soldiers led by Ensign Krylenko lynched him, and Krylenko took command. Kerensky fled, given false papers by the British agent Bruce Lockhart, and wound up in the United States, from which that other famous orator, Trotsky, had so recently come. Lenin issued an order: "Loot the looters" and the peasants were encouraged to kill landlords and seize their estates.

The Bolsheviks had proved to be a magnificent revolutionary political *Armée de Métier,* a small, well-trained, beautifully organized elite, led by a man who had studied not only the techniques of attaining power but—and in great detail— how to use it and for what purposes. Although "Bolshevik" means "majority," the Soviet Communist party which derived from Lenin's faction has always been a tiny minority in the vast state which succeeded czarist Russia. The only free election it ever won—there or anywhere else (to date)—was the Vladivostok city election just before the Union of Soviet Socialist Republics was finally and officially created as a state.

Lenin had always believed in war as a tool of revolution, but he was not always as optimistic and audacious as he now appears to history. After the failure of the 1905 uprising, which he saw gloomily through dark-colored glasses, and after his return to exile, he went through a period of depression, heightened when Marx's daughter and son-in-law, Laura and Paul Lafargue, committed suicide together, at last convinced of the failure of the Marxist movement. Lenin commented grimly: "If one cannot work for the party any longer one must be able to look truth in the face and die the way the Lafargues did."

Four years later he wrote Maxim Gorki: "A war with Austria would be a splendid little thing for the revolution. But the chances are small that Franz Josef and Nikolasha [Nicholas] will give us such a treat." Even as late as January 22, 1917, he cautioned an assemblage of Swiss workers: "Popular risings must flare up in Europe within a few years," but added, "we older men may not live to see the decisive battles of the approaching revolution." And when the first (February) uprising seized power in Petrograd, he glumly made no great effort to return but wired orders to the Bolshevik underground organization there: "Our tactics: absolute distrust, no support of the new government, Kerensky especially suspect, no rapprochement with other parties."

Thanks to a considerable degree to Parvus, Lenin was able to

Trotsky's forces storm the Winter Palace.

make use of the revolutionary potential of the military conflict. And if Parvus was a remarkably astute planner and contact man, a true conspirator at heart, Lenin had already reached a similar conclusion that violence was the key to success. Even during the 1905 revolution, when Lenin had dodged back to Russia and out again, just ahead of the police, he warned the army units summoned to restore order for the czar: "Go ahead and shoot. Summon the Austrian and German regiments against the Russian peasants and workers. We are for a broadening of the struggle; we are for an international revolution."

At the International Socialist Conference in Zimmerwald, Switzerland (September 5–8, 1915) Lenin declared: "Civil war is a splendid thing." He warned of the need, at times, for audacity and insisted: "The age of the bayonet is at hand."

As Sir Bernard Pares summed up the final, November 7 revolution:

> The Bolsheviks were a militant force, owing their power to the war and admirably adapted to war conditions. They had as leader the one man of genius, Lenin, who had a perfectly clear conception of his objects, and even of the tactics which were required to face every turn of fortune.
>
> By 1917 every old-established idea had been wiped out in hopeless discredit; the State had dwindled to the Empress and her group; the official Church had been demoralized by Rasputin; and the new Moses, descending from the mountain with his tablets, carried with him the support of the workers of the large towns, of the peasants, who had been rapidly expropriating the estates of the squires, and especially of the young, who saw the outlet for bravery and initiative which was given them in this new world.

The German envoy in Stockholm wired the Wilhelmstrasse one day after the Bolshevik's return: "Lenin's entry into Russia successful. He is working exactly as we would wish."

XVII

AN INCIDENT
OF CONSEQUENCE
AND PATHOS

THE CLASSIC GREEKS HAD A SAYING: "MULTIPLE DEATH IS not death." Stalin, who was an expert on the matter, observed: "A single death is an incident of consequence and pathos but the death of a million is a matter of statistics." Surely there are limits to mankind's comprehension of sadness; one's pain threshold, in dolorimeters, can be overwhelmed by tragedy's mass production. A holocaust is more appalling but perhaps less moving than cruelty to a single person or family because the normal mind cannot easily absorb or comprehend the meaning of terror beyond a certain scale.

It is therefore through the psychological optic of this peculiar human fallibility that the miserable and ultimately brutal final chapter of the Romanov dynasty must be viewed. It was a period in which they all behaved with touching dignity, grace, and simple affection in their relations with one another, with their pathetically restricted and nonimperial retinue, and even, when they found the slightest flicker of response, with the increasingly rough bullyboys sent to supervise their last, humiliating months on earth.

One forgets their stark and often unpleasant angularity when recalling the compassionless suffering they were forced to endure: the weak, indecisive, rather stupid czar; the willful, haughty, neurotic czarina; the beautiful but rather childish daughters who always behaved as if they were indeed years younger than the fact, until annealed by hardship; the sad little czarevitch, so often kept from bleeding his small life away, above all by the hypnotic Rasputin, only to have its final punctuation in a dreadful sea of blood.

It is particularly hard to reconcile the portrait of the imprisoned Alexandra, gray-haired, limned by advancing age, confined to a wheelchair with bad heart and painful rheumatism, with that of the bossy, arrogant empress who abandoned her modest German princely background and its rational religion to embrace Russia in a kind of literary passion for Eastern Orthodoxy's imagined mysticism. As Trotsky wrote,

> This woman adopted with a kind of cold fury all the traditions and nuances of Russian medievalism, the most meager and crude of all medievalisms, in that very period when the people were making mighty efforts to free themselves from it. This Hessian princess was literally possessed by the demon of autocracy. Having risen from her rural corner to the heights of Byzantine despotism, she would not for anything take a step down.

The time of troubles for Nicholas and his family really

began right after his enforced abdication to the Provisional Government dominated by Kerensky. On March 20, 1917, he implicitly repudiated the credo of absolutism which he had, in fact, never been qualified to practice, in sending a farewell message to his armies from Moghilev. He was escorted to Petrograd still believing he could live a quiet retired existence in Czarskoe Selo until he and his family were allowed to sail to exile in England. It therefore came as a shock when the new Petrograd commander, General Kornilov, called to inform him: "You are henceforth to consider yourself under arrest."

This restriction was not initially onerous. While the Provisional Government negotiated with London through Ambassador Sir George Buchanan and Kerensky even talked of personally accompanying the refugee Romanovs to Murmansk where they could board a British cruiser, Nicholas and his wife underwent questioning. They were kept apart, except at meals (which were attended by witnesses) and they were carefully supervised when walking in the palace grounds. But this condition endured for but a month. Kerensky soon felt satisfied that there had been no imperial treason (a charge frequently levied at Alexandra by malicious gossip). Thereafter they were allowed more privacy and more liberty— within the well-patrolled confines of their country residence.

The former czar felt decidedly comforted when Kerensky told him about preparations to send him to England where his relative and look-alike, King George V, would care for all of them. There seemed no reason to be alarmed by any threat to their physical safety. Apart from the Provisional Government's calm assurances, Kerensky had even legally abolished capital punishment in the new Russia.

Therefore, the Romanov family set about trying to adjust to their new circumstances. Nicholas sawed wood; the girls dug in the garden; Alexis played, often with his special sailor-protectors, Derevenko and his assistant, Nagorny; the

Imprisonment at Czarskoe Selo, 1917.

ex-czar read aloud evenings; the ex-czarina did needlework; the few friends and members of the once imperial retinue, including the sympathetic Swiss tutor of the czarevitch, Pierre Gilliard, did their utmost to maintain a cheerful atmosphere.

Some of the guards were ordinary soldiers, often infected with antipathetic feelings by the propaganda to which they had become inured, and sometimes they pushed Nicholas away with gun butts when he sought to walk past them. They always addressed him as "Mr. Colonel" (his official military rank, even when he had commanded at Stavka). Yet the circumstances were not dour.

Once a gang of ardent revolutionist troops arrived to demand, on behalf of the Petrograd soviet, that Nicholas be handed over for imprisonment in the fortress of St. Peter and St. Paul; but their mood was assuaged and crisis avoided. The most disagreeable incident, above all for Alexandra, was that cited earlier when another group of ruffians arrived, tore Rasputin's coffin out of the chapel in the park, levered out the remnants, and burned the entire foul mess on a pile of gasoline-soaked timber.

To try to ignore their total isolation—which even included inspection of all letters sent and received, the opening of parcels, the presence of two military eavesdroppers whenever the one permitted telephone was used—the sad little colony made the best of things. A family school was established. Nicholas was the geography and history instructor, Alexandra (quite properly) was in charge of religious courses, Gilliard taught French and acted as the principal. Gilliard, who later wrote his account of these events, said:

> The czar accepted all these restraints with extraordinary serenity and moral grandeur. . . . The fact was that his whole being was dominated by one passion, which was more powerful even than the bonds between himself and his family—his love of country.

Nicholas saw to it that prayers were uttered for both the Russian and the Allied forces and he was wholly dismayed to learn (from the few newspapers and magazines permitted him) that the Soldiers' Committee had refused to carry out orders to take the offensive. Gilliard reported that he bolstered his morale somewhat by remarking: "What gives me a little hope is our love of exaggeration. I can't believe that our army at the front is as bad as they say."

Despite the bravery the little group displayed, it was hard to avoid discouragement. As earlier stated, King George of England was forced, to his embarrassment, to accept the decision by his government (fearful of irritating Liberal and Labor voters) to withdraw the offer of asylum. Clemenceau, never personally interested in such a proposal, refused to tender a similar invitation on the part of France. Public rumors continued to circulate that "Citizen Romanov" and "the German woman" were conspiring to help the enemy; that the girls had led a lurid sex life; that the family gorged on delicacies. And finally Derevenko, the hitherto trusted sailor who seemed so devotedly to cherish and protect the czarevitch, took to drink, ordered the boy around in churlish bullying fashion, and eventually vanished.

Kerensky, once he had satisfied himself that the former czar and his czarina had always behaved in a correctly patriotic way, sought to protect his official wards and occasionally visited them to reassure himself of their well-being. "He is not a bad sort," Nicholas said of him. "He's a good fellow. One can talk to him. . . . He is a man who loves Russia and I wish I could have known him earlier because he would have been useful to me." As for Kerensky, he was to write of his charges: "The former emperor and the imperial family were no longer political enemies but simply human beings who had come under our protection. We regarded any display of revengefulness as unworthy of Free Russia."

When the Bolsheviks under Lenin attempted their unsuccessful July coup in 1917, Kerensky decided it was far too risky to leave the Romanovs near Petrograd. They represented a political target and temptation for those who might wish to slaughter them and also, potentially, for the Germans or other forces inimical to the Provisional Government. In early August Kerensky told Nicholas that the imperial family would be safer in a more remote part of the country. The former ruler hoped it might be possible for them to be sent to the Crimea, but on August 11 Kerensky came back and said a decision had been reached. They should take warm clothing with them—this clearly ruled out the Black Sea resort area with its mild climate. Nicholas said: "If you say we must move, it must be. We trust you."

In fact, although the Romanovs were not yet told of their actual destination, three days later they were packed off with their luggage and guards for Tobolsk in Siberia. Kerensky actually went to the railway station with them and warned the train guards: "Remember that one does not strike a fallen adversary." In fact, the choice of Tobolsk was politically reasonable from the Provisional Government's viewpoint because Siberia was a traditional place of political exile so that nobody could reasonably accuse Kerensky of betraying the revolution by sending the ex-czar there. Moreover, it was essential to act swiftly since, with his own political power again being menaced by Bolshevik extremists, he had been induced to restore the death penalty in Russia's wavering army. It was therefore questionable how long he would be able to protect the lives of the Romanovs so long as they continued to live near Petrograd and its increasingly left-wing soviet.

The ex-czar's entourage was assured that after a scheduled meeting of the Constitutent Assembly in November, Nicholas would be allowed to leave Tobolsk and, in fact, go wherever he desired. But no one, including above all Kerensky, could then foresee that the Bolsheviks would by then have seized all power and that Kerensky himself would be a fugitive, only able in the end to escape abroad thanks to an efficient British agent.

The train bearing the Romanovs eastward was disguised with placards lettered "Japanese Red Cross Mission" and bore the rising sun flag that Russians, to their misfortune, had already come to know so well in Korea and Manchuria. It was perhaps less comfortable than what czarist taste had become accustomed to on trips to and from *Stavka*, a wonderful affair with pale-blue silk saloon cars, thick carpets, silver plates and mugs; nevertheless it was equipped with sleeping cars and a well-supplied restaurant as well as a small retinue, thirty servants and the children's two spaniel dogs.

It was followed by a second train bearing a contingent of more than three hundred armed guards. When they all reached the town of Tyumen on the river Tura, they transferred to a ship which was to take them two hundred miles northeastward to their destination. En route they stared with fascination at the large village of Pokrovskoe where Rasputin had been born and which, in one of his weirdly striking phophecies, he had promised the empress she would see.

For two-thirds of a year the Romanovs lived in the house of the former provincial governor at the confluence of the Irtysh and Tobol rivers. Colonel Evgenyi Kobylinsky, the benevolent commandant of the detachment sent to oversee the former imperial family, initially permitted Nicholas quite a lot of freedom in this remote place. The more extreme guards protested and a tall wooden fence was built around the house. The Romanovs themselves were not allowed to leave their captors. They were able to contact servants or acquaintances of the czarist entourage; but nothing ever seemed to come from their inquiries. Finally, an unusual man showed up at Tyumen, where he based himself along the railhead.

His name was Boris Soloviev. When it became known he was in the approximate neighborhood, he had a magnetic appeal for Alexandra: for he was Grigori Rasputin's son-in-law. He had messages conveyed to Tobolsk indicating that he was deeply involved with a royalist group, built up by his personal efforts, and calling itself The Brotherhood of St. Ivan of Tobolsk after the town's best-known saint. He also sent word that "Grigori's friends and family" were active on behalf of the imperial family.

Just what Soloviev was after and on whose behalf has never been plain. He assuredly did not attempt any rescue that is known of; he had a murky and suspicious background and seems to have used a kind of medium's trick to win Matriona Rasputina as his wife. After the Romanovs had been moved from Tobolsk he was held briefly by the Bolsheviks, then released, deserted to the Whites, finally traveled to Vladivostok. Eventually he ran a restaurant in Berlin, acquiring a clientele that knew him—thanks to his self-promotion—as the man who had sought to save Russia's last czar. He has also been called a faker, seeking to appropriate funds to himself, a German agent, and a Bolshevik spy.

The chill winter ended with a new and exceedingly painful attack of hemophilia for Alexis. This was followed by a powerful German offensive which smashed the last remnant of a Russian army, assembled in crumbling units by Lenin's government, which was, in truth, far more interested in world revolution than in national war or salvation. To save his own Bolshevik goals, Lenin dispatched a delegation, in the end headed by Trotsky, to Brest-Litovsk and wound up by accepting the humiliating peace terms imposed by Ludendorff. This signed away most of the lands gained since the era of Peter the Great, one-fourth of the country's territory and three-quarters of the coal and steel on which it had hoped to build the proletariat's new world.

When Nicholas heard the news, he termed it "suicide for

Russia." Gilliard wrote afterward: "I then for the first time heard the czar regret his abdication." Quite obviously, and with the kaiser's approval, Ludendorff sought to dismember Russia without any thought of what effect this might have on the condition of the Romanovs, who were (at least in theory) warmly supported by all of Europe's royal dynasts, regardless of on whose side their armies were fighting. But all the minor German royal houses, taking a hint from the methods of their imperial master, the kaiser, nominated themselves for new crowns in the czar's former domain—Lithuania, Finland, and Latvia, for example.

That same spring so-called White divisions, commanded by renowned officers of the erstwhile czarist forces, began their own thrust against the Red units, moving from the Caucasus to the Don basin. This was the spark that ignited full civil and foreign intervention, including a British-White Russian thrust southward from Murmansk in the north and a Japanese drive from the maritime provinces of the Far East. At the same time prisoners taken earlier from the Austro-Hungarian armies and formed into Czechoslovakian units, which were to be transported to the Allied side via Asia, had begun their tedious eastward anabasis—which was to prove so fatal in weighing the Romanovs' dreadful destiny.

The chaos prevailing in torn-up, beleaguered Russia had induced Lenin to transfer the government to the old capital of Moscow from Petrograd which was too close to the Germans and also to the intervening British. On April 22, 1918, a representative of this Moscow regime arrived in Tobolsk with a troop of revolutionist cavalrymen. The town was already firmly controlled by the Bolsheviks, but they were split into rival factions, one from Ekaterinburg and another from Omsk.

The guard in charge of the Romanovs had also created its own soviet and sent off the two last commissars appointed by

Kerensky to supervise the imperial captives. Moscow's newly designated agent, who arrived amidst this confusion, was a man named Vassili Yakovliev. He was supplied with various documents and official orders authorizing him to shoot out of hand any persons who disobeyed him. He promptly informed the Tobolsk soviet and also the detachment safeguarding the Romanovs that the imperial family would shortly be transferred to another forced residence, but he would not say where.

At Yakovliev's first meeting with Nicholas and Alexandra, the former czar concluded that Yakovliev was a German agent whose real task was to hand them all over to the kaiser's troops for some unknown and unpleasant purpose. Alexandra thought it was likely the Germans wanted Nicholas in their hands so they could force him into signing the Brest-Litovsk treaty, thereby gaining for it some kind of legal status which would survive a Bolshevik overturn.

After several days of waiting, during which Yakovliev was in frequent but highly confidential contact with the central government, he appears to have received orders to transfer the Romanovs to Moscow. Both the ex-czar and his wife, who suspected what the destination was because of the amount of time Yakovliev said the journey would take (he did not state specifically its ultimate goal), became increasingly sure that the object was to urge him to endorse the Brest-Litovsk document, by one or another means. "I would rather cut off my right hand than sign such a treaty," said Nicholas.

Yakovliev apparently was deeply suspicious of the intentions of the local soviet of Ekaterinburg, principal city of the Urals, through which Moscow-bound trains normally had to pass. Ekaterinburg was a traditionally and fiercely revolutionary town, renowned for its miners, its blast furnaces, and a revolutionary reputation that had given the entire province the label "Red Urals."

Moreover, the Urals Regional Soviet had already asked

Moscow to send the Romanovs to Ekaterinburg and had also dispatched a detachment under its own commissar to Tobolsk, in order to sustain this request. In this atmosphere Yakovliev demanded access to Nicholas and his son, Alexis, who was still seriously sick and bedridden from his latest hemophiliac hemorrhages. When he became convinced that the illness was genuine, Yakovliev consulted Moscow by telegraph and was told to take Nicholas away with him but to leave the others behind until the boy was well enough to travel.

Alexandra indomitably insisted on accompanying her husband. The family gathered in sadness to spend the night by Alexis's bed. On April 26, 1918, the former czar and czarina embraced their children, their remaining friends and staff, and climbed aboard two springless horse-carts spread with straw. These were to carry them two hundred miles back to Tyumen, the railhead, on the first leg of their journey, a miserable, wracking ride.

It was Yakovliev's apparent intention to proceed from Tyumen eastward toward Omsk and then to double back from there by a circuitous route, thus avoiding the more direct trip through the vengeful, dubiously obedient city of Ekaterinburg, which had already demanded possession of the Romanovs. But, to his dismay, the plan failed, although at the start the train chugged promptly in the direction of the east.

Yakovliev did not know that the Urals Regional Soviet had already denounced him as "a traitor to the revolution" and had sent its own telegrams to all railway centers requesting that the Romanovs and their overseer be held. No counter-orders were dispatched from Moscow. Consequently, sixty miles from Omsk, the train was girdled by troops. Yakovliev was ordered by Yakov Sverdlov, president of the Central Executive Committee of the All-Russian Congress of Soviets in Moscow, Lenin's close friend, to take his prisoners to Ekaterinburg and turn them over to the Urals soviet.

Even today it is difficult to unravel this tale. Yakovliev's own record makes him seem a highly unreliable, untruthful, and suspicious person. Maybe he was simply carrying out instructions to bring the Romanovs back to Moscow by any possible means. Maybe this was done with the knowledge of the Germans who calculated that in the new capital Nicholas would be within reach of their formidable army. Maybe Sverdlov, aware of the possibility of a German plot, secretly encouraged Ekaterinburg to grab the former czar—and told Yakovliev nothing. Maybe Yakovliev himself was double-crossing everyone. In any case, Nicholas and Alexandra were given to the Urals Regional Soviet, and Yakovliev, after being threatened with arrest, was allowed to go free, soon deserting to Admiral Alexander Kolchak's White Army.

In Ekaterinburg the former rulers were billeted in the modest, old-fashioned, two-storied home of a merchant named Ipatiev, now bearing the unpleasant label of the House of Special Purpose. As soon as they arrived, they and their possessions were rigorously searched. This caused Nicholas to protest: "So far I have had to deal with decent people." He was sharply scolded and told that if he complained like that again he would be punished.

Life was decidedly more disagreeable than in Tobolsk, even after the children, when Alexis had recovered, were brought along to join their parents. The population was hostile from the start. The ex-czar was forced to carry his own luggage, and he was greeted at the door of his new residence with the words: "Citizen Romanov, you may enter." Once the four girls and Alexis arrived twelve people were crowded into five rooms. A high fence shut the house off from view. The upper rooms had their windows painted over to block all vision. Night and day the imperial captives were guarded by armed Bolshevik shock troops. One of their leaders took pleasure in calling the former emperor "Nicholas the Blood-Drinker."

Ipatiev house at Ekaterinburg where the imperial family was first interned and then murdered.

The last photograph of Nicholas II. Taken a few days before his death.

Food was simple; life was austere; the guards went out of their way to be rude and offensive; prayer became an increasing feature of the Romanovs' daily routine. When one of the Bolsheviks started to steal Alexis's gold chain, Nagorny, the good sailor, stopped him. He was executed for his pains. Finally, on July 4, a new set of guards, less offensive but more efficient and deadly, "Latvians" from the Bolshevik Cheka, moved in. They were called Latvians, but several were Hungarians, taken as prisoners of war and used for the toughest, most disagreeable secret police assignments. They were headed by a Russian named Yakov Yurovsky, of whom Nicholas noted in his diary: "This specimen we like least of all."

By early July, unknown to the Romanovs, the Czech Legion, consisting of forty thousand men, had turned westward from its journey toward the Pacific and had begun to fight the Bolsheviks as cobelligerents of the various White and interventionist forces. It had captured Omsk along the Trans-Siberian railroad and was heading toward Tyumen and Ekaterinburg.

The Czechs' sudden and hostile arrival in the area precipitated the Bolshevik decision to do away with the Romanovs, without even the pretense of a trial. The Urals Regional Soviet seemingly was advised by Moscow that it could take whatever action it wished with regard to the imperial family. Since Ekaterinburg was already in the process of being outflanked, the local government decided to massacre its hostages and erase all evidence. Yurovsky and Isaiah Goloshchekin, a Urals Presidium member and also a personal friend of Sverdlov, located an abandoned mineshaft fourteen miles away which they deemed well suited for the task. Another soviet member was assigned the job of buying many drums of gasoline and sulfuric acid.

Events were further urged toward a grim conclusion by

*In April 1918 the former emperor with his wife, son, and his four daughters was trans-
ferred from Tobolsk to Ekaterinburg in the Urals (today Sverdlovsk). After a few miserable
months, on July 16, they were ordered into this room; an armed guard entered and shot
them dead. Grand Duke Sergei was among other members of the family murdered during
the same period in this district. Fear of approaching White armies, which captured
Ekaterinburg a few days later, probably precipitated the slaughter.*

an anti-Bolshevik insurrection in Moscow of the rival (and anti-monarchist) Socialist Revolutionaries who started things off on July 6, 1918, by assassinating Count Mirbach, the German ambassador. Lenin replied with cold ferocity. He stamped out not only anyone suspected of being a Socialist Revolutionary but all types of known opposition. This, of course, provided an admirable official mood for the murder of the Romanovs which occurred just after midnight July seventeenth.

On the afternoon of the sixteenth Nicholas, a short, handsome, tired-looking fifty, strolled in the little Ipatiev garden with his four daughters. At seven o'clock Yurovsky told his Cheka men to disarm all the outside guards. Then he informed his Hungarian "Latvians": "Tonight we will shoot the whole family, everybody. Notify the guards outside not to be alarmed if they hear shots."

At ten-thirty the Romanovs went to bed. Yurovsky personally woke them up at midnight and instructed them to come downstairs, explaining that they must be swiftly moved elsewhere because the Czech Legion and White forces were nearing the town. They all dressed. Yurovsky then led them to a basement with an iron grill over the single window. Three chairs were brought for Nicholas, the worn-out, forty-six-year-old Alexandra, and weak, little Alexis. The four girls and five servants stood behind.

When the imperial family had placed themselves accordingly, Yurovsky led his entire Cheka squad in, all of them bearing revolvers. Historians disagree on minor details. According to Edmond Taylor: "Yurovsky hastily read out the sentence of death, then without further warning drew his revolver and fired point-blank at Nicholas. That was the signal for the massacre." According to Robert K. Massie in *Nicholas and Alexandra:* "He [Yurovsky] stepped forward and declared quickly: 'Your relations have tried to save you. They have failed and we must now shoot you.'" The shots were followed up by some kicks and bayonet thrusts.

As soon as all the victims, including Jimmy, the remaining spaniel, were dead, the bodies were wrapped in sheets, carried into a truck, driven to the abandoned mine, chopped up with axes and saws, soaked in gasoline, burned, and thrown down the shaft. One participant, who later became an ambassador, boasted: "The world will never know what we did with them."

On July 18 a telegram was sent to Moscow reporting the act. It was approved by the Presidium of the Central Executive Council. Sverdlov only told the Presidium that Nicholas had been shot, but both he and Lenin knew that the entire family was dead. One way or another it is virtually certain that the Ekaterinburg massacrers acted with the full advance knowledge and specific prior approval of Moscow. The night of July 18 five Romanov grand dukes and two grand duchesses were shot under similar conditions. On July 19 an official press bulletin in Moscow simply said that "sentence of death had been passed on Nicholas Romanov and carried out." On July 26 Ekaterinburg fell to the anti-Bolshevik Whites and Czechs who verified gruesome details. Six months later Sverdlov died and his name was shortly given to Ekaterinburg.

Trotsky reported:

> My next visit to Moscow took place after the fall of Ekaterinburg. Talking to Sverdlov, I asked in passing: "Oh, yes, and where is the czar?"
>
> "It's all over," he answered. "He has been shot."
>
> "And where is the family?"
>
> "And the family along with him. . . ."
>
> "And who made the decision?" I asked.
>
> "We decided it here. Ilyich [Lenin] believed that we shouldn't leave the Whites a live banner to rally around, especially under the present difficult circumstances."

Some years later Churchill wrote of the unhappy Nicholas:

> He made many mistakes, what ruler has not? He was
> neither a great captain nor a great prince. He was only a
> true, simple man of average ability, of merciful disposition,
> upheld in all his daily life by his faith in God.

The hecatomb brought about by World War I, for which
Nicholas with much vainglory and little judgment was certainly in part responsible, was far more than "a matter of
statistics" in the words of that cold, calm tyrant, Stalin. But
it held no more "consequence and pathos" than the brutal
murder of one family, the unfortunate Romanovs.

XVIII

YOU HAVE BEEN LISTENING TO YOUR WOMENFOLK AGAIN

THE FINAL TRAGEDY OF THE HABSBURG DYNASTY WAS THE exceptionally long life and, therefore, rule of Emperor Franz Josef who remained on the throne from the immediate aftermath of Metternich and the 1848 revolution until the end of 1916, when such men as Woodrow Wilson, Clemenceau, and the Russian Bolshevik leaders were exerting their influence on contemporaries and on future generations.

Franz Josef was in no sense a remarkable man in terms of intellectual ability. Nor was he endowed with the least bit of luck. His brother was shot in the foolish guise of

Emperor Maximilian of Mexico, trying to uphold the inane imperial dreams of Napoleon III. His son and heir, Rudolf, committed suicide with his mistress. His wife, the beautiful but moody Sissi, was murdered by an Italian anarchist. His nephew, who succeeded Rudolf as crown prince, was slain by the Serbian nationalist conspiracy that touched off World War I and disintegrated Europe's three leading imperial dynasties.

Yet Franz Josef was a man of character and stern probity. He managed to sustain the fabric of administration in an empire that had no national basis like those of Russia and Germany and no transoceanic domains like those of Britain. It was merely a potpourri assembled by a complex of royal marriages, awarded as dowries or left over as vestiges of past wars. The state felt no helpful, uniting sense of rising nationalism as in France or Italy—indeed it felt the reverse: a desire to tear down the structure of Habsburg rule. The sole unifying force of Austria-Hungary, if such it can be called, was the dynastic crown. And even this mattered less than elsewhere, since the same emperor, Franz Josef, wore two different crowns, one in Austria, another in Hungary, while the famous Bohemian crown of St. Wenceslaus and the Polish crown of Cracow were regarded as never having existed.

By a kind of historical momentum and without any originality or concession to changing times Franz Josef was able to keep this odd mélange going until his death, November 21, 1916; but thereafter things fell rapidly apart. The war had gone on too long to be supported by the shaky empire's resources. At first there had been high hopes that Serbia's destruction and initial advances into Russia, accompanied by Germany's startling victories in France, would permit a swift settlement that could consolidate the Habsburg position. But then everything began to go wrong.

Although Austria was the heart and brain of the empire, the German-speaking Austrians were a minority in the polyglot country and subjected more and more to the whims of other national blocs. These included the arrogant Magyars and various groups of Slavs, from Poland down to the frontier of Montenegro. Increasing restiveness was evident as the arts of political warfare were applied among these peoples, especially through Paderewski and Pilsudski among the Poles and through Masaryk and Beneš among the Czechoslovaks. And tens of thousands of prisoners who fell into Allied hands were turned against Vienna's rule with visions of their own promised lands of independence.

Moreover, it became increasingly difficult for the empire, being drained of its manpower, to feed itself. After Rumania joined in against the Central Powers and after successive offensives had failed to knock Italy out of the war, despite encouraging moments, only one splendid hope kept the shaky Habsburg apparatus fighting: this was the Bolshevik revolution which was clearly driving Russia out of the conflict.

Emperor Karl I, a grandnephew of Franz Josef, inherited the throne when that weary, stubborn old man died. Karl was not yet thirty, had held military commands in Italy, Galicia, and Rumania, and entertained fresh ideas, many of them sound. But events never gave him a chance to press through his novel and original concepts of how to achieve peace and bring about the obviously needed transformation of political rule from Vienna. He wanted a "truly federal" system to equalize the position and opportunities of his multilingual mass of subjects. But to have even a remote chance of succeeding at this late hour he knew that peace was the primordial precondition.

Karl was married to the Italian princess Zita of Bourbon-Parma, a very international family. Her two brothers, Princes Sixtus and Xavier, lived in France and considered themselves French citizens. But they were barred by law from serving in the French army because of the strongly anti-monarchical prejudice of the Third Republic. Therefore they had volunteered as stretcher-bearers in the forces of their cousin, King Albert of Belgium. In March 1917 Karl discreetly summoned his brothers-in-law to a most confidential family meeting: only himself, Zita, Sixtus, and Xavier. The place was Laxenburg, a Habsburg castle not far from Vienna; and the subject was peace.

The young emperor had already told the first cabinet meeting he attended, on January 12, 1917, that Austro-Hungarian war aims must be defined in order to prepare for any future negotiation. His own thought was that Vienna's absolute minimum demands must be a guarantee of the integrity of Habsburg territories, the acquisition from Montenegro of Mount Lovčen, dominating the important Adriatic harbor of Kotor, and ouster of the Karageorgević dynasty from Serbia. Although Karl had also outlined his concepts of maximum demands, it was clearly not these that were put forward at Laxenburg to his brothers-in-law, when they showed up via Switzerland, equipped with false documents.

Sixtus and Xavier, who knew the pope had blessed the effort, nonetheless made it clear that they could act only if they first confided in President Jules Henri Poincaré and Prime Minister Aristide Briand of France, their own government. Since Karl had already made his foreign minister, Count Czernin, privy to the secret, he agreed. Czernin then joined the little group and gave some professional counsel to the two secret envoys.

He did not know that Karl had written a letter for them to hand Poincaré in which the emperor proposed to use his influence on the Germans to get them to return Alsace-Lorraine to France and also to evacuate Belgium. For himself, he went no further than to promise restoration of Serbian sovereignty and perhaps to discuss granting Belgrade some kind of access across Habsburg territory to the Adriatic.

The suggestion that Vienna would attempt to persuade Berlin to withdraw in the west, above all from Alsace-Lorraine which it considered German, was rather venturesome since the keystone of Austrian policy had been adjusted to Germany's outlook almost since the terrible defeat at Sadowa. Indeed, Berlin proclaimed not long afterward: "Germany will never, no never, make any concessions on the subject of Alsace-Lorraine." But Karl felt the weakness of his country's position so keenly and was so painfully aware that a probable American intervention on the Allied side would prove fatal that he felt impelled to audacity. The text of the letter he gave Sixtus to show Poincaré (dated March 24, 1917) read as follows:

My dear Sixtus,

The third year of this war that has brought the world so much mourning and sorrow is coming to an end. All the peoples of my Empire are united more closely than ever in a common will: to preserve the integrity of the Monarchy even at the cost of the heaviest sacrifices. Thanks to their unity, thanks to the generous cooperation of all the nationalities of my Empire, the Monarchy has been able to withstand, it will soon be three years, the most severe assaults. Nobody can deny the achievements won by my armies, especially in the Balkan theater of war.

France has also shown magnificent power of resistance and dash. We all admire, without reservation, the traditional bravery of her army, and the spirit of dedication of the whole French people.

Although we are enemies at the present moment, I note with special pleasure that my Empire is not divided from France by any real clashes of interest, and that my lively sympathies for France, shared by the whole Monarchy, justify my hope that it will be possible to avoid in the future the repetition of the war for which I am not responsible. Therefore so that I can prove precisely the sincerity of my feelings, I beg you to let the President of the French Republic, M. Poincaré, know in a secret and un-

HOCHBEFRIEDIGT WEISS ICH DIE WÜN
SOEBEN IN ERGREIFENDEN WORTEN
ALLEN KRIEGSLEUTEN BIS ZUM JÜNG
MEIN HERZLICHSTER DANK U. GRUSS

*Franz Josef on his eighty-fifth
birthday in 1916.*

Raymond Poincaré, president of the French Republic at the time when Emperor Karl, through his brothers-in-law Sixtus and Xavier (and without knowledge of Wilhelm II), tried to enlist Poincaré's cooperation in bringing the war to an end.

official way that I shall support the just claims of France to Alsace-Lorraine in every way and with all my personal influence.

Belgium must be re-established as a sovereign state, retaining all its African possessions, notwithstanding the compensations she may receive for the losses inflicted upon her. The sovereignty of Serbia will be re-established and, as a token of our good-will, we are inclined to guarantee her an equitable and natural access to the Adriatic, and far-reaching economic concessions. Austria-Hungary, on the other hand, will demand as an indispensable condition that the Kingdom of Serbia dissociates itself from, and suppresses the tendency for the disintegration of the Monarchy, especially the *Narodna Odbrana,** that it shall faithfully and by all means in its power stop that kind of agitation in Serbia and outside her frontiers, and that it will make a pledge to that effect under the guarantee of the Entente Powers.

The recent events in Russia oblige me to withhold comment on that subject until the final formation of a legal government.

After having disclosed my ideas to you, I should like to ask you to let me know, after a previous consultation with the two Powers, the views of France and England, so that a basis for official and mutually satisfactory negotiations may be laid.

Hoping that in this way we shall soon be able, on both sides, to put an end to the suffering of so many millions of men and of so many families that live in sorrow and anxiety.

I beg you to believe in my kindest and most fraternal regards,

Karl

The French informed British Prime Minister Lloyd George of the letter on April 11, and he pointed out that it would be necessary to consult the Italians, so deeply involved in the Austrian fighting. No mention was made of Russia, which was already under a Provisional Government following the first (non-Bolshevik) revolution. Italy bluntly advised Britain it considered the entire affair a trick designed to split the Allies.

Meanwhile, Karl met with Kaiser Wilhelm at Bad Homburg on April 3. He argued that a peace without victory was better than possible disaster. Wilhelm was not impressed.

---

* *Narodna Odbrana* was the anti-Austrian propaganda organization based in Belgrade. Apparently the Vienna government did not yet know anything about the "Black Hand" which had supervised the assassination of Franz Ferdinand.

With his customary delicate tact he told his imperial ally: "You have been listening to your womenfolk again."

Despite the difficulties posed by Italy, and subsequently by Rumania, the two Bourbon princes pursued their efforts, even going to London where they lunched at 10 Downing Street. They assured the British that Karl and Zita were honestly pro-Allied, partly because the kaiser had insulted Zita while she was still a girl. But the British deduced from their questioning that the Austrian attitude had started to waver. Presumably this was because of the spread of military weakness among the Russian forces, bringing a new Viennese mood of optimism with respect to the eastern front. Lloyd George's private reaction was that Austria was the weak point of the Central Powers coalition. Therefore it should now be hit so hard that it would be forced out of the conflict anyway—on Allied terms. One consequence was a new Italian offensive, in August, which pierced the Austrian lines. But Vienna reacted with unexpected toughness, striking back in November and inflicting military disaster on Italy at Caporetto.

As a result, another secret negotiation was started, between the South African General Jan Smuts on behalf of Britain, and Count Albrecht Mensdorff-Pouilly-Dietrichstein, one of the most experienced and careful veterans of the Austrian diplomatic service. Smuts sought to persuade the Austrians to "free themselves from German domination" and promised them support if they did so. What he really was after, without openly saying so, was to encourage Vienna once again to seek a separate peace.

The Smuts-Mensdorff talks, in a suburb of Geneva, never resulted in any serious understandings. The Austrians indicated increasing worry that the policies openly enunciated by President Wilson, now a belligerent, meant the destruction and almost total dismemberment of the Habsburg empire that

Karl I.

would leave nothing but a tiny German-speaking core. Smuts countered:

> We had no intention of interfering in her interal affairs but we recognized that if Austria could become a really liberal empire in which her subject peoples would, as far as possible, be satisfied and content, she would become for Central Europe very much what the British Empire had become for the rest of the world.

This argument did not succeed in convincing Vienna, and Karl's peace initiatives finally petered out. In April 1918 Clemenceau, by then French prime minister, revealed the fact of the secret negotiations. The young Habsburg emperor's reputation was severely damaged as a consequence, not least among the Germans. To save himself, he journeyed to Wilhelm's headquarters at Spa, in Belgium, to plead his *mea culpa*. The price he had to pay was total: absolute subjugation to German interests of all Austro-Hungarian military, political, and economic policy. Karl was now tied firmly to the back of the tiger from which he had been seeking to dismount.

By 1918 the Austro-Hungarian casualty total had risen above four million; there were critical shortages, both for the troops and for the civilian population, of food and raw materials; many military sectors were lacking in arms and ammunition; the emperor's prestige had been severely shaken; and the propaganda battle, begun by western psychological warriors, had been reinforced by Bolshevik Russia. Revolutionary influence from the new soviet capital of Moscow electrified the various nationalist movements in the Habsburg domains, movements that had already been deeply stirred by Wilson's precepts.

Although the Central Powers had emerged triumphant in the east, imposing separate peaces by *Diktat*, on the Ukraine as well as on Russia, and finally on Rumania, the strain of protracted warfare had already proven far beyond the capacity of the disunited, strangely anomalous Habsburg empire. It was by no means either as homogeneous, as powerful, or as habituated to discipline as its dominating German partner. And the internal disruption stemming from the dual infections of Wilsonian and Leninist bacteria, was simply too much for the tottering administrative structure to bear.

The first successful revolt of internal nationalism came in the homeland of the Czechs and Slovaks. During the summer of 1918 the Allies had formally recognized Czechoslovakia as a cobelligerent. On October 18 Masaryk, in Washington, unfurling a new national flag, proclaimed official independence. But for many months the émigré committees led by Masaryk and Beneš had already been working with the Western partners, and the romantic story of the Czech Legion in Russia has already been referred to, including its fateful effect upon the imprisoned Romanovs at Ekaterinburg.

Considerably later (October 6) a National Council of Serbs, Croats, and Slovenes was established in Zagreb, principal city of Croatia, which had been subject to the Hungarian kingdom of the dual monarchy. The council announced union with independent Serbia, cut all ties with the Habsburg government, and, on December 4, proclaimed its own triune Slavic kingdom, with Belgrade as capital.

Meanwhile, on November 14, three days after Germany's final surrender, the Polish freedom movements merged and formed a coalition which, in January 1919, named Pilsudski as president and the brilliant pianist, Paderewski, as prime minister. Just before the final disintegration, Hungarian units in the imperial army began the equivalent of a sitdown mutiny, refusing as units to accept further orders.

Unconsciously the Habsburg empire had become an anomaly in the early twentieth century age of emotional national-

Franz Josef gazes at an Austro-Hungarian airship, as it and his dynasty vanish from sight.

ism. It was not yet aware of the potential for supranationalism and economic multinationalism that would characterize politics later in the century. The empire, at the time of its dissolution, was already a kind of common market for approximately fifty million people, but it was wholly ignorant of the reality of this fact.

Moreover, one of the very first moves of the new successor states—independent Hungary, Czechoslovakia, the kingdom of the Croats, Serbs, and Slovenes (now Jugoslavia)—was to erect customs barriers against Austria and against one another. Austria itself became an atrophied midget instead of an unwieldy giant. Vienna seemed like nothing so much as a kind of melancholic art museum from some earlier era.

The pact of Spa, which Karl signed with Wilhelm, had bound him most tightly to his senior partner at precisely the moment when the Austrian emperor most needed his freedom of action. This was the sad consequence of the well-meant but ineptly executed efforts to arrange separate peace negotiations.

Count Czernin, who lost his job as foreign minister when the French exposed Karl's irregular diplomatic endeavors, had already warned his counterpart in Berlin:

> If the monarchs of the Central Powers are not able to conclude peace during the next few months, the peoples will go over their heads and the waves of the revolutionary flood will sweep away everything for which our brothers and sons are still fighting and dying.

But the kaiser's regime, now in reality an outright military dictatorship, disregarded such cautions. It felt reassured by the collapse of the eastern front and, with vast potential food resources open in the Ukraine, prepared to stake everything on a brand-new victory bet in the west.

The long-pending disaster for Austria-Hungary became immutable when Bulgaria fell apart and surrendered, September 26, 1918. This severed all connections between Vienna and the Ottoman Empire, which gave up shortly afterward. A tough French and colonial army under General Franchet d'Esperey was marching northward from Salonika, together with the surviving Serbian forces that had been transported to the Greek port via Corfu when Austria originally overran their country. The last pretense of a Habsburg state was evaporating like rain in a hot desert. One Czech spokesman, in Vienna itself, declared: "We regard Austria as a centuries-old crime against humanity."

On October 4 Karl instructed his new foreign minister, Stephen Burian von Rajecz, to advise President Wilson that Austria accepted his Fourteen Points and would sue for peace on that basis. Wilson answered that "autonomy" was no longer sufficient. Therefore, on October 16, Karl published a manifesto that would transform his empire into a federation. But it was too late; and anyway Budapest insisted on maintaining the integrity of "Great Hungary," which included Croatia, part of Rumania, and Slovakia. The Viennese parliament abruptly formed itself into a Provisional National Assembly. On October 27, 1918, Karl informed the kaiser that Austria was forced to stop fighting.

One of the last acts of the last Habsburg emperor was to name a new prime minister of Hungary, Count Mihály Károlyi, a very rich landowner. Although his background and youth were those of a wealthy Magyar aristocrat with huge estates and much travel, he had later turned to politics, became a parliamentary deputy, and created a party advocating Hungarian independence and democratic reforms. As soon as Karl designated him, Károlyi formed a coalition between his own Liberals and the Social Democrats, which was approved by the advancing Franchet d'Esperey. The count's government severed ties with the emperor-king. Not long afterward, however, it was briefly replaced by the revolutionary movement of Béla Kun, a supporter of Lenin who had been taken prisoner during the war and was sent back to Budapest by the Bolsheviks to install a Marxist regime.

The disease that killed the Habsburg empire struck its heart, Austria, last. Karl attended mass in the imperial chapel at Schönbrunn on Sunday, November 10; it was his final public appearance. The next day his cabinet begged him to quit the throne and leave in order to prevent the menace of violent disorders. They gave him a draft renunciation document to sign. He showed it to Zita who stormed: "A king can never abdicate; he can only be deposed. I would rather die with you here. Then Otto would succeed us, and if he were deposed there will always be enough Habsburgs left."

In fact, what he did sign was not technically an abdication. As he explained to his remaining subjects:

> Since my accession to the throne I have unceasingly tried to spare my peoples the horrors of the war, for the outbreak of which I bear no responsibility. I have never hesitated to restore constitutional life and I have opened the way for my peoples to their independent political development. Since I am filled, now as before, by unchangeable love for all my peoples, I will not interpose my person as an obstacle to their free evolution.

Karl and his family promptly moved to his hunting lodge of Eckartsau, east of Vienna in the Burgenland. There, on November 13, he received a delegation sent by Károlyi asking that he also yield the Hungarian crown. In this case, as with Austria, he "renounced" rather than abdicated and made no commitment regarding his eldest son, Otto. However, the new Austrian constitution specifically banned the latter even from running for president of the republic. This was established while the ex-emperor was still at Eckartsau by one of the most laconic of history's declarations: "Article I—

German Austria is a democratic republic. All power emanates from the people. Article 2—The German-Austrian Republic is an integral part of the German Republic." Article 2 didn't last long. The victorious Allies sternly forbade an Anschluss between the two Teutonic states.

In March 1919 the republic expelled Karl and his family and expropriated his property. He went to Switzerland but twice managed to slip from there into Hungary and claim his throne. Both attempts failed and the second, on which he was accompanied by Zita, ended in their capture. Although the Communist revolution had been defeated and Admiral Horthy, a royalist, was in power, he refused to recognize Karl as sovereign and the Budapest parliament promptly voted to deprive the Habsburgs of all dynastic rights. As insurance against future trouble along the Danube valley, the British put pressure on the former emperor and he was forced to sail on an English ship and take up residence in a modest house at Funchal on the lovely island of Madeira, once adored by Sissi, Franz Josef's unhappy wife. There he died of lung trouble on April 1, 1922, aged thirty-five.

Karl had no chance to carve his niche in history. He might well have been the most intelligent of all Habsburg emperors. But he was young and inexperienced when thrust upon a battered throne in the midst of the bloodiest of all wars. He was an up-to-date and relatively enlightened man and no bigot, although his religious convictions and devoutness were markedly strong. He was unusual for a sovereign in openly abhorring violence of any sort, which made him a most eccentric wartime leader.

Unlike Franz Josef, the most experienced of all nineteenth-century monarchs, Karl had virtually no experience, outside of a brief army career, when he assumed the throne. But he was unorthodox, original in his outlook, and not afraid to try novel means of making peace and improving the lot of his patchwork country. In each endeavor he came to power both too late and too early to succeed. There was no escaping the grim vise of total military conflict; and Europe was not yet ready for non-national federation.

Wilhelm in July 1917.

XIX

NONE WOULD
HAVE BELIEVED
A PRUSSIAN KING
CAPABLE OF
SUCH CONDUCT

THANKS TO BISMARCK, THE BRILLIANT AND ENERGETIC GERman people, with their huge vigor, appetite for culture, and enormous zest for national development, had arrived at a moment of significant opportunity when, in 1888, Kaiser Wilhelm II, on his father's premature death, ascended the imperial throne. Thanks to Wilhelm, however, this great nation ultimately plunged down a cascade of disaster. It has not managed even yet to extricate itself from the terrible effects of that experience. The ambitious character and uncertain personality of Wilhelm brought a thunderous initial defeat in Europe's twentieth-century civil war. This, in turn, ultimately produced another madman at the German helm, so brilliant and yet so diabolical as to make the kaiser seem in retrospect a show-off schoolboy. And the price of Adolf Hitler's even more thunderous defeat has not yet been paid by a sundered people.

Wilhelm II was in many respects a moderately intelligent enthusiast who never truly overcame the complexes of his childhood: his hatred of his mother, his acute awareness of physical defect in an arm that prevented him from shining as the armored knight of his dreams, his uneasiness when surrounded by dominating personages, such as Bismarck, and his consequent preference for sycophants like Eulenburg. One result was his tendency—not novel among Prussian rulers— to leave administrative matters of a civilian nature in the hands of mediocrities or individuals whose personal ambitions inhibited any latent desire to speak up frankly to their sovereign. Another was the habit of giving greater authority in the state to the professional military (and naval) class than should normally have been their due, especially as a new century with new theories of governance dawned over Europe.

The upshot was that a vain, inadequate ruler, because of his own preferences, weaknesses, and idiosyncrasies, was kept largely isolated from the truth—about the world, his country, and himself. As the United States learned during the Watergate experience of the 1970s, not even the best-tested, strongest governmental institutions can function properly when the head of the entire apparatus is deliberately walled off from public opinion or reality. And by the time Kaiser Wilhelm inherited the reins of power in the German Empire, neither its administrative methods nor its adjustment to modern political habits were strong enough or of sufficiently long tradition to be able to survive the antics of a willful imperial oaf with excessive dreams of glory and far from excessive intellectual ability.

Once the Schlieffen Plan for *Blitzkrieg* had ground to a halt in France (resulting in Moltke's replacement as commander) and once the subsequent effort to shift military emphasis eastward, after Tannenberg and the Masurian lakes had failed to cripple Russia mortally (resulting in Falkenhayn's replacement as commander) it became evident that Germany was in for the one thing it had most hoped to avoid: a long war on two fronts. Despite sometimes astonishing initial successes, the Central Powers were slowly transferred into the position of defenders in a besieged bastion. Already by 1916 a good many alert Germans were aware that their empire was nearing a fatal crisis.

The kaiser, a moody, self-centered, mercurial man was insulated from or refused to recognize this important shift in public morale. Moreover, he had the fatal habit of believing almost everything he himself said. He sought to persuade his nation that he was actually in command of the vast and still vibrant German armies, rushing around restlessly on his imperial train between headquarters and his home in Potsdam while largely ignoring political affairs whose significance increased as the chances of all-out victory waned. Diplomacy, industry, finance, and the increasingly important role of propaganda were discounted by him. He even sneered at the rather unobtrusive Reichstag (parliament) as a "monkey-house." For Wilhelm, the army and sheer military power were all that counted; civilian subtlety, brains, and ingenuity were not worthy of his attentions.

While more and more Germans began, at first in a subdued fashion, to complain that they were poorly led and that the kaiser should install more effective guidance of the economic sinews and political administration of the empire, Wilhelm shifted his generals about. But he was never a wholly determined, steadfast man. After the first battlefield failures in 1914, his doubts about future success intermittently revived.

Thus, when in 1916 his intuition at last told him of the slippage in public support, he encouraged his chancellor, the plodding Bethmann-Hollweg, to put out feelers to see if the Allies might be in the proper frame of mind for a negotiated peace. Even massive old Hindenburg, by then chief of the General Staff, made no objection to this exercise. However, Ludendorff, a tough and fanatical advocate of winner-take-all, wanted a victor's settlement and his influence on Hindenburg was steadily growing.

Thus there was little significant room at the top for a serious negotiation when, in mid-December, Bethmann-Hollweg addressed a short note to the Allies. He stressed a willingness to discuss terms, even though, at that moment, the Central Powers were in the process of completing their conquest of fertile, oil-rich little Rumania. But on the very same day Ludendorff ensured that the chancellor's inquiry would have no prospect of succeeding. The general issued an army order: "Soldiers, in the consciousness of victory which you have won, the rulers of the Allied states have made an offer of peace."

This distorted boast achieved what its promulgator had hoped. Lloyd George, the angry new British prime minister, announced: "To enter into a conference on the invitation of Germany proclaiming herself victorious, without any knowledge of the proposals she has to make, is to put our heads in a noose." Shortly thereafter the Allies formally spurned the German suggestion.

When the United States' President Wilson proposed that both warring coalitions should indicate their ideas for the basis of a settlement, the Allies hastened to demand dissolution of the Habsburg and Ottoman empires plus return to France by the Hohenzollerns of Alsace-Lorraine. That ended the affair: neither Berlin nor Vienna could afford to negotiate on any such basis. Wilson, a visionary with prognathous jaw and pince-nez glasses, believed his visions, although they were as keenly disappointed during as after the war.

Ludendorff, the superhawk, almost immediately asked the kaiser to launch his fleet of U-boats on a new campaign of unrestricted attacks on all ships bringing cargo to Allied ports. He hoped in this way to isolate Britain and to deprive France and Italy of food and vital military supplies.

Even the kaiser realized that such a decision would bring with it the risk of enticing enraged neutrals into the war against Germany after their shipping began to suffer. And, above all, he feared the effect on the United States, which had already been angered when a limited submarine campaign against neutrals was temporarily unleashed in 1915. But Tirpitz and the other admirals expressed confidence that once the British were cut off from their supply lines they would be forced to sue for peace.

Moreover they were sublimely confident that whatever course America decided on, it would be unable to send any appreciable force across the ocean before the conflict had ended in a victory by the Central Powers. Hindenburg was persuaded by Ludendorff that Britain must be wounded where it hurt in order to restore sagging confidence to the kaiser's army. So, at a crown council early in January 1917 the decision was made in favor of indiscriminate submarine assaults—ensuring that the war would continue and that Germany would lose it in the end.

Lord Grey of Fallodon, who had seen the lamps going out all over Europe in 1914, commented in his memoirs that if Germany had accepted President Wilson's proclaimed intention of seeking to end the conflict by a "peace without victory," the Allies would have been forced to follow suit. He concluded: "They could not have risked the ill-will of the government of the United States, still less a *rapprochement* between the United States and Germany." But Wilhelm, who paid more heed to the opinions of those in uniform than to civilian counselors, cheerfully followed the road desired by Ludendorff. Washington broke relations with Berlin shortly afterward and on April 6, 1917, declared war.

The kaiser's wobbling, indecisive policy, which culminated in this massive miscalculation, earned him no heightened respect among the growing circle of doubters in Germany. Princess Blücher, an Englishwoman by birth who never lost her pro-British sentiments even though she spent the entire conflict in an enemy land, wrote of the bewildered German sovereign: "I think people in England hardly realize the covert scorn with which people speak of him here."

Indeed, as subsequent memoirs and recollections show, on and off throughout the conflict Wilhelm displayed a lack of any true faith in his country's ability to win. He certainly contributed nothing himself except a yen for being photographed in bemedaled uniform among his generals at places described as front-line sectors. In most cases these were no more dangerous to his physical well-being than a seat in an autobus.

"The kaiser is daily growing more and more the shadow of a king," Princess Blücher confided to her secret journal in July 1917, when even a discouraged Reichstag mustered its courage and passed a resolution seeking to encourage peace negotiations by pledging German renunciation of all conquered territory. But the Reichstag didn't count for much— either in Germany or abroad.

By that time Wilhelm was the virtual political prisoner of his own highest officers, headed by Hindenburg and Ludendorff. This came about simply because he was unable to take the initiative and appoint strong civilian leaders to whom he might delegate overall political authority and preserve the institutional state. He bragged to Admiral Georg von Müller, chief of his naval cabinet: "The Reichstag can do what it likes. I have the nation and the army behind me."

The worse the situation became, the greater his vanity swelled. He boasted (in the face of the Reichstag resolution): "Where my bayonets are on guard, the land will under no circumstances be returned." And after the German army gained control of the province of Courland (in Latvia), from Russia, he announced, taking himself quite seriously: "I will take the Duchy of Courland, I, the victor by the strength of my sword."

Throughout 1917 the two Russian revolutions provided a period of respite and reinforced Berlin's hopes, especially after the momentous political warfare decision to send Lenin home with the intention of disintegrating Russia and terminating the war on the eastern front. This strategy worked exceedingly well at the start.

Under the cruel Brest-Litovsk treaty, Germany gained control of huge and critically important lands between the Baltic and the Black seas and was simultaneously able to transfer westward more than a million men and three thousand artillery pieces. Then, having bound Karl, the flagging Austro-Hungarian emperor-king, to his own doomed strategy, Wilhelm and his generals prepared for their long-postponed triumph.

As Empress Zita said: "He was completely under the thumb of his generals. This, I think, was largely because he was such a dreamer. He believed in his dreams and one of them, unfortunately, was that of final victory." What Zita did not realize was that the kaiser actually preferred to be "under the thumb of his generals" because he was incompetent to walk, think, or act alone.

The last massive German offensive began with a series of probing operations against the British portion of the Allied line around St. Quentin in Flanders. In some respects this resembled the great Hitler offensive in 1944 which aimed to thrust between Eisenhower's armies, capture Antwerp, and cut off their supply base.

Ludendorff wanted to shove the British into the channel and smash France before American reinforcements could make their presence in Europe effective. Hitler managed to surround, but not conquer, Bastogne. Ludendorff, who conceived the kaiser's earlier plan, managed to capture ninety thousand men, thirteen hundred guns, and two million bottles of whiskey. But although the excited Wilhelm happily announced: "The battle is won; the English have been utterly defeated," Ludendorff was stopped near Soissons.

The final great push, dubbed "the Kaiser's Battle," was then mustered from German positions deep inside France and aimed in the direction of Rheims. Both Ludendorff and the commander in chief of all Allied forces, Marshal Foch, agreed on its significance. The German said: "If my offensive at Rheims succeeds, the Germans have won the war." The Frenchman agreed: "If the German offensive at Rheims succeeds, the Germans have won the war." It failed.

Despite the submarine campaign against surface shipping, some five hundred thousand American troops had already been convoyed to France and constituted a sufficiently strong reserved force to enable Foch to stop the Germans' forward movement and, within a week, to shove it backward. As the Germans broke, Wilhelm complained in puzzlement: "It's very strange that our men cannot get used to tanks."

After a dinner with his top officers at headquarters in Spa, the kaiser gloomily spoke to them (according to Müller): "His Majesty spoke of himself to a small circle as a defeated warlord to whom we must show consideration." Ludendorff tried unsuccessfully to resign, then collapsed. It was left to Hindenburg to withdraw from the pressure of Foch's mounting counteroffensive to defensive positions and to hold out for what he hoped might be an honorable peace.

On March 3, 1918, the Brest-Litovsk *Diktat* had been accepted on Russia's behalf by Trotsky. A few weeks later Adolf Joffe arrived in Berlin as the first Soviet ambassador.

Karl and his family in exile in Switzerland, 1919. He had always been opposed to the war and in 1917 had written to Wilhelm: "We are fighting against an enemy which is more dangerous than the Entente—against international revolution which finds its strongest ally in general starvation."

He arrogantly refused to present his credentials to the kaiser in person and he even invited to his maiden dinner party two guests who patently could not come: Rosa Luxemburg and Karl Liebknecht, the outstanding German Marxist leaders, who were at the time serving jail sentences for treason. But Joffe actively promoted the Communist cause. He built up the nucleus of a revolutionary apparatus (later guided by Karl Radek, a close friend of Lenin). This was installed clandestinely in key points for the expected propitious moment when Germany would be socialized.

The Götterdämmerung began to accelerate. On September 13 the kaiser favored defining German surrender conditions through the diplomatic medium of Holland. On September 26 Bulgaria ceased fighting, isolating the German-Austrian forces from Turkey. On September 28 Ludendorff arrived at Hindenburg's GHQ office in Spa and urged that an armistice be arranged immediately by any kind of new German government able to win the security of Wilson's pledged Fourteen Points. On October 3 the kaiser's cousin, Prince Max of Baden, was named chancellor. The supreme command hoped thereby to make Germany a credible interlocutor with the Allies.

That night Prince Max asked for a cease-fire on the basis of Wilson's stipulated conditions. The American president replied, however, that all occupied territory must first be evacuated and also inquired on whose behalf Baden was acting. The kaiser interpreted this query as confirmation that the Allies intended to do away with both the House of Hohenzollern and the monarchy as an institution.

Prince Max, not only related to the kaiser but also a grandson of Russian Czar Nicholas I, was an urbane liberal who had included Socialist leaders in his cabinet, sought "revolution from above," and was determined to press for peace, using Switzerland as his communications channel with the Allies. He was not dissuaded by Wilhelm's vacillations. Nor, after Wilson stated on October 24 that Germany must "surrender," not negotiate, unless the "military leaders and monarchical autocracy" were first shelved, was Baden by any means as upset as Ludendorff. The embittered general publicly denounced Wilson's statement as "unacceptable to us soldiers." Wilhelm himself objected hollowly: "A descendant of Frederick the Great does not abdicate." Nonetheless, as Princess Blücher observed: "As for the mood of the people, the heroic attitude has completely disappeared."

The kaiser wobbled to the end. On October 27 he accepted Ludendorff's resignation. On October 28 the High Seas Fleet mutinied. On October 29 Wilhelm developed the weird theory of a "European Monroe Doctrine" which envisaged "Japanese divisions arriving via Serbia [a curious geographical concept] on the western front to help throw out the Americans." Finally the sensible Prince Max formally called upon Wilhelm to give up the throne in favor of his twelve-year-old grandson (whose father, the crown prince, was possibly even more unpopular than the emperor himself).

On November 1 the High Seas mutiny spread to the naval ports. Three days later open revolution started to engulf all north Germany, with soldier and worker councils taking over one city after another much as the early soviets had gathered up power amid Russia's turmoil. Hindenburg warned the new minister of the interior that, if the kaiser was ousted, "the army would not hold together . . . but would simply stream back home like a horde of marauding bandits."

Prince Max, as chancellor, had no conceivable freedom of action, poised as he was between chaos and disaster. In response to an ultimatum from the increasingly irate Socialists, he warned the kaiser that civil war would break out if he didn't leave promptly. Wilhelm was still muttering to his generals that he must lead his troops against the revolutionists, but General Wilhelm Groener (known as the good Swabian), speaking for the overwrought Hindenburg, advised his sovereign that such an operation was impossible. "Sire," he told the kaiser, "you no longer have an army."

On November 7 revolution engulfed Munich. Its leaders, headed by a former journalist named Kurt Eisner, proclaimed Bavaria a Socialist republic. That same day all railway lines leading to Berlin were severed in order to protect the capital within a kind of isolation ward. On November 8 a German armistice commission, headed by Matthias Erzberger, arrived at Marshal Foch's mobile headquarters aboard a train in the forest of Compiègne, to sue for formal peace. With a stony face, Foch had his terms read out. They were designed, as he wished, "to put Germany at the mercy of the victors."

When the news was received at Spa, Wilhelm realized he had no choice but abdication; yet he still procrastinated and talked of yielding the imperial crown of Germany while simultaneously retaining the king of Prussia's crown. These delays, arising successively in the military headquarters at a Belgian resort from which the Germans had not yet withdrawn, were no longer acceptable to Prince Max who could see the shapeless tide of anarchy preparing to overwhelm his tottering government and all that was left of German order.

He announced from a balcony of the Berlin chancellery that the kaiser and the crown prince respectively would renounce the throne and the succession and that Friedrich Ebert, a conservatively inclined Social Democrat, had accepted the post of Imperial Chancellor under a regency that would shortly be set up to assume interim charge of Germany's fate. The kaiser greeted news of his cousin's action as "Barefaced, outrageous treason"; but there was nothing he could do about it.

Groener had already let it be known that he thought Wilhelm's only honorable course was to go to the front and somehow manage to get himself killed. The kaiser, despite a lifetime of posturing and playing soldier, disapproved of this idea when it was timidly conveyed to him. He reasoned that it was unsuitable for both humanitarian and religious reasons.

Hindenburg now reentered the picture, having regained his composure. He warned the kaiser that he was no longer safe at Spa. He added:

> I cannot accept the responsibility of seeing the emperor hauled to Berlin by insurgent troops and delivered over as a prisoner to the revolutionary government. I must advise Your Majesty to abdicate and proceed to Holland [which was only about forty miles away].

At dawn on November 10, the day before an armistice terminating World War I was announced, Wilhelm slipped away aboard his white and gold special train. He left no message for Hindenburg or his faithful generals, only a letter for the unpopular crown prince. This said in part:

> Dear Boy. Since the field marshal can no longer guarantee my security here and since he also will no longer take the responsibility for the loyalty of the troops, I have decided, after severe inward struggle, to leave the collapsed army. . . . I recommend that you remain at your post and hold the troops together until they start the march back home. . . . Your stricken father, Wilhelm.

Thus he departed from history and from a battlefield for whose creation he bore the major responsibility, an ignoble, posturing playactor to the end.

The kaiser crossed the Dutch border at Eysen where a bewildered sentry telephoned The Hague. Queen Wilhelmina consulted her cabinet and, some hours later, sent a special train to the frontier for the imperial party. They were taken to Amerongen where the Dutch-English Count Godard Bentinck placed his seventeenth-century house at Wilhelm's disposal. "Now," said the ex-emperor as he and his host drove up to the portal, "for a cup of really hot, strong English tea."

Behind him he had left his army, his wife, his family, his nation, and all the minor German sovereigns and princes who saw they had no choice but capitulation to the evolving insurrection. However, the surprisingly efficient General Groener telephoned Ebert in Berlin and asked if the new chancellor was prepared to restore order. When Ebert answered affirmatively, Groener promised to maintain discipline in the defeated army, to bring it home, to cooperate with the regular officers in suppressing Bolshevism, and to help ensure internal security. Hindenburg would remain in command.

Wilhelm signed a formal act of abdication only on November 28—both as German emperor and Prussian king. He took up sawing wood as a form of exercise and stimulated his mind by reading, primarily in English and often aloud. His favorite author was P. G. Wodehouse.

The neutral Dutch refused an Allied demand for his extradition and helped him buy Doorn House, near Amerongen, as a permanent residence, which he filled with possessions the new government allowed him to have sent from Berlin. Following the death of his wife, Dona, he married a minor German princess, Hermine of Reuss, who was almost thirty years younger than he. He died in 1941, after having congratulated Hitler for capturing Paris. The old man was given a military funeral in occupied Holland—at the Führer's command.

Emil Ludwig, German-born historian and biographer, commented accordingly on the end of the last Hohenzollern ruler:

> Two hundred years earlier his forebear, the young Frederick the Great, had planned to escape over the frontier and had only been detained by a chance.
>
> Then his father's will had been that that prince should be shot for a deserter. Now the news that the Supreme War

The ex-kaiser feeds the wild ducks at Doorn, in Holland, where he bought a small estate and lived until the middle of the Second World War, much in the comfortable manner of an English country gentleman.

Lord had foresaken his country, in uniform, at the moment of her greatest need, evoked in the people neither hate nor rage, only an immense disappointment; for except the higher nobility, who knew the emperor's character, none of his enemies would have believed a Prussian king capable of such conduct.

It destroyed (temporarily) the belief of the Prussians in the military basis of their State, which had been instilled into them for centuries as a maxim of morals and honor, and a great illusion fell shattered round the heads of millions. Prussia and Germany became republics not because the time was ripe, but because all their princes had become degenerate and defenseless, and vacated their twenty thrones without a blow. Thus ended the dynasty of the Hohenzollerns, at the height of their power, after rising from lords of the manor to emperors, from rulers of 1,000,000 to 66,000,000, from a vassal state to the heads of Germany.

XX

A PACK OF TRICKS
WE PLAY
ON THE DEAD

MY JUDGMENTS ON THESE THREE GREAT DYNASTIES THAT
endured so long and in many respects so influenced the
course of mankind may be excessively hard, but after all
I am a Jeffersonian Democrat not predisposed to monarchy
and not unbiased. Yet, at the same time, I think it only just
to give the descendants of these impressive and now power-
less lineages a chance to make their own comments from their
isolated cupboards of retirement. And, when measuring their
human, sympathetic, tender recollections of immediate ancestors and their own vanished youth, let us never forget

what René Descartes, the great French philosopher, wrote of "madmen [who] try to make people believe they are kings, but they are only poor men who dress their nakedness in gold and purple."

Prince Nicholas of Greece, who married one Romanov grand duchess (Helene, called Ellen) and was the son of another (Olga), observed in his memoirs: "To be born a prince is an accident but not always a privilege and by no means a career." And, as it turned out, it was neither privilege nor career for those who were finally destined to bear the eagles of Habsburg, Hohenzollern, and Romanov to their doom.

It is interesting, looking back across the centuries, to realize how few outstanding people these three long-lived dynasties produced: only Charles V for the Habsburgs, Peter the Great for the Romanovs, and Frederick the Great for the Hohenzollerns can without challenge be included in humanity's talent club. Nor was the autocratic system they represented very often hospitable to political originality.

Fate struck down Archduke Franz Ferdinand, the Austrian heir. The mild liberalism of Russia's Czar Alexander II ended in a whiff of dynamite. Peter the Great murdered his own son, and Friedrich Wilhelm I of Prussia almost murdered his heir—who survived to become known as Frederick the Great.

The autocratic system did not even very often welcome exceptional counselors. Perhaps the only giants of this group were Metternich, who saved the Habsburgs, and Bismarck who made the Hohenzollerns. Potemkin doesn't count; all he really succeeded in doing was to mislead and fool Czarina Catherine of Russia.

Yet, if beneath the purple, gold, and ermine that garbed them, hiding their "emperor's new suit," they collectively represented astonishing mediocrity, they produced few heroes, they also produced no Neros or Caligulas. Maybe the worst moral offenders among them were the greatest—like the

Romanovs' Peter and Catherine. Most were plodding, honorable people with a sense of decency (up to a point) and a sense of style and decorum, who were simply beyond the depth of their capacity (like Nicholas II) and who managed to be sustained a long time on little more than remarkably steadfast public acceptance of the kingly concept. And, one may add, among these three great families there were few cases of regicide or, until the end, any truly earthshaking revolutions.

Like the patterns set by their own slowly evolving families, the final dynasts of this interwoven triangle played archetypal roles as if cast for the impending melodrama by a percipient director. Kaiser Wilhelm was a vain, military-minded Hohenzollern; Czar Nicholas was a rather gentle, handsome, helpless fool, at least politically betrayed by a distressed, dominating wife urged on by a scheming, lascivious monk; and Franz Josef, who remained almost until his throne turned to dust, was a decent, rather unimaginative *Pechvogel*. Tragedy followed him throughout life without actually embracing him.

Franz Josef was succeeded by Emperor Karl, who held his crown but two years, when the empire disintegrated. Not long after that Karl himself died of tuberculosis probably and despair certainly in far-off Madeira. But Karl's son, Archduke Otto, is still very much on the scene, an active, energetic, lean, and studious man who spends much time seeking to bring about European unity. He feels the Pan-European idea, which he sees as an ultimate successor of the souped-up nationalism that reached its apogee early this century, had already displayed green shoots in the polyglot Habsburg empire before World War I. In a letter to me, the Habsburg heir wrote:

> If an imaginative solution had been found earlier to the national problem, things might have been fundamentally different. There is no question that Austria-Hungary showed

a remarkable resilience in the critical years of the First World War. After all, the multinational old state resisted for four and a half years the overwhelming power of its foes. The successor states, the so-called national countries, did not resist when Hitler came or their resistance crumbled within a matter of days or hours.

The great problem, nevertheless, with such a hypothetical question, is this: Was it possible for the people of the middle of the 19th century, when the decisive errors were committed, to foresee the development of nationalism as it took place? It is a little bit the same question as the one one might ask rightly about the social policies in the industrial revolution. Then too, humanity had to face unprecedented problems and did not successfully meet them. The same might be said of the national problem, which is also something relatively very modern.

We are too prone to forget that the national question truly developed only in the course of the 19th century. It took many decades to begin developing certain elements of a solution—the most remarkable of these being the so-called Moravian Agreement of 1906, which, I feel, has been the most successful attempt so far to tackle the problem, which may certainly arise anew in Europe, either as a consequence of political changes in Central Europe or as the logical consequence from the vast movement of people which is far from ended.

I have had long talks with contemporary representatives of the Romanovs, Hohenzollerns, and Habsburgs who lead comfortable, discreet lives which they admit are certainly happier in the sense of personal relationships with family and friends than could ever have been the case had history turned down a different and more grandiose avenue. And I may add that all of them retain tender remembrances of their exalted forebears.

The lovely Princess Olga of Greece and Denmark (wife of Prince Paul, who ruled Jugoslavia seven years after his cousin, the king's, assassination) is Romanov by both paternal and maternal descent. She shows it by the beauty of her features which the Russian imperial family transmitted to generation after generation of its womenfolk.

As a child, she spent regular summer holidays in Russia until World War I with her cousins, the tragic grand duchesses and the boy czarevitch who were slaughtered like animals in 1918. She recalls with affection the handsome, sad eyed Czar Nicholas, who looked almost the twin of King George V of England, and describes him as gentle and by nature good. She admits, however, that he was influenced far too greatly by Czarina Alexandra and showed me a handwritten letter from her own father, Prince Nicholas, to her mother, sent from the czar's military headquarters (Stavka) in 1916, in which he wrote:

> She mixes a good deal in politics. You cannot conceive what is said about her and I fear with every good reason! The girls [the czar's daughters] are pretty and do hospital work with her, dressed as nurses. Alix comes and goes from Czarskoe to the Stavka and the result of these journeys is always a change of ministers or high functionaries which drives everybody frantic.

(The letter, incidentally, to avoid chance of interception, was sent by courtesy of French Ambassador Paléologue.)

With respect to the influence of Rasputin on the czarina and, therefore, through her, on the czar, both Princess Olga and Prince Paul (whose mother also was Russian and who was born in that country) agree that when women of the royal family of Hesse abandon the Lutheran creed for Orthodoxy, because of the custom that queens assume the religion of their husbands' countries, they can become passionately overwhelmed by exposure to the Eastern faith.

Prince Paul, who was an unusually cultivated, open-minded

man who made no secret of his admiration for Marshal Tito, present tenant of his old palace in Belgrade, believed that in the end, the Russian empire foundered not only because of growing military disasters and economic hardship and not only because of Rasputin's malevolent political influence, but because Russia under the last czar was governed by total paradox. "It was an autocracy without an autocrat," as Princess Olga observes.

The point they make is that modern social institutions had not yet been created, but the strong, firm hand required to make the nation function without them was not the hand of Nicholas II. He was a good-natured man, but weak. He offered Russia neither the determination of his grandfather to put through an extensive reform program nor the willful resolution of his father, the reactionary Alexander III. Autocracy, constructed as totalitarian, yet conducted by vacillation, is highly susceptible of disastrous collapse.

Princess Olga thinks the greatest of the Romanov rulers was: "Certainly Peter the Great. He produced things. He left his mark. But I suppose Catherine the Great was also very significant." Her husband added: "Remember, she was not a Romanov."

Olga believes Russia had been greatly weakened in 1914 by the way it staged a premature offensive against the Germans on the eastern front in order to honor its alliance with France when the French were on the verge of collapse during the first big German drive. But she admits that "You must look back on the situation. Things were going worse and worse, even before the Japanese war [1905]. The rich people and the great landowners were always traveling and paying no attention to their national obligations. And poor little Nicholas, the emperor!"

Paul thought that "Nicholas was just not an autocrat: He was a weak man. He was the son of an autocrat [Alexander III] and the children of autocrats are usually nothing but mollycoddles." Paul suggested there was little doubt that the process of modernization of Russia in the nineteenth century and bringing its institutions up to date had been greatly set back by the reaction after the assassination of Czar Alexander II in 1881. "Poor Emperor Nicholas," says Olga. "He wanted so much to have a moderate kind of government and a constitutional monarchy. But he wasn't strong enough to bring it about."

I said it was too bad he was so indecisive because his wife had a much stronger character, and when for understandable and tragic reasons (her son's hemophilia) she fell under the influence of Rasputin, she was able to push for unwise appointments and policies. Olga agreed. She repeated: "When a Hesse [member of the Hessian royal family] changes religion, mysticism always gets ahold of them."

Princess Olga said of Empress Alexandra: "I remember her as a half invalid and very tender. She was always nice with children but she was agonizingly shy before crowds. My mother told us this. She would blush all over her neck and face even when she had to shake hands. She was warm and kind with us—but I could see that she could easily and often turn very cold."

She added: "My grandmother decided to emancipate her sons, the grand dukes, too soon and they all became adventurers much too early. They even had mistresses at home."

I said I had a feeling Nicholas II had suffered at a disadvantage because Kaiser Wilhelm had continually gotten the better of him. She said: "Everybody loathed the kaiser [at which Paul nodded]. He was an unbearable bounder. For me the Hohenzollerns were an inferior lot—except for Frederick the Great."

At this point Paul added with a faint smile. "The Hohenzollerns were just tough soliders. But the Coburgs brought a brilliant, sly quality into the bloodstream and they were also very ambitious. This mixture made the kaiser a more complicated man than he seemed. But all the Coburgs were tricky. Look at Ferdinand, the Bulgarian fox. You could never trust him for thirty seconds."

It is notable of the Habsburgs, who produced no ruler of true quality save Charles V (some people argue, also Joseph II), that during their final century of rule, despite the stern, simple appearance of Franz Josef, who dominated most of that period, the family became notable for eccentricity and scandal. There were distinct traces of insanity that cropped up from time to time and popular legend added the touch that both the competent Joseph II and the flighty Crown Prince Rudolf came to unfortunate ends because they were not as devoutly and extremely Roman Catholic as the others. It is a little more likely that this interwoven accident of fate and religiosity had more to do with their final tragedies than the hot, dry Föhn wind which blows over Vienna from the Alps and is said to encourage suicidal and violent acts among those stricken with headaches and morosity by its tiring effects.

Archduke Otto feels that because he is banned from the nonexistent Austro-Hungarian throne (and is ever forbidden to run for president in Austria) is no reason to abandon the cause of European federation, which he regards as the mission of the last Habsburg emperors, a mission that failed. Today, a resident of Munich and Innsbruck, he is chairman of the Pan-European Movement which seeks to bring the continent together: a spare, rather bald man of sixty-four, with slate-colored eyes, a short gray mustache, and an impeccable knowledge of English.

He told me that "very definitely" he regarded Europe's advance toward unity as the main purpose of his life. "It is the only task of long-range significance as I see it. If we don't succeed, all the rest will go the wrong way. It is an enduring task that requires much patience. Clearly, it would be an error to forecast or to fix a time limit for its completion. You can't keep looking at your watch."

I then inquired whether he thought there might have been any way that the Habsburg empire could have become the kernel of a confederated or federated Europe. He said: "Certainly. There were quite a number of studies along such lines during the nineteenth century. One can go back even further. Already during the time of the Holy Roman Emperor Charles V this idea was alluded to.

"Soon after the 1848 revolution Prince Schwarzenberg was prime minister after Franz Josef became emperor and he was much more modern on this subject than Metternich, who had just gone out. Later when Franz Ferdinand was the heir, he had a special group of advisers headed by a Transylvanian Rumanian named Aurel Popovici. Popovici, a political writer, was quite fascinating on this subject.

"He foresaw the inevitable expansion of Russia. He predicted that if a community of nations was not enlarged in time, the Russians would extend their power as far as the Bavarian Alps. Popovici died in Geneva during World War I and next year [1977] we are going to erect a monument to him there. [Popovici, 1863–1917, wrote a book in 1906 called *The United States of a Greater Austria* in which he proposed renewing the Habsburg monarchy on the basis of national spirit by federating its fifteen small nation states within a federal monarchy.]

"Franz Ferdinand had his own special workshop and also thought a lot about these problems himself. Popovici, as a Rumanian, wanted more than a triune kingdom ruled from Vienna and including autonomous German, Magyar, and Slavic states. The triune kingdom thought mainly of the South Slavs, as linked to Austria and Hungary. But their view also had certain ties to the Slavic community in Bohemia.

"The Austrian Ausgleich with Hungary provoked thought about a similar arrangement with the crown of Saint Wenceslaus in Bohemia. But once the Ausgleich had taken place, it prevented such a development with Bohemia because the central European Slavs were tied both to the Hungarians and to the Austrians. Furthermore, the Poles [part of whom were under Vienna until after World War I] objected to an independent Bohemian kingdom for their part. They felt that this interfered with their own future. Moreover, the Poles had great traditional power in the Habsburg administration. For example, for years there was always a Polish finance minister—although when Poland regained its independence it was never brilliant at finance."

Obviously, against this background of intra-Slavic rivalries, Otto considered the 1906 Moravian Ausgleich a particular success in arranging at least some pattern of relationships with Vienna (and also Budapest, the subordinate capital). I asked the archduke whether he thought that either Rudolf, who committed suicide at Mayerling, or Franz Ferdinand, whose assassination brought the whole imperial edifice down, had had any chance of moving the Habsburg empire toward a valid new concept of federation. He replied: "Yes, especially Franz Ferdinand. Maybe Rudolf at an earlier stage. He was a very intellectual man, but there was an element of imbalance in his personality. One fundamental difficulty of the Austro-Hungarian empire was the collision of two ideas—Rudolf, who favored even more power for the Hungarians; and Franz Ferdinand, who favored a triune kingdom with the Slavs. The empire had a parliament based on a broad vote and popular representation, but the balance of the non-Austrian national groups was not freely allowed. Yet coalitions among national groups blocked the crown from imposing its power.

"Consequently the Austrian parliament was one of the greatest impediments to the modernization of the country. We must think of the region under the Habsburgs as a united Europe in which all areas would be represented; but they were not protected, in terms of nationality blocs, the way the different states of America are protected in the U.S. Senate.

Your Senate is a marvelous example of such protection.

"Hungary did not apply equal representation so liberally as Austria. Its electoral system had no secret ballot—so there was no real protection. The upshot of these contradictions was that a coalition of German speakers and the Poles, often aided by Ruthenians, ran most things. Franz Ferdinand and Popovici studied these contradictions carefully and much documentation exists.

"Rudolf, for his part, had been a brilliantly intelligent but apolitical ideologue. He was what you might call an archaic liberal. He would have been for proportional representation if he had known about it. His was a human tragedy: a wasted life followed by a needless death.

"Franz Ferdinand came later. His was a more serious political tragedy. Sarajevo was really a great crime designed to prevent precisely the evolution Franz Ferdinand wanted. He was murdered because he was a friend of the southern Slavs and neither the Russians nor the Serbs could tolerate this. The Pan-Serbs feared him because they wished to extend their own rule over the people he wished to benefit and 'Apis' [Dimitrijević, head of Serbian military intelligence], who was paid by the Russian military attaché, arranged for the assassination. One might say that Mayerling was a mini-tragedy, that Sarajevo was a maxi-tragedy."

I asked Otto how his father, who became Emperor Karl I, succeeding Franz Josef because of the Sarajevo murder, would have viewed Franz Ferdinand's program. The archduke answered: "He would have followed Franz Ferdinand's line. He agreed very strongly on the theory of federation." I then wondered whether Franz Josef had been so hostile to his nephew and (since Rudolf's suicide) heir, Franz Ferdinand, only because he disliked the latter's morganatic marriage. "No," he said categorically. "Franz Josef was of a different temperament than that of Franz Ferdinand. Franz Ferdinand was most outspoken. He was a tough-talking man. Emperor

Franz Josef's dislike for him went far beyond his marriage. Their temperaments were simply incompatible."

I asked if he thought that monarchy, which was such an old profession, is now disappearing as a governing form. He said: "I believe in the cyclic movement of history. Institutions are born, they mature, and then they decay. Actually, after the eighteenth century, monarchies were in a condition of decay. I once devised a formula—and I believe it still—that when kings ceased to die on the battlefield for their subjects, monarchy entered its period of decline. The original idea that the king could do no wrong only became an outward manifestation of pomp and circumstance.

"Monarchy is understood in the Holy Scriptures. You come across it first in Judges. Then they become kings. But the judicial function was too much disregarded and led to ultimate decay. The disease lasted a long time but it was fatal. The autumnal storm suddenly blows away the sickening leaves overnight. This doesn't mean that ideas fundamental to monarchy are dead. But the kaleidoscope has changed. Only today. After all, man is the least changeable element in nature and gives permanence to certain concepts."

What did he think had been the Habsburgs' greatest contribution to history? "Their greatest contribution was to be an integrating factor among several nationality and language groups," he observed. "The Habsburgs were Spanish in Spain, Austrians in Austria, Dutch in Holland, Germans in Germany. A European dynasty always. They were not in the least bit like the Bourbons who were a typical French dynasty and always nationalistic rather than multinational. I remember riding in an airplane in Spain and Ximenez Caballero, a Spanish poet, pointed out of the window first at La Granja, emphasizing that architecturally it was a purely French castle; and then at El Escorial, a Habsburg creation, describing it as truly Spanish. I can even think of a third typical architectural instance. Look at Klosterneuburg, an edifice which represents Spanish ideas developed in Austria.

"For me Charles V was without doubt the greatest Habsburg and he was also a deliberate federator. One might say that his great heritage had come from Burgundy which also had a federative tradition. There was a desire to join together various peoples and language groups.

"But France, by contrast, was always on the defensive. Its hexagon was surrounded by Habsburgs. They were everywhere—in Spain, Holland, Burgundy, Austria. They imposed the habit of defensiveness and therefore nationality. Every nation is born with the idea of resisting someone else and that is the way France as a nation was born.

"Even in our European work now we still must be more careful in dealing with the French than with any of the others. The French are emphatically a nation state; the Habsburgs never were. Indeed it was the task of the Habsburg dynasty to resist nineteenth-century nationalism. It had to choose deliberately to be an anachronism. But what was anachronistic in the nineteenth century no longer is today.

"The Habsburg reaction was instinctive. A holding position that could be the foundation for a new 'Europe' in future generations. But this is what is beginning to happen now. Take the case of migratory labor in Europe. This increasingly helps to mix nationalities and there is a permanent development because men seeking jobs bring their families along."

Otto said that the 1906 Moravian Ausgleich (agreement) was "a great chapter at the end of the Habsburg era. It hugely lessened tensions between the Czechs and the Germans. It became the basis of the nationality coexistence in Bukovina and also for coexistence between Czechs and Poles in Galicia.

"The extremes three generations ago were between the French national state and the Habsburg international state. Burgundy was a first international formula which was transmitted on to the Danube by Emperor Maximilian's grand-mother."

Had Otto's father, the Emperor Karl, succeeded in 1917 in arranging a separate peace through Empress Zita's two Bourbon-Parma brothers or through General Jan Smuts, he thought the case for internationalism might still have been saved. But this was not to be; and "the ideological split and crusading spirit that followed World War II set back the 'European' idea by a generation."

Prince Louis Ferdinand of Prussia, claimant to the Hohenzollern throne were it ever again to exist, is a pleasing contrast to the conventional portraits of his father, the crown prince, and his grandfather, Kaiser Wilhelm II, as they are generally limned by historians and memorialists. One Berlin story recounted that, shortly before World War I, when the kaiser was invited to a hunting party in Prussia a guest was warned: "For God's sake don't shoot him by mistake or we'll have something worse," meaning the crown prince, Louis Ferdinand's father.

But the present Hohenzollern heir is a modest, pleasant man, both interesting and agreeable, with a passion for music (he composes and plays the piano) and a far more liberal outlook (for his generation—he is now sixty-nine) than his immediate forebears. He lives in Wümmehof, near Bremen, in a comfortable house like that of many another prosperous German (or American), near most of his seven children and nine grandchildren. His wife, Grand Duchess Kira of Russia, died some time ago, but he continues to lead a seemingly happy life with his children, horses, dogs, and friends, traveling when opportunity arises.

Louis Ferdinand is over six feet tall but not powerfully built. He is exceptionally friendly and speaks remarkably good English, although he says his Spanish is better, and he also speaks French, some Italian, and a bit of Russian. He has a long nose, long ears, and a kindly expression, and he is clearly a genuinely simple and modest man with no apparent trace of the Hohenzollern arrogance. He said the republic, after World War I, had given him legal permission to use the title "Prince of Prussia" as a family name—"like Müller or Schmidt," he explained, but not as a sign of rank. But he makes no bones about the fact that he still considers himself claimant to the throne and that is his "principal business." When I asked if business is good, he said, "Not yet," with a twinkle and a smile.

He was in the United States and subsequently Argentina from 1929 to 1934. When he arrived in New York, he was met by Poultney Bigelow, a retired U.S. diplomat who was a great friend of the kaiser and had played with him as a boy. Bigelow introduced him to Governor Franklin Roosevelt with whom they lunched at Hyde Park. He liked Roosevelt immensely and thought he was a charming, intelligent, liberal man.

Bigelow also introduced him to Henry Ford, who gave him a salesman's job. He said Ford was a curious, dried-up fellow, but extremely nice to him and, although he hated Roosevelt, was involved in anti-Semitism, and was a prohibitionist (all characteristics disliked by the young Hohenzollern), he was an industrial genius and the prince admired him.

Louis Ferdinand fell head over heels in love with Lili Damita, the famous and beautiful Hollywood actress of that era, and he wanted to marry her. This produced a spate of telegrams from both his grandfather, the kaiser, and his father, who were living separate lives of exile in Holland. Ford and Bigelow put pressure on him, and he agreed to go to Argentina where Ford gave him another job.

He became heir to the crown prince in 1933 when his brother Wilhelm married someone disapproved of by the family, "because she was not considered up to our standards," and his grandfather, the ex-kaiser, insisted he withdraw. Prince Wilhelm was killed at the very start of the German invasion of France in 1940. The crown prince himself died in 1951, so Louis Ferdinand became the claimant.

I asked why he was called Louis Ferdinand and not Ludwig Ferdinand. (Ludwig is the German version of Louis.) He said both he and one of his sons were actually christened Louis Ferdinand, "which is really a nickname for one of my ancestors, a nephew of Frederick the Great, who was an excellent composer of romantic music as well as a good soldier. He got into romantic trouble and died in 1806 fighting Napoleon, virtually committing suicide by leading a totally foolhardy charge. This nephew of Frederick the Great was called Ludwig Friedrich Christian, Prince of Prussia, but was known to everybody as Louis because French was the fashionable language in the time of Frederick the Great and Louis was considered more 'chic' than Ludwig." The prince said he was the first member of the family actually to be christened Louis.

I asked if there was any active monarchist movement nowadays. He said: "There are a few hundred and they put out occasional publications. But I have never encouraged them and I hold that such a movement will only damage the cause of our family. I keep out of party politics completely. I am loyal to the legal democratic state as long as it remains free and democratic. I was against the Hitler dictatorship [unlike some of his family] and I oppose any dictatorship."

He said he had been brought up primarily at Potsdam, spending childhood winters at the imperial palace in Berlin and passing many of his summers at the resort seaside town of Zoppot near Danzig (now Poland). His father and grandfather fled to Holland in 1918, but his mother remained in Germany. He studied at Berlin University and graduated in 1929. After that he had his sentimental journey to the United States and Argentina.

He continued: "Then my grandfather, for whom I had great respect, said, 'You will have to come back to Germany because someday you will be the heir to our family claims.' I returned and got a job with Lufthansa. I married Grand Duchess Kira and settled down. As a matter of fact, my grandmother was also a Romanov, the Grand Duchess Anastasia who was wife of the duke of Mecklenburg."

I asked if he felt that the Hohenzollern heritage meant anything more to him than in a family sense and a proud tradition. It was only later that he told me that he regarded himself as a theoretical "claimant." At this point he said: "I am just a German citizen with all the rights of other citizens. I can run for any office in the republic, including the presidency [unlike Otto in Austria]. But I refuse to join any party. As a matter of fact, I am on very good terms with the Social Democrats, and when Willy Brandt was mayor of Berlin he came to the wedding of my daughter with all his local government Socialist ministers.

"But despite my political inactivity many Germans still consider the head of our family as pretender to the throne. I don't advocate any change in the political system now or in the future, but I don't exclude the possibility and we keep this in mind always. In politics nothing can be excluded."

I asked him which direction the eagle in the Hohenzollern coat of arms looked—east or west. (The double-headed Romanov and Habsburg eagles look in two directions.) He answered: "The eagle looks to the east. But you know the Hohenzollerns didn't have an eagle in their coat of arms until they went to Brandenburg. They used to have a dog." (I believe the eagle they now have derives from the Polish royal family emblem and prior to that from the German Order of Teutonic Knights. The latter certainly looked only eastward to conquests.)

I asked him which Hohenzollern, to his mind, was the greatest. He said: "Without any doubt Frederick the Great. He was an all-round genius. He was a fantastic military leader, but he was also a writer, a philosopher, a flautist, and a composer. He composed some lovely music for the flute and also wrote symphonies. He made the flute the instrument of his century. It had been played only a little before. Johann Joachim Quantz, his flute teacher, played a great part in this. So you can see that Frederick was a universal spirit, a kind of Renaissance man."

I asked what he thought had brought about the end of the empire—by which I meant, while this was obviously World War I's result, could the empire have continued indefinitely had there been no war? He said: "I am convinced it would have continued. There was no social upheaval here when the war ended; there was simply a kind of hunger strike when people were unable to go on. This situation would have been avoided.

"I consider it was a very great tragedy that my great grandfather, the Emperor Friedrich III, died only three months after he ascended the throne. He and his empress, Queen Victoria's daughter, would certainly have speeded up the rate of reform in Germany and advanced toward a parliamentary and more liberal system of government. And there was another thing: Friedrich III's entourage was made up of older men, and my grandfather changed this completely when he moved in because there was such a generation gap between them and my grandfather and his advisers. Unfortunately there were no more liberals in the newer group.

"There were two tragedies involved—Friedrich III's premature death which was the *real* tragedy and World War I. But I am certain there would have been no World War I had Friedrich lived. And, had he lived, this might have given my grandfather much more time to mature, to travel around the world as he wished and to get to know new people.

"When I asked my grandfather for permission to travel to the U.S.A., he told me, 'I always wanted to travel a bit, but they wouldn't let me; so you go ahead.' He was hemmed in by a certain group of east German feudal landowners, the

Junkers. Many of them were very cultivated, but they had closed minds. They stood between the throne and the people.

"Personally I have always felt that had there been equal access to privileges—had liberals and Social Democrats been granted titles as in Britain and felt a part of the entire structure in a personal sense, there never would have been a revolution here. The British are very wise on this kind of thing. But my grandfather, although he did grant titles to industrialists and occasionally to intellectual or artistic leaders, had no access to liberal and Socialist political people. They were closed off by the Junkers."

I said it has often been observed that Wilhelm II weakened the institutions of government by heeding the military too much and the civilians too little, thereby thwarting desired progress toward democratic institutions. His grandson replied: "I can't truly judge if that theory is correct. I find my grandfather has been accused of being too despotic, and yet I think he was not despotic enough from what some people tell me. He made no decisions for the government without consulting Bülow, his chancellor. But Bülow was much too lazy. He never even read the text of the famous interview the kaiser gave to the *London Daily Telegraph* which got him into so much trouble; and yet he approved of it when the kaiser sent it to him—without having read it.

"My grandfather's self-respect was so hurt by this incident and he was so offended by Bülow that after that he tended to let others rule entirely. He didn't really mix into things enough. There was a crack in his psychological self-respect following that affair. He had considered Bülow an admirable man and a great friend. And yet this same Bülow told the Reichstag that he knew nothing about the interview in the *Telegraph*—which had actually been submitted to him. My grandfather was immensely hurt by this and in a pitiful state. This was a great psychological crisis for him—his betrayal by a dear friend. That betrayal by Bülow killed something inside of him. Until then he had been a gay and lively man, interested in everything. After that he became a mere shadow of himself."

I said he had obviously known his grandfather well—he interrupted and said above all in Holland after his exile—and I wondered if he could recall his strengths and weaknesses as a human being. Louis Ferdinand said: "Certainly he was easily influenced. And of course in Holland, during his later exile, he was quite isolated and believed everything he was told. He trusted people too much. Perhaps I might say he was too decent [a charge rarely made by history about the kaiser].

"We were always told to regard everyone with the highest respect and to avoid too much respect for one's self, which leads to arrogance. And my grandfather had had a very severe youth.

"But I don't think his weak arm seemed to bother him, and I doubt if it gave him many of the complexes historians have attributed to him. After all, he rode well and, indeed, he played tennis.

"I don't think it is fair, either, to say that there was a coldness between him and his mother which affected his political outlook. Grandfather loved England, and he was the favorite grandchild of Queen Victoria. He was never anti-British, although he was very disappointed by the outbreak of war with England. Personally I am convinced he didn't want the war, although he did make very strong speeches in public.

"I was very fond of him. He was a really warmhearted man. Of course I was far to the left of him in my thinking, but he never minded this because he had great wisdom. And I wasn't at all militarily minded. I am not at all in the military tradition personally.

"I think that my grandfather was an able, intelligent, warm man who had a lot of bad luck. He was the most intelligent of all the sovereigns of his time. Actually I think the French, who are very intelligent, liked him more than the Germans."

(I think most French over the age of sixty would shiver at this thought.)

I asked him where he thought the kaiser had gone wrong in his calculations and estimates of the world. He said: "Well, the generation of leaders and advisers who had been helpful to his own father dropped out completely when Friedrich III died. They had included very good people like Bismarck. But the most experienced of them dropped out and inexperienced young ones came in. This younger generation moved in just about the same time as my grandfather, and I think the sudden change undoubtedly was not helpful to him.

"Bismarck was certainly our greatest statesman, but he had very bad manners and he became increasingly overbearing with age. Frankly I don't think his dismissal by my grandfather was a great tragedy. Russia was already on the other side [meaning pro-French] because of the Berlin Congress of 1878.

"Had Bismarck stayed he would not have helped. He already wanted to abolish all the reforms that had been introduced. He was aspiring to establish a kind of shogunate and hoped to treat our family in the same way the Japanese shoguns treated the Japanese emperors isolated in Kyoto. My grandfather had no other choice but to dismiss him."

Did he think—as I had asked Otto—that monarchical government was still viable in today's world? He said: "Definitely so. Of course I am talking for my own sake, the way I personally see things. I have just come back from Copenhagen where my cousin, a Danish prince, had his funeral. The system there is conducted with great tact, simplicity, and charm. There is no pomp; the queen is accompanied by no security policemen or protective cars and the royal cars stop at every red light. That is real democracy. I think the monarchic system can be as resilient as any other."

I asked how he would have played things differently had he been sovereign. He said: "I would have tried to establish a more open society the way the British and the Danes have done and to give equal opportunity for titles, advances, etc., to all members of the social community. A monarch could have done this. My grandfather was too cut off to realize what he should have done for the workers and so-called proletariat."

He said the dispatch of Lenin to Petrograd by Hindenburg and Ludendorff had been "a horrible mistake. Ludendorff and Hindenburg did that virtually alone because my grandfather was entirely out of the picture by then. He was sitting there almost like a prisoner.

"But you know that at the end, in October 1918, he wanted to stay in Berlin. He was forced by the high command to go back to headquarters in Spa because they feared he might take an initiative on his own. Had he stayed in Germany it might have avoided revolution and we might have had a negotiated peace. Then the high command made him get out to Holland.

"Grandfather told me once he had made all preparations to help get Czar Nicholas out if possible." (He obviously refers to the guarantee that a British cruiser originally planned to carry out the Romanovs would have its safe passage guaranteed by the Germans.)

Louis Ferdinand said the death of Franz Ferdinand, the Habsburg heir, in 1914 "struck my father heavily because they were great friends. And when he saw the Serbian reply to Austria's ultimatum he wrote a marginal note on his copy of the document and in his own handwriting, 'First class. War unnecessary.' Germany was pulled into that war by Austria.

"I categorically refuse the theory that my grandfather was responsible for that war. It wasn't at all like Hitler in World War II. Hitler had isolated Germany from everyone by fighting the Catholics, the Jews, and everybody you can imagine. His idiotic policy led to no other alternative but war."

It is obvious from talks with members of the three imperial dynasties that in all probability each would have been better off had newer generations or other princes come to power. Otto von Habsburg considers the great tragedy for his family was the assassination of Franz Ferdinand. This not only allowed a brutal Viennese bureaucracy to push through World War I but terminated all progress toward the first true federative, multinational state on a big scale and in modern times. Louis Ferdinand, the genial musician, wisely sees the sad importance of Friedrich III's death after only a three-month rule. And there is no doubt that another progressively inclined Alexander II would have made Russia a more effective czar than Nicholas.

As can be understood from earlier chapters of this book, I by no means accept the fully favorable interpretations of some of these dynastic forebears as iterated by their sentimental descendants. There is some indication that Franz Ferdinand was not in any way the modern, realistic liberal some now hold him to have been. As for Kaiser Wilhelm, gentled by time, he certainly made a great dent on his grandson's heart; but there is much evidence that this was the exception, in his human relationships, not the rule. The prince's theory that Bismarck wished to establish a Prussian shogunate and thereby earned his discharge is quite fascinating.

The assassination of Franz Ferdinand—if for no other reason than that it provoked a cataclysm and ended a global way of life—and the premature end of Friedrich III were certainly unforeseen accidents; but history is made up of accidents and if institutions cannot survive them they are useless. There is no future for the If-Lincoln-Had-Not-Been-Shot school of historical thinking.

At least the dynasts gained the love of their families, as is amply evident and I feel like a villain for commenting acerbly on the ancestors of charming people who have been helpful, friendly, and hospitable to me, showing warmhearted consideration. They quite clearly cherish deep affectionate attachments, as human beings, for these departed rulers. Was the same true for the families of their successors, Stalin and Hitler?

André Malraux once said to me: "Had the Maréchal de Saxe met Napoleon in heaven he might have said: 'I never lost a battle.' But Napoleon could have replied: 'Yes, but have you ever made a woman dream?' " The descendants of the imperial dynasts, all of whom lost the last battle, still dream of them with tenderness, despite the evidence of history. And what is history? Voltaire wrote: "History is after all only a pack of tricks we play on the dead."

PICTURE
CREDITS

THE BETTMANN ARCHIVE   Pages 120, 126, 127, 139, 176
THE COOPER-BRIDGEMAN LIBRARY   Pages 21, 24, 62–63,
    70–71, 73, 76, 108, 117, 130–31, 147, 180, 220, 253, 274, 338,
    343
THE MANSELL COLLECTION   Pages 65, 212, 231, 300, 311,
    363
MONDADORI PUBLISHING COMPANY, INC.   Pages 31 (*top*),
    84, 116
NEW YORK PUBLIC LIBRARY PICTURE COLLECTION
    Pages 31 (*bottom*), 93, 144, 172, 205 (*top and bottom*), 209,
    261, 327, 329
NOVOSTI   Pages 34–35

RADIO TIMES HULTON PICTURE LIBRARY Pages 64, 68, 69, 92, 100, 101, 102, 111, 118, 119, 123, 128, 129 (*top and bottom*), 132, 133, 145, 155 (*top*), 162, 163, 165, 169 (*top and bottom*), 171, 173, 174–75, 183, 186, 188 (*bottom*), 192, 193, 199, 204, 216, 223, 225, 238, 250, 254, 255, 259, 265, 266, 288, 291, 292, 293, 295 (*top and bottom*), 326, 352–53, 369
TIME-LIFE PICTURE AGENCY Pages 80–81, 346–47

A History of the Modern World, Second Edition, revised by R. R. Palmer and Joel Colton. Copyright 1950, © 1956 by Alfred A. Knopf, Inc. Reprinted by permission of the publisher. Pages 22, 41–42, 52–53, 107, 115.

Brooklyn Eagle, July 1914. Page 226.

The illustrations on the pages listed below are to be found in the following archives.
Kunsthistorisches Museum, Vienna, page 24;
The Prado, Madrid, page 27;
Louvre, Paris, page 51, 77;
Historische Staat Museum Beethoven, pages 66–67;
Bildarchiv d. Ost Nationalbibliothek, Vienna, pages 68, 69, 111;
Giraudon, pages 88–89;
Heeresgeschichtliches Museum, Vienna, pages 108–9;
Friedrich Krupp Gemeinschaftesbetriebe, pages 246–47.

Fall of Eagles was produced by the British Broadcasting Corporation and was created by John Elliott.
The programs in the series were written by the following authors:

"Death Waltz," Hugh Whitemore
"The English Princess," John Elliott and Elizabeth Holford
"The Honest Broker," John Elliott
"Requiem for a Crown Prince," David Turner
"The Last Tsar," John Elliott
"Absolute Beginners," Trevor Griffiths
"Dearest Nicky," Jack Pulman
"The Appointment," Troy Kennedy Martin
"Dress Rehearsal," Jack Pulman
"Indian Summer of an Emperor," Robert Muller
"Tell the King the Sky Is Falling," John Elliott and Elizabeth Holford
"The Secret War," Ken Hughes
"End Game," Keith Dewhurst

Maps redrawn by Vincent Torre

INDEX

Italic numbers refer to pages with illustrations.